EATINGWELL

Secrets *of*

{ *for great healthy food* }

Low-Fat

Cooking

EatingWell

Secrets of

{ for great healthy food }

Low-Fat Cooking

100 Techniques &

200 Easy Recipes

from the Magazine
of Food & Health

EatingWell BOOKS

A Division of EW Communications L.P.
Box 1001, Ferry Road, Charlotte, Vermont 05445-1001

EATING WELL: The Magazine of Food & Health®, is a registered trademark of EW Communications L.P.
For subscription information, write to EATING WELL, P.O. Box 52919, Boulder, CO 80322-2919
or call (303) 604-1464.

Library of Congress Cataloging-in-Publication Data

Eating well secrets of low-fat cooking : from the magazine of food & health / editor, Susan Stuck.
p.   cm.
Includes index.
ISBN 1-884943-11-X (hardcover) — ISBN 1-884943-12-8 (softcover)
1. Cookery.   2. Low-fat diet—Recipes.   I. Stuck, Susan.   II. Eating well.   III. Title: Secrets of low-fat cooking.
TX714.E236 1997   96-41794
641.5'638—DC20   CIP

Editor: Susan Stuck   **Managing Editor:** Wendy S. Ruopp   **Editorial Director:** Scott Mowbray
Nutrition Editor: Elizabeth Hiser   **Test Kitchen Director:** Patsy Jamieson   **Test Kitchen Manager:** Susanne Davis
Recipe Development & Analysis: Thy Tran   **Recipe Tester:** Jennifer Armentrout
Proofreaders: Kathleen Bond Borie, Anne Treadwell   **Support:** David Grist, Kristina Machanic

Design Director: Joannah Ralston   **Associate Art Director:** Elise Whittemore-Hill
Principal Photographer: Lori Landau   **Digital Prep Technician:** Jess L. Richardson

Front cover: Technique 24 (*page 52*) and West Indian Squash Soup (*recipe on page 39*)
Back cover: Technique 28 (*page 62*), Clay-Pot Chicken with a Spice Rub (*recipe on page 63*)

Distributed by
Artisan, a Division of Workman Publishing
708 Broadway, New York, NY 10003

Printed and bound in Canada by
Metropole Litho Inc., Montreal, Quebec

CONTENTS

Introduction

TO MAKE GREAT-TASTING, LOW-FAT FOOD, it helps to have a few tricks up your sleeve. For more than six years, EATING WELL has redefined the way to cook, creating innovative methods that do not depend on butter, cream and other high-fat ingredients to make food delicious. The Test Kitchen staff—working with the magazine's editors and outside experts—has developed and fine-tuned an extensive repertoire of fat-cutting tips and techniques, which are gathered for the first time in this comprehensive book.

When EATING WELL, The Magazine of Food & Health, first appeared on newsstands in 1990, skeptics wondered if low-fat food wasn't just one more flash in the nutrition fry pan. "It will last as long as oat bran," they said; "here today, gone tomorrow." Fat, however, has edged out all others as *the* dietary issue. In fact, limiting fat to reduce heart disease and cancer risk will remain a priority as long as these diseases remain our number one and number two killers.

EATING WELL recipes have always followed established, sensible guidelines for healthy eating: no more than 30 percent of calories in the overall diet should come from fat, and meals should contain modest portions of meat in combination with plenty of grains, vegetables and fruits. Nutrition Editor Elizabeth Hiser makes sure that the cooks in the EATING WELL Test Kitchen not only watch the total amount of fat in a recipe, but also pay particular attention to the source of fat. Saturated fats, the type of fat that raises blood cholesterol, should make up less than a third of the total fat in a healthy diet.

Instead of feeling hindered by the fat restrictions, the Test Kitchen staff has been invigorated by the challenge. High-fat creamy soups, pasta dishes, hearty stews, cakes, pies and fancy desserts are all reworked with enthusiasm, even gusto. (Over the years, they have thrown in the towel only once, and that was for oysters baked in heavy cream.) As Test Kitchen Director Patsy Jamieson says, "It's easy to make food taste good if you add enough cream or butter. It's far more interesting to cook without them."

At EATING WELL, standards for flavor are just as high as standards for nutrition. Our low-fat food does not taste *almost* as good as high-fat food; it tastes as good, and from time to time it tastes better. To create these delicious dishes, we like to draw from a diverse collection of ingredients.

Our recipe developers have been known to raid the global pantry in search of inspiration. Mediterranean influences are strong throughout this book; the various cuisines of that region all favor vegetables and grains and use heart-healthy olive oil as a cooking medium. You will find foods from Asia too: the Asian emphasis on vegetables, with meat used as a condiment, make this cuisine a natural for low-fat cooking. We have streamlined the recipes so you don't need an armload of exotic ingredients to make them.

Don't think that American classics have been neglected in any way: barbecued pork, burgers, potato salad, strawberry shortcake, even brownies, are all here.

The beauty of low-fat cooking is that it doesn't require complicated kitchen theatrics or peculiar equipment. It's just a matter of using everyday cooking skills in a new way. You have to be aware of fat and think about flavor. With these 200 thoroughly tested recipes, we have done that thinking for you. By sharing the techniques we use, you will soon be creating your own healthy, delicious recipes.

—*Susan Stuck*

Using This Book

FOR THIS BOOK, EATING WELL'S EXPERTISE in fat-busting has been distilled into 100 nifty techniques. Each chapter contains anywhere from four to 11 of these techniques. The first part of the book covers savory cooking: it begins with EATING WELL salads and salad dressings, then moves on to soups, pastas and pizzas, meats, vegetables, and ends with imaginative ways to cook with healthy beans and grains.

The second half covers all aspects of low-fat baking: tricks to boost flavors, the best way to effectively use high-fat ingredients in small quantities, clever uses for fruit puree, making the most of egg whites, and more. Knowing that chocolate makes our lives just a little more enjoyable, we have devoted a whole chapter to making it a healthier choice.

The chapters open with a short summary of the techniques to be covered and a list of the recipes in that chapter. Every chapter contains several different techniques on how to reduce fat, each one described in a concise paragraph. All techniques are followed by one, two or several recipes that put the technique into action.

Many of the techniques are illustrated. Have you been confounded by wordy directions for rolling out a pie crust? We show you how in three clear photographs on page 166. When we talk about browning butter to bring out its flavor, we show you just the right shade of brown on page 154.

F Look for the Fat Savings that accompanies every technique: this is a summary of how much fat you actually save by using the technique.

N Recipes are followed by a Nutrition Bonus highlighting a particular nutritive benefit.

? Leafing through the book, you will see a number of big green question marks in the lefthand corner of yellow-tinted boxes. These boxes answer a variety of commonly asked questions regarding cooking and nutrition. They teach you to identify the leanest cuts of meat or how to beat egg whites to greatest heights; they explain the healthfulness of the Mediterranean diet or how to avoid the salmonella risk.

Between some chapters you will find the "Mini-Courses." These two-page articles cover a range of topics in sweet and savory cooking, everything from identifying new salad greens to providing tips for storing herbs and spices to roasting fruits so their intrinsic flavors are enhanced. In addition, most Mini-Courses include recipes: you will find dynamite marinades and simple herb sauces and an extraordinary spice cake on these pages.

A menu section on page 202 features healthy, seasonal menus that can be made with the recipes in the book. The recipes were not created specifically for these menus, so in some cases you may need to double the recipes; in others, you may have leftovers. The extensive glossary, beginning on page 204, is divided into two parts to cover both cooking and nutrition terms. An exhaustive index at the back allows you to find techniques, ingredients and, of course, all 200 of those irresistible EATING WELL recipes.

MAKING SENSE OF THE NUMBERS

TODAY'S NUTRITION ADVICE CAN BE summed up this way: Eat more plant-based foods, and eat less fat. That simple rule needs to be understood before you can choose your new, healthier diet—even when you base that diet on EATING WELL recipes. As you plan your meals, keep in mind that you need a total of at least five fruits and vegetables a day—the five-a-day rule. (Even though this minimum seems quite reasonable, health experts say that this is far more than most people now eat.) Then calculate the limit of the amount of daily fat that you ought to observe (see Fat guidelines below). Having this basic knowledge, you will be able to make better use of the nutritional fine print in the *Secrets of Low-Fat Cooking* recipes.

The breakdown of calories, protein, fat, saturated fat, carbohydrate, sodium, cholesterol and dietary fiber for one serving that follows each recipe in this book is, therefore, not just of interest to nutritionists and diet fanatics. Everyone should make this part of their recipe browsing, because it is easier to *think* that one is eating a healthier diet—by eating an extra apple here, cutting back to low-fat milk there—than to do so over the long term. Here is an explanation of the nutrition information for our recipes.

---

70 calories per serving: 3 grams protein, 6 grams fat (1.8 grams saturated fat), 3 grams carbohydrate; 145 mg sodium; 7 mg cholesterol; 1 gram fiber.

CALORIES: Calorie needs vary enormously among individuals; contributing factors include age, gender, genetics and activity levels. On average, most moderately active people need about 15 calories per pound each day to maintain their present weight.

PROTEIN: Few Americans have to worry about getting enough protein, because the typical diet provides two to three times the amount required. In fact, eating smaller amounts of high-protein foods helps lower fat intake because fat and protein often occur together in foods.

FAT: Minimizing the amount of fat in each recipe helps people stay below the recommended limit—30 percent of total daily calories from fat. Reducing fat in the diet not only lowers risk of heart disease and cancer, but it is the best way to maintain a healthy weight because fat is the most concentrated source of calories.

Easier than counting calories and calculating percentages is to use EATING WELL's simple shortcut method to estimate your fat limit: divide your ideal body weight (or the weight you would *like* to be) by 2. For example, an average person with an ideal weight of 150 pounds should eat no more than 75 grams of fat per day. (People at risk for heart disease may want to restrict fat to 20 percent of calories. If so, divide ideal weight by 3 to calculate fat limit in grams.) This helps put the grams of fat in a recipe in perspective.

We are mindful of not only the amount, but also the source of fats. Most recipes specify monounsaturated oils—usually olive or canola oil. Saturated fat should make up less than a third of total fat.

Saturated fats raise blood cholesterol, and although both polyunsaturated and monounsaturated fats lower blood cholesterol when they replace saturated fats in the diet, evidence suggests that monounsaturates are the healthier of the two.

SATURATED FAT: Experts say that saturated fat is the component of the diet that needs to be limited more than any other because it is the main culprit contributing to heart disease, our number one killer. It is recommended that calories from saturated fat should be limited to 10 percent or less of total calories. Although all fats contain some saturated fatty acids, animal products generally contain more than plant products, with the exception of palm and coconut oils.

CARBOHYDRATE: In a healthy diet, foods high in complex carbohydrates outnumber high-fat foods while offering more vitamins, minerals and dietary fiber. Simple sugars add to the carbohydrate counts in nutritional analysis, but don't contribute much in the way of nutrition.

SODIUM: Our recipes vary greatly in sodium content but contain the minimum amount that we judge necessary to enhance food flavor.

CHOLESTEROL: It is recommended that intake of dietary cholesterol be kept below 300 milligrams per day. Fat (particularly saturated fat), rather than dietary cholesterol, is most implicated in raising blood cholesterol.

DIETARY FIBER: The average fiber intake in the United States is about 11 grams per day; the recommended amount is 20 to 35 grams. Besides its well-known contribution to intestinal health, fiber helps protect against colon cancer and heart disease.

Equipment
for the Health-Conscious Kitchen

LOW-FAT COOKING DOES NOT REQUIRE a new set of saucepans or expensive, hard-to-find gadgets. Beyond a sharp knife and a handy wooden spoon, the cooks in the EATING WELL Test Kitchen have found the six pieces of equipment they most often use in low-fat cooking are:

NONSTICK SKILLET

If you are serious about low-fat cooking, invest in a top-quality nonstick skillet. Virtually all manufacturers of high-quality cookware now produce heavy nonstick skillets. Look for a skillet that is heavy, ovenproof and has a superdurable coating with a textured bottom surface. Heavy pans made from stainless steel or hard anodized aluminum provide even heating without hot spots, and they don't warp. An ovenproof skillet allows you to start a recipe on the stovetop and finish it off in the oven without having to switch pans.

The new generation of nonstick coatings offers toughness and durability that the original Teflon coating lacked; brand names to look for include Autograph, SilverStone Select or SupraSelect. The textured bottom surface is another recent innovation; the interior of this type of pan has either a circular groove or square-pocket pattern, which allows you to deglaze, something that cannot be done in smooth-bottomed pans. Follow the manufacturer's instructions regarding the care and handling of a nonstick skillet.

KITCHEN SCALE

While we try to give volume measurements wherever practical, you will find some ingredients in our recipes are listed by weight. In the EATING WELL Test Kitchen, we prefer electronic scales over spring-loaded scales for their convenience and accuracy with small quantities—plus they are so compact they fit neatly into a drawer. When buying a scale, look for one that has a capacity of at least 4 pounds and a wide weighing base.

INSTANT-READ THERMOMETER

It's a fact of life—raw meat and eggs can be bearers of pathogens. The safest way to be sure that food is sufficiently cooked is to take its temperature. An instant-read thermometer allows you to take the temperature of cooked meat and eggs quickly and accurately.

WIRE WHISK

Translating one stroke into many, a wire whisk is ideal for mixing salad dressings, beating eggs, making sauces. We also find that for baked goods, it blends dry ingredients—the flour, spices and leavenings—quite nicely so they don't have to be sifted together. Look for a whisk with a dozen or more stainless-steel wires. The wires should be neither too rigid nor too flexible.

FOOD PROCESSOR

For pureeing, chopping, slicing, grating, blending, even kneading, the food processor saves valuable time in the kitchen, and about 25 percent of the recipes in this book ask for the processor. We suggest buying a processor with a large workbowl.

PARCHMENT PAPER

This strong paper is useful for lining baking sheets and cake pans to prevent sticking. While less-expensive wax paper will often do instead, parchment is essential for cookies that tend to stick, such as meringues. Find it at kitchen-equipment shops.

Apricot Dressing, page 18,
on mixed bitter greens

THE TECHNIQUES

1 Using tea to reduce oil in basic vinaigrette

2 Choosing mellow vinegars

3 Adding fruit juices to extend salad dressings

4 Substituting cottage cheese and buttermilk
for sour cream

5 Relying on buttermilk for easy dressings

6 Grating fresh tomatoes as a base

7 Making low-fat homemade mayonnaise

8 Adding body with versatile nonfat yogurt

9 Tempering raw garlic by mashing it with salt

10 Roasting garlic to use as a fat substitute

TECHNIQUES
1-10
SALADS
& Salad
Dressings

**A MIX OF TENDER GREENS, WEDGES
OF RIPE TOMATO, SLICES
OF CRISP CUCUMBER:**
more healthy food can-
not be found. The
trick is to keep it healthy
by not drowning it in a
high-fat dressing.

Sure, there are countless
commercial salad dressings—
many of which are quite low
in fat—but there isn't one that has the bright fresh
flavor of homemade dressing. By reducing the oil
and stretching the basic dressings with a variety
of ingredients (anything from roasted garlic to
apricot nectar to tea), the EATING WELL Test
Kitchen is able to keep flavor at a maximum and
hold fat to a bare minimum.

1 Use tea to reduce oil in a basic vinaigrette.

The three-to-one oil-to-vinegar ratio of a classic vinaigrette yields 10 grams of fat and 90 calories in a single tablespoon. Ouch. But how to cut back on the oil and still have enough dressing for a salad? Equal amounts of vinegar, oil and, believe it or not, strong brewed tea produce a mellow vinaigrette that is neither bland nor overly acidic.

F FAT SAVINGS: A 60% reduction in fat over a traditional vinaigrette. Commercial bottled vinegar-and-oil dressings vary greatly in fat—anywhere from 1 to 13 grams per tablespoon.

To add a hint of garlic to the vinaigrette, spear a garlic clove onto a fork. Use the fork to vigorously whisk vinegar, oil, tea and seasonings until well blended.

? WHY USE EXTRA-VIRGIN OLIVE OIL?

In these salad dressing recipes, you might notice that whenever olive oil is called for, "extra-virgin" is recommended. The words "extra-virgin" and "cold pressed" on the label of the olive oil bottle refer to a low-acid oil that has not been refined by heat or solvents. This type of olive oil tastes much better than lower-grade oils, which have been scrubbed of flavor, color and aroma. As all oils are extremely concentrated in fat and calories, it makes sense to use one that brings the most flavor to the recipe.

Basic Vinaigrette

A hint of garlic, a little mustard and a touch of fresh herbs lightly flavor an elegantly simple dressing that is perfect on a mesclun salad.

1 clove garlic, peeled
2 tablespoons olive oil, preferably extra-virgin
2 tablespoons red-wine vinegar *or* lemon juice
2 tablespoons strong brewed Earl Grey tea
1 teaspoon Dijon mustard
  Salt & freshly ground black pepper to taste
1 tablespoon chopped fresh parsley *or* chives

Skewer the garlic clove onto the tines of a fork, and use to vigorously blend oil, vinegar or lemon juice, tea and mustard. Taste and season with salt and pepper. Just before serving, stir in fresh herbs.

Makes about ⅓ cup.

45 calories per tablespoon: 0 grams protein, 5 grams fat (0.7 gram saturated fat), 0 grams carbohydrate; 2.5 mg sodium; 0 mg cholesterol; 0 grams fiber.

N NUTRITION BONUS: Olive oil has been part of the heart-healthy traditional Mediterranean diet for centuries.

Greens & Gorgonzola Salad

1 ounce Gorgonzola cheese
2 tablespoons strong brewed tea, such as Earl Grey *or* orange pekoe

1 tablespoon white-wine vinegar
1 tablespoon olive oil, preferably extra-virgin
1 tablespoon finely chopped shallots
1 teaspoon Dijon mustard
  Salt & freshly ground black pepper to taste
3 cups washed, dried and torn red leaf lettuce
3 cups washed and dried watercress sprigs

In a salad bowl, mash the cheese with a whisk. Add tea, vinegar, oil, shallots, mustard, salt and pepper and whisk to combine. Add lettuce and watercress and toss well. Garnish with a grinding of black pepper.

Makes 4 servings.

70 calories per serving: 3 grams protein, 6 grams fat (1.8 grams saturated fat), 3 grams carbohydrate; 145 mg sodium; 7 mg cholesterol; 1 gram fiber.

 NUTRITION BONUS: A tiny amount of full-flavored cheese, such as Gorgonzola, will flavor a large amount of healthful greens.

TECHNIQUE 2 Choose mellow vinegars as a way to cut oil in a dressing.

Flavorful, lower-acid vinegars, such as balsamic vinegar, high-quality red-wine vinegar and raspberry vinegar, allow you to get away with less oil in a dressing. Why? The mellower the vinegar, the less oil you need to counteract the acidity.

FAT SAVINGS: These dressings have half the fat of traditional vinaigrettes.

Maple-Balsamic Vinaigrette

Serve on any mixed green salad.

2 tablespoons olive oil, preferably extra-virgin
2 tablespoons balsamic vinegar
2 teaspoons pure maple syrup
2 teaspoons grainy mustard
  Salt & freshly ground black pepper to taste

In a small bowl, whisk oil, vinegar, maple syrup, mus-

? WHAT IS BALSAMIC VINEGAR?

Made in Northern Italy from Trebbiano grape juice and aged like wine, balsamic vinegar is dark, sweet and complex. The finest balsamics are a handmade product, and are aged for anywhere from 12 to 100 years in a series of smaller and smaller casks made of different woods. This traditional balsamic is extremely expensive. Most of the balsamics sold in the United States are commercially produced; they are less concentrated and less complex than the traditionals, but offer the same balance of sweet and tart.

tard, salt and pepper until blended. (*Alternatively, combine ingredients in a small jar, secure the lid and shake.*)

Makes about ⅓ cup.

45 calories per tablespoon: 0 grams protein, 5 grams fat (0.7 gram saturated fat), 2 grams carbohydrate; 6 mg sodium; 0 mg cholesterol; 0 grams fiber.

NUTRITION BONUS: Bottled salad dressings usually contain hydrogenated (artificially saturated) oils. Olive oil is high in monounsaturated fat, which does not raise "bad" LDL blood cholesterol as saturated fat does.

Raspberry Vinegar Dressing

Try with spinach or watercress salad.

3 tablespoons raspberry vinegar
1 tablespoon honey
2 tablespoons olive oil, preferably extra-virgin
  Salt & freshly ground black pepper to taste

In a small bowl, whisk vinegar and honey until blended. Whisking continuously, slowly add oil. Season with salt and pepper. (*Alternatively, combine ingredients in a small jar, secure the lid and shake.*)

Makes about ⅓ cup.

55 calories per tablespoon: 0 grams protein, 5 grams fat (0.7 gram saturated fat), 3 grams carbohydrate; 0 mg sodium; 0 mg cholesterol; 0 grams fiber.

NUTRITION BONUS: When selecting greens, keep in mind that richness in color means richness in nutrients.

Basil Vinaigrette

The best thing for tomatoes from the garden.

- 3 tablespoons olive oil, preferably extra-virgin
- 2 tablespoons red-wine vinegar
- 2 tablespoons balsamic vinegar
- 2 tablespoons fresh lemon juice
- 2 tablespoons grainy mustard
- 2 teaspoons minced garlic
- 1½ teaspoons sugar
  Salt & freshly ground black pepper to taste
- ¼ cup finely chopped fresh basil

In a small bowl, whisk oil, vinegars, lemon juice, mustard, garlic, sugar, salt and pepper. (*Alternatively, combine ingredients in a small jar, secure the lid and shake until blended.*) Just before serving, stir in basil.

Makes about ⅔ cup.

45 calories per tablespoon: 0 grams protein, 4 grams fat (0.5 gram saturated fat), 3 grams carbohydrate; 8 mg sodium; 0 mg cholesterol; 0 grams fiber.

TECHNIQUE

3 Add fruit juices to extend salad dressings without adding fat.

The juice of mildly acidic citrus fruits is a natural for fresh-tasting salad dressings. Look for other fruit nectars and juices that have some acidity; apricot nectar and cranberry juice are two excellent choices.

F FAT SAVINGS: At 1, 2 or 3 grams of fat per tablespoon, these dressings are a real boon for people on very low-fat diets.

Apricot Dressing

This is good with a salad of bitter greens or on a couscous salad.

- ⅓ cup apricot nectar
- 3 tablespoons minced dried apricots
- 3 tablespoons balsamic vinegar
- 3 tablespoons coarsely chopped fresh parsley
- 2 tablespoons olive oil, preferably extra-virgin
- 2 teaspoons minced garlic
- 2 teaspoons grainy mustard
- 1 teaspoon sugar
  Salt & coarsely ground black pepper to taste

In a small bowl, whisk apricot nectar, apricots, vinegar, parsley, oil, garlic, mustard, sugar, salt and pepper. (*Alternatively, combine ingredients in a small jar, secure the lid and shake until blended.*)

Makes about ¾ cup.

35 calories per tablespoon: 0 grams protein, 2 grams fat (0.3 gram saturated fat), 4 grams carbohydrate; 5 mg sodium; 0 mg cholesterol; 0 grams fiber.

N NUTRITION BONUS: Apricot nectar boosts the carotenoid content of a green salad even higher.

Asparagus with Tangerine & Sesame Seed Dressing

This dressing is also good on mixed Asian salad greens, such as baby bok choy, pea shoots or mizuna.

- 1 teaspoon peanut oil *or* olive oil
- 1 tablespoon sesame seeds
- 2 tablespoons chopped shallots
- 1½ teaspoons grated tangerine zest *or* orange zest
- 1 cup fresh tangerine juice *or* orange juice
- 1 tablespoon sherry vinegar *or* rice vinegar
- 1½ teaspoons reduced-sodium soy sauce
- 1½ pounds asparagus, trimmed
- 2 tablespoons chopped fresh chives *or* scallion greens

1. In a small saucepan, heat oil over low heat. Add sesame seeds and stir until lightly toasted, about 20 seconds. Add shallots and stir until soft, about 1 minute. Add citrus zest and juice, vinegar and soy sauce. Simmer until reduced to ½ cup, about 6 minutes.

2. Place asparagus in a large steamer set in a large pot over simmering water. Cover and cook just until tender, about 5 minutes. Just before serving, stir chives or scallion greens into the sauce. Divide asparagus among 4 salad plates, spoon on the sauce and serve.

Makes 4 servings.

95 calories per serving: 6 grams protein, 3 grams fat (0.3 gram saturated fat), 15 grams carbohydrate; 75 mg sodium; 0 mg cholesterol; 2 grams fiber.

NUTRITION BONUS: Asparagus is a good source of folic acid, a B vitamin now known to be important for reducing the risk of strokes and heart attacks.

Ginger-Orange Dressing

Spinach, watercress or Belgian endive are good matches for this zesty dressing.

¼ cup fresh orange juice
4 teaspoons vegetable oil, preferably canola
1 tablespoon minced scallions
1 teaspoon minced peeled fresh ginger
½ teaspoon grated orange zest
¼ teaspoon minced garlic
Salt & freshly ground black pepper to taste

In a small bowl, whisk orange juice, oil, scallions, ginger, orange zest, garlic, salt and pepper until well blended. (*Alternatively, combine ingredients in a small jar, secure the lid and shake until blended.*)

Makes about ⅓ cup.

35 calories per tablespoon: 0 grams protein, 3 grams fat (0.2 gram saturated fat), 1 gram carbohydrate; 1 mg sodium; 0 mg cholesterol; 0 grams fiber.

NUTRITION BONUS: Add orange sections to your salad for a boost of vitamin C and folic acid.

Salad of Mâche & Beets with Cranberry Dressing

2 tablespoons cranberry juice
2 tablespoons red-wine vinegar
2 tablespoons minced shallots
1 tablespoon grainy mustard
2 tablespoons olive oil, preferably extra-virgin
Salt & freshly ground black pepper to taste
6 small beets, cooked, peeled and cut into thin sticks
1 hard-boiled egg, peeled (*see box, page 99*)
9 cups mâche *or* Boston lettuce

1. In a small bowl, whisk cranberry juice, vinegar, shallots and mustard. Slowly whisk in oil. Season with salt and pepper. Pour half of the dressing into a separate bowl and set aside. Marinate beets in the remaining dressing for at least 1 hour and up to 6 hours.

2. Just before serving, use a rubber spatula to press egg through a coarse strainer into a small bowl. Add the mâche or Boston lettuce to the reserved dressing and toss. Arrange on 6 salad plates. Divide the marinated beets over the mâche or lettuce and garnish with some of the sieved egg and a grinding of black pepper.

Makes 6 servings.

85 calories per serving: 3 grams protein, 6 grams fat (0.9 gram saturated fat), 6 grams carbohydrate; 80 mg sodium; 36 mg cholesterol; 1 gram fiber.

NUTRITION BONUS: Beets are rich in fiber, iron and potassium.

Cranberry juice enlivens the dressing for a salad of mâche (also known as lamb's lettuce) and beets.

Jícama Slaw

¼ cup fresh apple cider
1½ tablespoons olive oil, preferably extra-virgin
1 tablespoon cider vinegar
2 teaspoons Dijon mustard
1 clove garlic, minced
2 cups grated jícama
1 cup grated carrots
1 cup grated Granny Smith apple
Salt & freshly ground black pepper to taste

In a salad bowl, whisk apple cider, oil, vinegar, mustard and garlic. Add jícama, carrots and apples; toss to coat. Season with salt and pepper.

Makes about 4 cups, for 4 servings.

150 calories per serving: 1 gram protein, 5 grams fat (0.8 gram saturated fat), 25 grams carbohydrate; 25 mg sodium; 0 mg cholesterol; 2 grams fiber.

 NUTRITION BONUS: Jícama is a good source of vitamin C.

TECHNIQUE 4 — Substitute cottage cheese and buttermilk for sour cream.

If you find that nonfat or reduced-fat sour cream lacks the dairy flavor of the full-fat version, try pureeing 2 parts low-fat (1%) cottage cheese and 1 part buttermilk.

F FAT SAVINGS: One cup of full-fat sour cream contains 48 grams of fat. A blend of ⅔ cup low-fat cottage cheese and ⅓ cup buttermilk contains 2 grams of fat.

Beet & Citrus Salad with Creamy Dressing

½ cup low-fat cottage cheese
¼ cup buttermilk
1½ tablespoons prepared horseradish
1 tablespoon fresh lemon juice
1 teaspoon Dijon mustard
½ teaspoon sugar

? WHAT IS BUTTERMILK?

Despite its high-fat name, buttermilk is a great asset for the low-fat cook. Years ago, buttermilk was the liquid left after churning butter. Today's commercial buttermilk is no longer a by-product of butter-making: it is nonfat or low-fat milk that has bacteria added to it, which thickens the milk and imparts a mild acidity.

¼ teaspoon hot-pepper sauce
3 medium-large red beets (about ¾ pound)
1 large grapefruit
1 large navel orange
1 large bunch watercress, trimmed and rinsed
2 tablespoons thinly sliced scallion greens

1. In a blender or food processor, combine cottage cheese, buttermilk, horseradish, lemon juice, mustard, sugar and hot-pepper sauce; process to a smooth puree. Transfer to a bowl, cover and chill until serving time.

2. Trim beets if necessary, leaving 2 inches of stem; save greens for another use. Drop the beets into boiling salted water; boil until they can be pierced through but are not tender, 15 to 25 minutes. Drain, then cover with cold water and cool to room temperature, about 30 minutes.

3. Peel the beets and cut into thin slices. Stacking a few slices at a time, cut into strips ½ inch wide.

4. With a sharp knife, remove skin and white pith from grapefruit and orange. Cut the grapefruit segments from their surrounding membranes. Cut orange in half, then across into very thin semicircles.

5. Arrange watercress on 4 salad plates. Top with the beets, then the citrus segments. Stir the dressing, drizzle over the salads and sprinkle with scallions.

Makes 4 servings.

100 calories per serving: 7 grams protein, 1 gram fat (0.2 gram saturated fat), 18 grams carbohydrate; 285 mg sodium; 2 mg cholesterol; 4 grams fiber.

N NUTRITION BONUS: Watercress and citrus fruits contain phytochemicals that protect against cancer.

For more recipes using low-fat cottage cheese, see pages 102, 138 and 183.

TECHNIQUE 5

Rely on buttermilk for a low-fat salad dressing that keeps well.

Buttermilk, with its pleasant dairy tang, marries well with fresh herbs, and it has enough body to make a creamy dressing that coats greens quite nicely.

F FAT SAVINGS: Just because a commercial dressing is labeled "made with buttermilk" is no guarantee that it is lower in fat. Commercially prepared buttermilk dressings range from 3 to 10 grams of fat per tablespoon; ours contain 1 or 2 grams.

Poppy Seed Dressing

This dressing is perfect for a melon salad.

½ cup buttermilk
½ cup nonfat sour cream
2 tablespoons honey
1 tablespoon fresh lemon juice
½ tablespoon poppy seeds, toasted

In a small bowl, whisk buttermilk, sour cream, honey, lemon juice and poppy seeds until smooth. (*The dressing can be stored, covered, in the refrigerator for up to 4 days.*)

Makes about 1 cup.

20 calories per tablespoon: 1 gram protein, 1 gram fat (0.1 gram saturated fat), 3 grams carbohydrate; 20 mg sodium; 1 mg cholesterol; 0 grams fiber.

N NUTRITION BONUS: Fruit salads help you and your family reach the five-a-day goal.

Creamy Herb Dressing

A lovely dressing for Boston or butter lettuce.

¾ cup buttermilk
¼ cup reduced-fat mayonnaise
¼ cup chopped scallions
3 tablespoons chopped fresh dill
1 tablespoon chopped fresh parsley

1 tablespoon fresh lemon juice
1 tablespoon prepared horseradish
Salt & freshly ground black pepper to taste

In a blender, combine buttermilk, mayonnaise, scallions, dill, parsley, lemon juice, horseradish, salt and pepper. Blend well until smooth. (*The dressing can be stored, covered, in the refrigerator for up to 4 days.*)

Makes about 1 cup.

10 calories per tablespoon: 1 gram protein, 1 gram fat (0.1 gram saturated fat), 2 grams carbohydrate; 50 mg sodium; 1 mg cholesterol; 0 grams fiber.

N NUTRITION BONUS: Reduced-fat mayonnaises vary in fat content from 1 to 5 grams per tablespoon. (Regular has 11.) Be sure to compare labels.

For more recipes using buttermilk,
see pages 22, 116, 136, 154, 157 and 180.

Buttermilk is the base for easy Poppy Seed and Creamy Herb dressings.

6 Grate juicy fresh tomatoes as a base for low-fat dressing.

When you grate red-ripe tomatoes the juice is thicker than if you had squeezed them, making it just right for a fresh-tasting salad dressing.

F FAT SAVINGS: Half the fat of a commercial French dressing, with none of the too-sweet, canned-tomato taste.

To grate a tomato, set a small-holed grater over a shallow bowl. Grate cut side of tomato halves, pressing with your palms to flatten the skin as the flesh is grated. Discard the skin.

Fresh Tomato Vinaigrette

Toss this summery dressing with romaine or spinach.

- 2 vine-ripened tomatoes, halved and seeded
- 1 small clove garlic, peeled
- 1 tablespoon red-wine vinegar
- 1 tablespoon olive oil, preferably extra-virgin
- 1 tablespoon finely chopped fresh parsley
     or basil
     Salt & freshly ground black pepper to taste

Grate tomato halves over a small bowl. Skewer the garlic clove onto the tines of a fork, and use to vigorously mix vinegar into the tomato juice. Still mixing, slowly drizzle in oil. Add parsley or basil and season with salt and pepper.

Makes about ½ cup.

30 calories per tablespoon: 1 gram protein, 3 grams fat (0.5 gram saturated fat), 2 grams carbohydrate; 4 mg sodium; 0 mg cholesterol; 1 gram fiber.

N NUTRITION BONUS: Leave out the oil for a fat-free homemade dressing.

7 Make homemade mayonnaise with buttermilk and very little oil.

Start with buttermilk, an egg, some cornstarch and a few seasonings and cook gently to thicken. Whisk in oil and lemon juice. *Voilà!* It's mayonnaise. The mayo is great on its own or as a base for exciting flavor variations.

F FAT SAVINGS: With just 1 gram of fat in a tablespoon, this glossy golden mayonnaise has one-tenth the fat of the homemade original. And it tastes better than commercial low-fat mayos.

Amazing Mayonnaise

- 1 tablespoon cornstarch
- 1½ teaspoons dry mustard, preferably Colmans
- 1 teaspoon sugar
- ½ teaspoon salt, or more to taste
     Pinch of cayenne
- ¾ cup buttermilk
- 1 large egg
- 2 tablespoons fresh lemon juice
- 1 tablespoon olive oil, preferably extra-virgin

1. In a medium saucepan, whisk cornstarch, mustard, sugar, salt and cayenne. Add ¼ cup of the buttermilk and whisk to a smooth paste. Whisk in egg and the remaining ½ cup buttermilk until smooth.

2. Set the pan over medium-low heat and cook, whisking, until the mixture comes to a simmer and thickens. Continue to whisk for 15 seconds, then remove the pan from the heat.

3. Whisk in lemon juice and oil. Transfer the mayonnaise to a small bowl and press a piece of plastic wrap directly on the surface to prevent a skin from forming. Let cool. (*The mayonnaise can be stored in the refrigerator for up to 3 days; whisk briefly before using.*)

Makes about 1 cup.

20 calories per tablespoon: I gram protein, I gram fat (0.2 gram saturated fat), I gram carbohydrate; 90 mg sodium; 14 mg cholesterol; 0 grams fiber.

Ⓝ NUTRITION BONUS: Our mayonnaise does *not* contain raw egg yolks like the classic homemade mayonnaise.

Aioli

This Provençal classic is excellent on new potatoes, fresh tomatoes or in a vegetable sandwich.

- 2 cloves garlic, crushed and peeled
- ½ teaspoon salt
- ½ cup Amazing Mayonnaise

Mash garlic to a paste with salt (*see page 25*) and stir into mayonnaise.

Makes about ½ cup.

20 calories per tablespoon: I gram protein, I gram fat (0.3 gram saturated fat), 2 grams carbohydrate; 220 mg sodium; 14 mg cholesterol; 0 grams fiber.

Sesame-Ginger Dressing

Mix with shredded napa cabbage for an Asian slaw, or use for a chicken or pasta salad.

- 1 clove garlic, mashed
- ½ cup Amazing Mayonnaise
- 1 tablespoon minced fresh ginger
- 1 tablespoon chopped scallions
- 1½ teaspoons rice-wine vinegar
- 1 teaspoon soy sauce
- 1 teaspoon sesame oil
- ½ teaspoon Dijon mustard
- ½ teaspoon honey

Rub the inside of a small bowl with garlic; discard garlic. Add mayonnaise to the bowl along with ginger, scallions, vinegar, soy sauce, oil, mustard and honey; stir to blend.

Makes about ⅔ cup.

20 calories per tablespoon: I gram protein, I gram fat (0.3 gram saturated fat), 2 grams carbohydrate; 100 mg sodium; 10 mg cholesterol; 0 grams fiber.

Curried Mayonnaise

Use when making chicken or tuna salad.

- 2 teaspoons curry powder
- ½ cup Amazing Mayonnaise
- 1 teaspoon honey

Toast curry powder in a dry skillet over very low heat for 1 minute; transfer to a small bowl. Add mayonnaise and honey; stir to blend.

Makes about ½ cup.

25 calories per tablespoon: I gram protein, I gram fat (0.3 gram saturated fat), 2 grams carbohydrate; 90 mg sodium; 14 mg cholesterol; 0 grams fiber.

Watercress Dressing

Toss with cooked potatoes for an easy potato salad.

- 1 clove garlic, mashed
- ½ cup Amazing Mayonnaise
- ⅔ cup chopped watercress leaves
- 1 teaspoon fresh lemon juice
- ¼ teaspoon freshly ground black pepper

Rub the inside of a small bowl with garlic; discard garlic. Add mayonnaise to the bowl along with watercress, lemon juice and pepper; stir to blend.

Makes about ¾ cup.

15 calories per tablespoon: I gram protein, I gram fat (0.2 gram saturated fat), I gram carbohydrate; 60 mg sodium; 9 mg cholesterol; 0 grams fiber.

Ⓝ NUTRITION BONUS: These mayonnaise variations also make great dips for crudités—and are far better for you than the standard sour cream dips.

Coleslaw

Just the thing for your next picnic.

1 cup Amazing Mayonnaise (*page 22*) *or* commercial reduced-fat mayonnaise
¾ cup reduced-fat sour cream
3 tablespoons cider vinegar
1 tablespoon Dijon mustard
1 teaspoon sugar
Salt & freshly ground black pepper to taste
9 cups shredded green cabbage, preferably Savoy (1 small head)
1 large green bell pepper, quartered, cored and very thinly sliced
2 cups grated carrots

In a large bowl, whisk mayonnaise, sour cream, vinegar, mustard and sugar. Season with salt and pepper. Add cabbage, bell pepper and carrots and toss until well combined.

Makes about 8 cups, for 8 servings.

110 calories per serving: 4 grams protein, 5 grams fat (2.2 grams saturated fat), 14 grams carbohydrate; 220 mg sodium; 36 mg cholesterol; 3 grams fiber.

Ⓝ NUTRITION BONUS: Our low-fat mayonnaise dresses up carrots and cabbage, a well-matched pair in terms of nutrition *and* protective phytochemicals.

TECHNIQUE 8 Add body, flavor and not a gram of fat to salad dressings with versatile nonfat yogurt.

In the EATING WELL Test Kitchen, more empty yogurt containers go into the recycling bin than any other kind. Yogurt is so handy in so many recipes that we make sure there is always some in the refrigerator. It adds body and rich dairy flavor to salad dressing, but its sharp tang often needs sweetening with a little sugar or honey.

Ⓕ FAT SAVINGS: Full-fat yogurt contains 8 or 9 grams of fat per cup; nonfat yogurt, of course, contains none.

Honey-Mustard Dressing

A perfect foil for a salad of mixed bitter greens including arugula, chicory, escarole, radicchio and/or watercress. If you like, double the recipe and keep on hand in the refrigerator for 3 or 4 days.

½ cup nonfat yogurt
1 tablespoon cider vinegar
2 teaspoons Dijon mustard
2 teaspoons honey
Salt & freshly ground black pepper to taste

In a small bowl, whisk yogurt, vinegar, mustard, honey and salt until blended. Add a generous grinding of pepper and whisk again. (*Alternatively, combine all ingredients in a small jar, secure the lid and shake until blended.*)

Makes about ½ cup.

15 calories per tablespoon: 1 gram protein, 0 grams fat, 3 grams carbohydrate; 15 mg sodium; 1 mg cholesterol; 0 grams fiber.

Ⓝ NUTRITION BONUS: Check the label to see if yogurt contains live, active cultures; these friendly bacteria are good for your digestive tract.

TECHNIQUE 9 Temper the bite of raw garlic by mashing it with salt before incorporating into a dressing.

A lot of oil in a dressing tends to mellow the assertiveness of raw garlic. But in lower-oil dressings, minced raw garlic can be unpleasant. If you love the warmth and depth garlic lends to salads, but don't want that bite, try mashing whole garlic cloves and salt before adding to a dressing. Kosher salt works best because of its coarser grain. You will find the mashing technique useful in any number of recipes that call for garlic.

Ⓕ FAT SAVINGS: Commercial garlic-flavored salad dressings have up to 9 grams of fat in a tablespoon; none has the great garlicky flavor found in the homemade dressing for the low-fat summery salad that follows.

To mash garlic, sprinkle peeled cloves with kosher salt. With the flat of a large knife, mash to a fine paste. Use knife to scrape garlic into a mixing bowl.

Tuna & Tomatoes Provençale

This salad is perfect for those hot summer days when tomatoes are abundant and cooking is out of the question.

- 2 cloves garlic, crushed and peeled
- ½ teaspoon salt, preferably kosher
- 2 tablespoons olive oil, preferably extra-virgin
- 2 tablespoons balsamic *or* red-wine vinegar
- 2 tablespoons lemon juice
- ½ teaspoon freshly ground black pepper
- 2 6-ounce cans solid white tuna in water, drained and flaked
- ½ cup diced roasted red peppers (from a jar, *or see Technique 24, page 52*)
- ¼ cup chopped pitted black olives
- ¼ cup chopped fresh basil
- ¼ cup chopped fresh chives *or* scallion greens
- 2 tablespoons drained capers
- 4 large vine-ripened tomatoes
    Several fresh basil leaves for garnish

1. Mash garlic and salt into a paste; transfer to a large bowl. Add oil, vinegar, lemon juice and black pepper. Whisk until well blended.

2. Add tuna, red peppers, olives, chopped basil, chives or scallions and capers. Toss gently to combine.

3. Slice tomatoes ½ inch thick and arrange on a serving platter. Sprinkle tuna mixture evenly over tomatoes. Let stand 20 minutes to let flavors meld. Garnish with whole basil leaves just before serving.

Makes 6 servings.

120 calories per serving: 19 grams protein, 2 grams fat (1 gram saturated fat), 6 grams carbohydrate; 620 mg sodium; 28 mg cholesterol; 1 gram fiber.

Ⓝ NUTRITION BONUS: If you are counting grams of fat, check the tuna label. Albacore tuna can contain anywhere from 1 to 7 grams in 2 ounces, depending on the catch.

TECHNIQUE 10

Roast garlic to replace fat in robust dressings.

After 45 minutes in a hot oven, a head of garlic is transformed to a sweet, aromatic, almost buttery substance that is easy to incorporate into salad dressings.

Ⓕ FAT SAVINGS: A Caesar salad made with a roasted-garlic dressing has one-fifth to one-fourth the fat of the standard Caesar salad. Roasted garlic helps cut fat in potato and pasta salads too.

1. Slice the tip off a head of garlic, exposing the cloves. Set on a square of aluminum foil, sprinkle with 1 tablespoon water and pinch edges of foil together. Roast for 45 minutes in a 400°F oven.

2. Unwrap the roasted garlic and let cool slightly. Squeeze the soft garlic from the cloves into a mixing bowl or food processor.

Caesar Salad

Ever since Tijuana restaurateur Caesar Cardini invented this salad in 1924, it has been popular on menus. Over the years, the dressing has grown remarkably heavy with too much oil and cheese. This revised version has only 7 grams of fat per serving.

ROASTED GARLIC DRESSING

  2 heads garlic
 ¼ cup defatted reduced-sodium chicken broth *or* water
  3 tablespoons red-wine vinegar *or* cider vinegar
  2 tablespoons olive oil, preferably extra-virgin
  2 teaspoons Dijon mustard
  3 anchovy fillets, rinsed and coarsely chopped
  2 teaspoons Worcestershire sauce
     Salt & freshly ground black pepper to taste

SALAD

 10 cups torn romaine lettuce (2 small heads)
  2 cups Garlic Croutons (*see box, above*)
 ½ ounce Parmesan cheese, shaved with a vegetable peeler
  3 anchovy fillets, rinsed and halved lengthwise (optional)
     Freshly ground black pepper to taste

Garlic Croutons

  2 cloves roasted garlic
  2 teaspoons olive oil, preferably extra-virgin
  1 tablespoon fresh lemon juice
 ¼ teaspoon salt
 ¼ teaspoon pepper
  2 cups ½-inch bread cubes, cut from country-style bread

Preheat oven to 375°F. In a bowl, mash roasted garlic with oil. Stir in lemon juice, salt and pepper; add bread cubes and toss. Spread the croutons on a baking sheet. Bake until golden, 15 to 20 minutes. Set aside to cool.

Makes about 2 cups.

40 calories per ⅓ cup: 1 gram protein, 2 grams fat (0.3 gram saturated fat), 5 grams carbohydrate; 140 mg sodium; 0 mg cholesterol; 0 grams fiber.

Ⓝ NUTRITION BONUS: Garlic may not lower cholesterol, but it is loaded with natural protective chemicals.

TO MAKE ROASTED GARLIC DRESSING:
Roast garlic as described on page 25. Squeeze the garlic cloves from their skins into a blender or food processor. Add chicken broth or water, vinegar, oil, mustard, anchovies and Worcestershire sauce; blend until smooth. Season with salt and pepper. (*The dressing can be stored, covered, in the refrigerator for up to 2 days.*)

TO MAKE SALAD:
In a large salad bowl, combine lettuce with the dressing and toss well. Add the croutons, Parmesan and anchovy fillets, if using. Grind pepper over the top, toss once and serve.

Makes 6 servings.

150 calories per serving: 5 grams protein, 7 grams fat (1.3 grams saturated fat), 17 grams carbohydrate; 360 mg sodium; 4 mg cholesterol; 2 grams fiber.

Dressing only: 30 calories per tablespoon: 1 gram protein, 2.5 grams fat (0.3 gram saturated fat), 1 gram carbohydrate; 60 mg sodium; 1 mg cholesterol; 0 grams fiber.

Ⓝ NUTRITION BONUS: This salad does not contain a raw egg like many traditional Caesars.

Garlic-Lemon Dressing

Try this garlicky blend on a Greek salad of tomatoes and cucumbers sprinkled with feta cheese.

2	large heads garlic
⅓	cup fresh lemon juice
4	teaspoons olive oil, preferably extra-virgin
¼	cup coarsely chopped parsley
	Salt & freshly ground black pepper to taste

1. Roast garlic as described on page 25. Let cool slightly.

2. Squeeze the garlic cloves from their skins into a blender or food processor. Add lemon juice, oil and 3 tablespoons water and blend until smooth. Transfer to a small bowl, stir in parsley and season with salt and pepper. (*The dressing can be made 1 day in advance and stored, covered, in the refrigerator.*)

Makes about ⅔ cup.

35 calories per tablespoon: 1 gram protein, 2 grams fat (0.3 gram saturated fat), 5 grams carbohydrate; 5 mg sodium; 0 mg cholesterol; 0 grams fiber.

Potato Salad

Old-fashioned potato salads made with full-fat mayonnaise have up to 12 grams of fat per cup. This crowd pleaser has only 4 grams per cup.

2	heads garlic
3	pounds red potatoes, scrubbed and cut into 1-inch pieces
1	tablespoon white-wine vinegar
⅓	cup Amazing Mayonnaise (*page 22*) *or* commercial reduced-fat mayonnaise
⅓	cup nonfat plain yogurt
2	tablespoons Dijon mustard
	Salt & freshly ground black pepper to taste
4	hard-boiled eggs, peeled (*see box, page 99*)
1	cup chopped celery (3-4 stalks)
1	4-ounce jar sliced pimientos, drained and rinsed
½	cup pitted black olives, rinsed and chopped
2	tablespoons chopped fresh parsley
2	tablespoons chopped fresh chives *or* scallion greens, plus more for garnish

Paprika for sprinkling

1. Roast garlic as described on page 25.

2. Meanwhile, place potatoes in a large saucepan and cover with cold water. Season with salt and bring to a boil. Cook, covered, over medium heat, until the potatoes are tender, 7 to 9 minutes. Drain well, then place them in a large bowl. Toss gently with vinegar and let cool.

3. When the garlic is cool enough to handle, squeeze the cloves from their skins into a blender or food processor. Add mayonnaise, yogurt and mustard; blend until smooth. Season with salt and pepper.

4. Add the dressing to the potatoes and toss to coat. Finely chop 3 hard-boiled eggs and add to the potatoes, along with celery, pimientos, olives, parsley and chopped chives or scallion greens. Stir gently to mix. Season with salt and pepper. Transfer to a serving dish and sprinkle with paprika. Slice the remaining egg and arrange the slices decoratively on top. Garnish with additional chopped chives or scallions.

Makes about 10 cups, for 10 servings.

195 calories per serving: 6 grams protein, 4 grams fat (0.8 gram saturated fat), 34 grams carbohydrate; 176 mg sodium; 85 mg cholesterol; 2 grams fiber.

Ⓝ NUTRITION BONUS: A low-fat potato salad is a tasty way to boost a meal's complex-carbohydrate count.

For more recipes using roasted garlic, see pages 108 and 125.

Greenskeeping

SELECTION AND STORAGE

Start with the best-looking head of lettuce or bunch of greens you can find. The leaves should be vibrant, crisp and blemish-free; stems or core ends should look freshly cut, not dried out, wilted or discolored.

Remove rubber bands or twist ties. Pull off any bruised or wilted leaves. Place greens in a plastic bag that has been punctured with a few holes and store in the coldest, most humid part of the refrigerator—usually the bottom crisper drawer.

WASHING AND DRYING

A bit of grit will ruin the best of salads. Always wash lettuce leaves and other greens in a large bowl or a sinkful of cold water. Swish the leaves for several seconds, then lift out and put in a colander. Drain the water and begin again, repeating the steps until the water is clear. For many greens, one or two washings is sufficient, but for spinach or greens from your garden, several washings might be required.

Always dry salad greens—either by wrapping in clean kitchen towels or whirling in a salad spinner—because wet greens water down the salad dressing, rapidly diluting its flavor. This is particularly important for salads with low-oil dressings.

THE NEW GREENS ON THE BLOCK

MESCLUN

Not one particular type of lettuce, but a mixture of many baby greens. The beauty of mesclun is that you can buy as little as you like and there is no waste. A quick rinse, a few revolutions in the salad spinner and it's ready to eat.

ARUGULA

Also called rocket, an appropriate name given its peppery, fired-up flavor, which becomes more pronounced in older greens. Spiciness also varies considerably from bunch to bunch.

ESCAROLE

A close relative of the chicory tribe with a similar bitterness but the leaves are broader. The tender interior leaves are best in salads, the tougher outer leaves are lovely sautéed or stirred into soups.

BELGIAN ENDIVE

The tight heads of pearly, furled leaves resemble small torpedoes. Belgian endive is blanched—grown in darkness—to preserve its white color and mildly bitter flavor.

MIZUNA

A mild peppery flavor and pretty feathery leaves are making this Asian green increasingly popular with American consumers.

CHICORY

Also called curly endive, the spiky, curly leaves are dark green at the end and fading to nearly white at the stems. The very dark outer leaves can be tough; use the interior ones for salads. The taste is bitter but pleasant. The heads are often quite large.

RADICCHIO

This "green" is actually red and white. The compact heads of radicchio store well, and the unusual color adds interest to salads. It too is a chicory family member with a pleasant bitterness.

Tuscan Ribollita, page 36

THE TECHNIQUES

11 Skimming the fat from canned broth, and boosting the flavor with aromatic herbs and spices

12 Adding a creamy finish with evaporated skim milk

13 Stirring in reduced-fat sour cream for the illusion of richness

14 Thickening soup with bread

15 Giving soup a satiny smooth texture with rice

16 Pureeing vegetables for a hearty soup base

TECHNIQUES 11-16

SOUPS

GOOD FOR THE HEART AS WELL AS THE SOUL, A HOT bowlful of homemade soup can be the best antidote for a cold raw day. And on a steaming summer night, a cold soup can be most refreshing.

While soups that have a clear broth are generally low in fat, creamy soups do need some creative reworking to bring the fat levels into the healthy range. The first step with all soups is to skim the fat from the broth. Next, look for a way to thicken or enrich cream soup without resorting to high-fat dairy products like cream or egg yolks. Using techniques developed in the EATING WELL Test Kitchen, you can once again enjoy satisfying chowders, rich bisques and other creamy soups, and your broths will have added flavor dimensions.

11 Skim the fat from canned broth, and boost the flavor with aromatic herbs and spices.

Store unopened cans of broth in the refrigerator: the fat will congeal on the surface, enabling you to remove it easily. Then you can build homemade flavor into the broth by infusing it with garlic, herbs and spices.

F FAT SAVINGS: For every 14-ounce can of broth added to a recipe, you will save 3 grams of fat by skimming.

1. Pour chilled broth through a strainer into a saucepan.

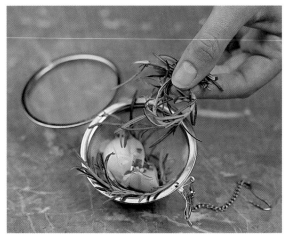

2. Pack aromatic herbs and spices into a tea ball to use for infusing the broth with flavor.

Tortellini in a Rosemary-Scented Broth

2   cloves garlic, unpeeled
2   sprigs fresh rosemary
¼   teaspoon red-pepper flakes
5½ cups Homemade Chicken Broth (*page 34*)
    or defatted reduced-sodium canned chicken broth (three 14-ounce cans)
1   8- *or* 9-ounce package low-fat fresh *or* frozen cheese tortellini
2   tablespoons freshly grated Parmesan cheese (optional)
    Freshly ground black pepper to taste

1. Crush garlic cloves with the flat of a chef's knife (do not peel). Tuck the garlic, rosemary sprigs and red-pepper flakes into a tea ball (or cheesecloth bag) and place it in a large saucepan. Add chicken broth and bring to a boil. Boil, uncovered, until reduced to 4 cups, 15 to 20 minutes, skimming off any froth that rises to the surface. Remove the tea ball.

2. Meanwhile, cook tortellini in a large pot of boiling salted water, following package directions. Drain the tortellini and add to the infused broth. Ladle into bowls and serve with Parmesan, if desired, and a grinding of black pepper.

Makes about 5 cups, for 4 servings.

220 calories per serving: 15 grams protein, 3 grams fat (0.6 gram saturated fat), 32 grams carbohydrate; 1,125 mg sodium; 25 mg cholesterol; 0.5 gram fiber.

N NUTRITION BONUS: Chicken broth *does* make you feel better. One reason is that it is rich in minerals that help restore your fluid balance when you have been feeling out of sorts.

Aromatic Middle Eastern Soup

2   cloves garlic, unpeeled
1   teaspoon whole coriander seeds
1   teaspoon whole cumin seeds
1   teaspoon black peppercorns
⅛   teaspoon red-pepper flakes
¼   teaspoon turmeric
1   cinnamon stick
5½ cups Homemade Chicken Broth (*page 34*)
    or defatted reduced-sodium canned chicken broth (three 14-ounce cans)
1   tablespoon olive oil
1   large *or* 2 medium onions, chopped (1½ cups)
½   cup basmati rice *or* bulgur
1   lemon

1 8-ounce can chickpeas, drained and rinsed
   Freshly ground black pepper to taste
¼ cup slivered fresh mint leaves for garnish

1. Crush garlic cloves with the flat of a chef's knife (do not peel). Crush coriander, cumin and peppercorns with a heavy saucepan. Tuck the garlic, crushed spices, red-pepper flakes and turmeric into a tea ball (or cheesecloth bag) and place it in a large saucepan. Add cinnamon stick to the pan and pour in broth. Bring to a boil. Boil, uncovered, until reduced to 4 cups, 15 to 20 minutes, skimming off any froth.

2. Heat oil in a large heavy pot over medium heat. Add onions and cook, stirring, until softened and very lightly colored, 3 to 5 minutes. Add rice or bulgur and stir for 1 minute.

3. Pour in the reduced broth (including the tea ball and the cinnamon stick) and bring to a simmer. Cover and simmer over low heat until the rice or bulgur is tender, 15 to 20 minutes.

4. Cut 4 slices from the lemon and reserve for garnish. Juice the remaining lemon to flavor the soup. Stir chickpeas into the soup and heat through. Remove the tea ball and cinnamon stick. Season to taste with the lemon juice and black pepper. Ladle into bowls and garnish with lemon slices and mint.

Makes about 5 cups, for 4 servings.

235 calories per serving: 10 grams protein, 5 grams fat (0.7 gram saturated fat), 40 grams carbohydrate; 1,000 mg sodium; 5 mg cholesterol; 5 grams fiber.

Ⓝ NUTRITION BONUS: Served with whole-wheat flatbreads, this soup makes a well-balanced low-fat meal.

TECHNIQUE 12 Add a creamy finish with evaporated skim milk.

Evaporated skim milk, from which about half of the water has been removed, has a consistency similar to light cream.

Ⓕ FAT SAVINGS: By choosing ¾ cup fat-free evaporated skim milk instead of the same quantity of light cream, you save 375 calories and 55 grams of fat. Canned corn chowders have about 20 grams of fat per serving.

Corn Chowder

Red peppers, corn and fresh herbs bring color and texture to this slightly spicy version of a familiar chowder.

1½ teaspoons vegetable oil, preferably canola
  2 large onions, chopped
  1 stalk celery, chopped
  1 red bell pepper, cored, seeded and diced
  3 cloves garlic, minced
  ½ teaspoon ground cumin
3½ cups Homemade Chicken Broth (*page 34*) *or* defatted reduced-sodium canned chicken broth (two 14-ounce cans)
  1 tablespoon chopped fresh thyme *or* 1 teaspoon dried thyme leaves
  1 bay leaf
  2 cups corn kernels, fresh (2 large ears) *or* frozen
  1 large potato, peeled and diced
  2 tablespoons cornstarch
  1 12-ounce can evaporated skim milk
     Salt & freshly ground black pepper to taste
     Pinch of cayenne

1. In a large heavy saucepan, heat oil over medium-low heat. Add onions and cook for 5 minutes, until softened. Add celery, red pepper, garlic and cumin and cook for 2 to 3 minutes. Add chicken broth, thyme and bay leaf and bring to a boil. Reduce heat to low and simmer, uncovered, for 10 minutes. Add corn and potatoes, return to a simmer and cook until all the vegetables are tender, 5 to 10 minutes.

2. Place cornstarch in a small bowl and slowly add evaporated milk, stirring until smooth. Stir the mixture into the vegetables and return to a simmer. Cook, stirring, for 2 minutes, until the chowder has thickened. Discard bay leaf. Season with salt, pepper and cayenne. Serve immediately.

Makes 6 cups, for 6 servings.

150 calories per serving: 8 grams protein, 2 grams fat (0.2 gram saturated fat), 28 grams carbohydrate; 410 mg sodium; 2 mg cholesterol; 3 grams fiber.

Ⓝ NUTRITION BONUS: Corn and potatoes are two ingredients that nudge the complex-carbohydrate content of the diet in the right direction.

13 Use reduced-fat sour cream for the illusion of richness.

Soups don't have to contain lots of cream to be considered creamy. A small quantity of reduced-fat sour cream added to a soup near the end of cooking provides a lush, velvety consistency. Be careful, however, not to let the soup come back to a boil after adding the sour cream.

F FAT SAVINGS: Switching to reduced-fat sour cream has a dramatic effect on the fat count of a recipe. One cup of heavy cream contains nearly 90 grams of fat, a cup of full-fat sour cream has almost 50: the reduced-fat version of sour cream has 16 grams of fat per cup.

Creamy Cremini Mushroom Soup

The pudgy brown mushrooms called cremini are generally firmer and richer-tasting than common white mushrooms.

1½	teaspoons extra-virgin olive oil
1	large onion, chopped
1½	teaspoons chopped fresh thyme *or* ½ teaspoon dried thyme leaves
1	pound cremini mushrooms, sliced
½	cup all-purpose white flour
3½	cups Homemade Chicken Broth (*right*) *or* defatted reduced-sodium canned chicken broth (two 14-ounce cans)
1	cup reduced-fat sour cream
1	cup low-fat milk
	Salt & freshly ground black pepper to taste
	Fresh lemon juice to taste
	Dry sherry to taste (optional)

1. In a Dutch oven or soup pot, heat oil over low heat. Add onions and cook, stirring until soft and translucent, 5 to 7 minutes. Add thyme and cook for 1 minute more. Stir in mushrooms, cover pot and steam until the mushrooms exude their moisture, about 5 minutes.

Homemade Chicken Broth

If you intend to add pieces of chicken to your soup, remove the breast pieces after 20 minutes of cooking. Cut off the meat and return the bones to the pot.

1	large stewing chicken (5-6 pounds) *or* 2 smaller roasting chickens (2½-3 pounds each), quartered
4	large carrots, cut into chunks
1	large onion, quartered
6	cloves garlic, unpeeled
10	black peppercorns

1. Pour 5 quarts water into an 8- to 10-quart pot. Add chicken pieces, heart, neck and gizzard; bring to a boil over high heat. Skim impurities from the surface. Reduce the heat to medium-low and add remaining ingredients. Simmer, covered with the lid slightly ajar, for 1½ hours, skimming as necessary. Strain the broth through a fine sieve set over a bowl. Discard the vegetables and bones.

2. Refrigerate for at least 2 hours. Skim the fat from the surface. (*The broth can be stored, covered, in the refrigerator for up to 2 days or in the freezer for up to 6 months.*)

Makes about 4 quarts.

2. Sprinkle flour over the mushrooms. Increase heat to medium and cook, stirring, for 3 to 4 minutes. Gradually whisk in chicken broth, scraping up any flour that clings to the pan. Simmer, stirring occasionally, until thickened and smooth, 5 to 7 minutes.

3. Combine sour cream and milk; whisk into the mushrooms. Season with salt and pepper. Gently heat until the soup is hot but not boiling. Just before serving, stir in lemon juice and sherry, if using.

Makes about 7½ cups, for 6 servings.

160 calories per serving: 7 grams protein, 6 grams fat (4 grams saturated fat), 19 grams carbohydrate; 380 mg sodium; 16 mg cholesterol; 2 grams fiber.

N NUTRITION BONUS: A serving of full-fat cream of mushroom soup has 275 calories and 24 grams of fat.

Shrimp Bisque

A very simple stock made from shrimp shells, vegetables and white wine adds complexity to the soup's flavor base.

¾   **pound medium, shell-on shrimp**
1   **carrot, peeled and sliced**
1   **stalk celery (with leaves), sliced**
1   **onion, chopped**
½   **cup dry white wine**
½   **teaspoon black peppercorns**
1   **bay leaf**
1   **tablespoon olive oil**
¼   **pound mushrooms, sliced (about 1½ cups)**
½   **green bell pepper, cored, seeded and chopped**
¼   **cup chopped scallions**
2   **tablespoons chopped fresh parsley**
¼   **cup all-purpose white flour**
1½   **cups low-fat milk**

¼   **cup reduced-fat sour cream**
¼   **cup dry sherry**
1   **tablespoon fresh lemon juice**
    Salt & freshly ground white *or* black pepper
    Dash of hot sauce

1. Peel and devein shrimp, reserving the shells. Cut the shrimp into ¾-inch pieces; cover and refrigerate.

2. In a large heavy saucepan, combine the shrimp shells with carrots, celery and about half of the onions. Pour in wine and 3 cups water. Add peppercorns and bay leaf and simmer over low heat for about 30 minutes. Strain through a sieve, pressing on the solids to extract all of the juices; discard the solids. Measure the shrimp stock and add water, if necessary, to make 1½ cups; set aside.

3. In the same saucepan, heat oil over medium heat. Add mushrooms, green peppers, scallions, parsley and the remaining onions. Cook, stirring, until the mushrooms are soft, about 5 minutes.

4. Sprinkle the vegetables with flour and cook, stirring, until the flour starts to turn golden, 2 to 3 minutes. Slowly stir in milk and the reserved shrimp stock. Cook, stirring to loosen any flour sticking to the bottom of the saucepan, until the bisque returns to a simmer and thickens, about 5 minutes.

5. Add the reserved shrimp and cook until they turn opaque in the center, about 2 minutes more. Add sour cream, sherry and lemon juice; stir over low heat until heated through; do not let it come to a boil. Taste and adjust seasonings with salt, pepper and hot sauce.

Makes about 6 cups, for 6 servings.

190 calories per serving: 15 grams protein, 5 grams fat (1.7 grams saturated fat), 14 grams carbohydrate; 480 mg sodium; 94 mg cholesterol; 1 gram fiber.

Ⓝ NUTRITION BONUS: The old-fashioned version of this luxurious bisque contains 275 calories and 21 grams of fat; our healthier version cuts out 85 calories and 16 grams of fat.

Creamy, rich Shrimp Bisque tastes like it was made with full-fat cream.

14 Thicken soup with bread.

While there is nothing new about this technique—it has a decidedly medieval ring to it—adding bread is a nifty trick for the low-fat cook. Cubes or slices cut from a French or Italian-style loaf add no fat to the soup and make it very hearty and satisfying.

F FAT SAVINGS: These main-course soups have well under 10 grams of fat per serving.

Portuguese Açorda

- 2 cloves garlic, unpeeled
- 12 sprigs cilantro
- ¼ teaspoon red-pepper flakes
- 5½ cups Homemade Chicken Broth (*page 34*) *or* defatted reduced-sodium canned chicken broth (three 14-ounce cans)
- ½ pound day-old country-style bread
- 1 tablespoon olive oil

1. Crush garlic cloves with the flat of a chef's knife (do not peel). Separate cilantro leaves from stems and set the leaves aside for garnish. Tuck the garlic, cilantro stems and red-pepper flakes into a tea ball (or cheesecloth bag) and place it in a large saucepan. (*See Technique 11, page 32.*) Pour in chicken broth and bring to a boil. Boil, uncovered, until reduced to 4 cups, 15 to 20 minutes, skimming off any froth.
2. Meanwhile, cut bread into 1-inch cubes. (You will have about 4 cups.) Heat oil in a large heavy pot over medium heat. Add the cubed bread and cook, stirring, until it is lightly toasted, 3 to 5 minutes.
3. Remove the tea ball from the reduced broth. Pour the broth over the bread. Remove from the heat, cover and let stand for 1 minute to allow the bread to soften.
4. Cut the reserved cilantro leaves into slivers.
5. With a wooden spoon, mash the bread slightly so

that it thickens the soup. Ladle into bowls, sprinkle cilantro over the top and serve immediately.

Makes about 5 cups, for 4 servings.

210 calories per serving: 10 grams protein, 3 grams fat (0.5 gram saturated fat), 34 grams carbohydrate; 1,060 mg sodium; 0 mg cholesterol; 2 grams fiber.

Variation: To make this soup a little more substantial, you can slip a poached egg into each bowl, which adds 5 grams of fat per serving.

N NUTRITION BONUS: Keep canned chicken broth in a cool pantry or refrigerator so the fat will congeal and be easy to remove.

Tuscan Ribollita

A hearty soup from Tuscany, ribollita is delicious with a nice Chianti.

- 1 cup dried cannellini beans, soaked overnight in water, then drained
- 1 tablespoon extra-virgin olive oil, plus additional oil for drizzling over soup
- 1 small red onion, chopped
- 2 stalks celery, chopped
- 1 large carrot, chopped
- 6 cloves garlic, minced
- ¼ cup chopped fresh parsley
- 1 28-ounce can plum tomatoes, juice reserved, chopped
- 1 tablespoon chopped fresh thyme *or* 1 teaspoon dried thyme leaves Salt & freshly ground black pepper to taste
- 1 large potato, peeled and diced
- 1 pound zucchini, sliced (3 small zucchini)
- 1 pound cabbage *or* winter kale
- ½ pound green beans, trimmed and cut into 1-inch segments
- 4 cups Homemade Chicken Broth (*page 34*) *or* defatted reduced-sodium canned chicken broth
- 1 pound country-style bread, thinly sliced

1. Place soaked beans in a large saucepan and add water to cover by 3 inches. Bring to a boil, skim any foam and reduce the heat to a bare simmer. Cook, partially covered, until tender, about 1 hour. Drain, reserving beans and bean-cooking liquid separately.

2. Heat oil in a large soup pot over low heat; add onions, celery, carrots, garlic and parsley and gently cook until the onions are soft, about 10 minutes. Add tomatoes and thyme. Season with salt and pepper. Bring to a simmer and cook for 5 minutes.

3. Meanwhile, in a food processor, puree about ½ of the cooked cannellini beans together with the reserved bean-cooking liquid. Add the puree to the pot along with potatoes, zucchini, cabbage or kale, green beans and the reserved whole beans. Add chicken broth and 3 cups water. Cook, uncovered, until the vegetables are tender, 30 to 40 minutes. Taste and adjust seasonings. (*The* ribollita *can be prepared ahead to this point and stored, covered, in the refrigerator for 2 days. Reheat before continuing.*)

4. In a large pot (6- to 8-quart capacity), place a layer of bread slices. Add a few ladlefuls of soup, then another layer of bread. Continue in this manner until the pot is full, finishing with soup. To serve, ladle into bowls and drizzle a teaspoon of fine olive oil over the top of each.

Makes about 4 quarts, for 12 servings.

185 calories per serving: 8 grams protein, 3 grams fat (0.2 gram saturated fat), 34 grams carbohydrate; 280 mg sodium; 0 mg cholesterol; 5 grams fiber.

Ⓝ NUTRITION BONUS: This soup is rich in cancer-fighting chemicals from the cabbage, garlic, beans and tomatoes.

TECHNIQUE **15** Use rice for a satiny smooth soup.

Take advantage of the starchy nature of white rice to make a soup that is glossy, smooth and rich-tasting. Cook a small quantity of rice along with broth until the grains are very soft and tender, then puree with the broth until very smooth.

Ⓕ FAT SAVINGS: The original inspiration for the following recipe was a curry soup thickened with coconut milk; by omitting the coconut milk, we cut out almost 50 grams of fat, or 12 grams of fat per serving.

Chicken Curry Soup

1 tablespoon vegetable oil, preferably canola
1 large onion, chopped
4-5 cloves garlic, crushed
3 slices fresh ginger, peeled and lightly crushed
3 tablespoons curry powder, preferably Madras
½ cup raw white rice
2 bone-in chicken breasts (about 1 pound), skinned and trimmed of fat (*see Technique 27, page 60*)
4 cups Homemade Chicken Broth (*page 34*) *or* defatted reduced-sodium canned chicken broth
1 vine-ripened tomato, seeded and chopped
Salt & freshly ground black pepper to taste
Fresh lemon juice to taste
Finely chopped fresh cilantro *or* chives for garnish

1. In a Dutch oven or soup pot, heat oil over low heat. Add onions, garlic and ginger; stirring occasionally to prevent browning, cook until the onions are soft and translucent, 5 to 7 minutes. Add curry powder and rice; cook for 5 minutes longer.

2. Add chicken breasts, chicken broth and 3 cups water. Bring to a boil, then lower heat to medium. Stirring frequently, simmer just until the chicken breasts are no longer pink in the center, about 30 minutes. Transfer chicken to a plate to cool.

3. In a food processor, puree soup in batches until smooth, adding water as needed for a creamy texture. Return soup to cleaned pot and heat again to a simmer.

4. Shred the chicken meat into small strips and add to the soup along with tomatoes; cook 3 minutes more. Season with salt and pepper. Just before serving, stir in lemon juice. Ladle into bowls and garnish with cilantro or chives.

Makes about 8 cups, for 6 servings.

200 calories per serving: 21 grams protein, 4 grams fat (0.5 gram saturated fat), 19 grams carbohydrate; 425 mg sodium; 43 mg cholesterol; 2 grams fiber.

Ⓝ NUTRITION BONUS: You will find that this creamy smooth soup makes a satisfying low-fat *and* low-calorie weeknight supper.

Cool Beet Soup with a Chile-Cilantro Swirl brightens a summer meal.

Cool Beet Soup with a Chile-Cilantro Swirl

1   pound (4 medium) closely trimmed beets, scrubbed but not peeled, sliced
1   medium leek, split, washed and sliced
¼   cup coarsely chopped peeled fresh ginger
2   plum tomatoes (½ pound), sliced
1   teaspoon coarse kosher salt, plus more to taste
1   quart cranberry juice
1   cup tightly packed sliced cilantro
1   mild chile, such as Anaheim *or* poblano, seeded and sliced
1   small hot chile, such as jalapeño *or* serrano, seeded and sliced
2   scallions, trimmed and sliced
½   cup low-fat plain yogurt
1   tablespoon raspberry vinegar *or* other fruit vinegar

1. In a pot, combine beets, leeks, ginger, tomatoes and 1 teaspoon salt. Pour in cranberry juice and 2 cups water; bring to a boil. Lower the heat to medium-low and simmer, covered, until the beets are very soft, about 1 hour.

2. Transfer the mixture in two or three batches to a blender or food processor and blend to a smooth consistency. Press through a medium-mesh sieve into a large bowl. Taste and add salt if necessary. Let cool, then cover and chill.

3. In a blender or food processor, puree cilantro, mild and hot chiles, scallions, yogurt, vinegar and salt to taste until smooth.

4. Ladle the chilled soup into wide shallow bowls. Drizzle swirls of the chile-cilantro mixture on the soup just before serving.

Makes about 8 cups, for 8 servings.

120 calories per serving: 2 grams protein, 1 gram fat (0.1 gram saturated fat), 28 grams carbohydrate; 335 mg sodium; 1 mg cholesterol; 2 grams fiber.

Ⓝ NUTRITION BONUS: Although beets are not known for being rich in one particular nutrient, they contain a range of vitamins and trace minerals.

TECHNIQUE

16 Puree vegetables for a substantial soup base.

Slow-cooking vegetables until they are soft makes them easy to puree in a food processor or blender. This puree then becomes the satiny-smooth base for very low-fat soups.

Ⓕ FAT SAVINGS: Because the soup base is so thick and rich, the only added fat comes from a little oil in which to cook the vegetables and a sour cream or yogurt swirl added at the end. The result is a soup with no more than 5 grams of fat per serving.

West Indian Squash Soup

This rustic vegetable soup makes a great starter for a Creole meal.

- 1 tablespoon olive oil
- 1 onion, chopped
- 2 stalks celery, chopped
- 1 carrot, chopped
- 3 cloves garlic, finely chopped
- ½ Scotch bonnet chile (*or* other very hot fresh chile), seeded and finely chopped
- 5½ cups Homemade Chicken Broth (*page 34*) *or* defatted reduced-sodium canned chicken broth (three 14-ounce cans)
- 1½ pounds butternut squash, peeled, seeded and cut into 1-inch pieces (4 cups)
- ¼ cup finely chopped fresh parsley
- 2 bay leaves
- 2 sprigs fresh thyme
- 1 tablespoon brown sugar, plus more to taste
- ½ cup reduced-fat sour cream, plus 3 tablespoons for garnish
  Salt & freshly ground black pepper to taste
  Chopped chives for garnish
  Cayenne for garnish

1. Heat oil in a Dutch oven or soup pot over medium heat. Add onions, celery and carrots; cook until soft but not brown, 3 to 4 minutes. Add garlic and chiles and cook for 1 minute more. Stir in broth, squash, parsley, bay leaves, thyme and brown sugar. Bring to a boil, then reduce heat to medium-low and simmer until the vegetables are very soft, 25 to 30 minutes. Discard the bay leaves and thyme sprigs.

2. Puree the soup in a blender or food processor, in batches if necessary, until very smooth. Add a little water if the soup is too thick. (*The soup can be prepared ahead to this point and stored, covered, in the refrigerator for up to 2 days.*)

3. Return the soup to the pot and stir in ½ cup sour cream; heat gently without boiling. Adjust seasonings, adding brown sugar, salt and pepper.

4. To serve, ladle the soup into bowls. Garnish each portion with a ½ tablespoon dollop of sour cream, some chives and a dusting of cayenne. Serve at once.

Makes about 7 cups, for 6 servings.

140 calories per serving: 5 grams protein, 5 grams fat (2.7 grams saturated fat), 20 grams carbohydrate; 510 mg sodium; 9 mg cholesterol; 1 gram fiber.

Ⓝ NUTRITION BONUS: This soup is rich in beta carotene and other carotenoids.

Leek & Potato Soup

- 1½ teaspoons olive oil
- 3 leeks, trimmed, washed and thinly sliced (3 cups)
- 2 cloves garlic, minced
- 1½ teaspoons chopped fresh thyme *or* ½ teaspoon dried thyme leaves
- 5½ cups Homemade Chicken Broth (*page 34*) *or* defatted reduced-sodium canned chicken broth (three 14-ounce cans)
- 1¼ pounds all-purpose potatoes (about 3 medium), peeled and cut into small chunks
- ½ cup reduced-fat sour cream
  Salt & freshly ground black pepper to taste

1. In a Dutch oven or soup pot, heat oil over low heat. Add leeks and cook, stirring, until softened, about 10 minutes. Add garlic and thyme; cook for 2 minutes more. Pour in chicken broth, increase heat to medium and bring to a boil. Reduce heat to low and simmer, uncovered, for 10 minutes.

2. Pour the soup through a strainer set over a large bowl. Puree the leeks in a food processor or blender until smooth, adding some of the broth if necessary. Return the puree and broth to the saucepan. Add potatoes and simmer, covered, until potatoes are soft, 10 to 15 minutes. Remove from the heat and mash potatoes thoroughly with a potato masher.

3. Stir in sour cream, salt and pepper. Return to low heat and heat until hot, but not boiling. Serve hot or chilled.

Makes about 6 cups, for 6 servings.

170 calories per serving: 6 grams protein, 3 grams fat (1.9 grams saturated fat), 30 grams carbohydrate; 590 mg sodium; 7 mg cholesterol; 2 grams fiber.

Ⓝ NUTRITION BONUS: Reduced-fat sour cream is often thickened with carrageenan, which is derived from Irish moss, a seaweed.

Lasagne al forno, page 49

THE TECHNIQUES

17 Adding bulgur to lower the fat in
   meatballs

18 Boosting flavor with wine and herbs for
   carbonara

19 Choosing the right ricotta

20 Adding breadcrumbs to pesto

21 Roasting eggplant for a fat-free sauce

22 Replacing meat with mushrooms

23 Prebaking pizza crusts for crispness

24 Roasting red peppers for a low-fat sauce

25 Spritzing pizza with olive oil

26 Using a bean puree for a pizza sauce

TECHNIQUES
17-26
PASTA & PIZZA

LASAGNE, SPAGHETTI AND
MEATBALLS, MANICOTTI
AND PIZZA ARE SUCH
fixtures on the American menu
that they hardly seem Italian
anymore. Originally, pastas
and pizzas were built on a foundation
of grains and vegetables. Americanization
of these dishes has transformed them from
the epitome of healthy food to one of the worst of-
fenders in our diet: common to all are too-gener-
ous amounts of oil and mozzarella, ground meat
and sausage—heavy doses of fat and saturated fat.

The good news from the EATING WELL Test
Kitchen is that creamy fillings and flavorful sauces
need not be lost in makeovers of these favorites.
The techniques presented here are varied, but the
overall direction is to return the recipes to their
healthful roots.

17 For low-fat meatballs, add bulgur and bake, don't fry.

High-fat meatballs require adjustments in ingredients and cooking methods to bring them within healthy-eating guidelines.

1. Stretch ground beef and/or sausage with bulgur: for every half pound of ground meat, add ⅔ cup soaked bulgur (from ⅓ cup dry bulgur). This step alone will cut the fat in half.

2. Don't add more fat to the recipe by frying the meatballs; instead bake them on a rack set over a pan: the fat they exude will drip into the pan.

3. Once they are cooked through, blot the meatballs on paper towels to remove more fat.

F FAT SAVINGS: Traditional spaghetti-and-meatball recipes contain up to 55 grams of fat per serving. You save almost 75% of the fat.

? WHAT IS BULGUR?

Wheat kernels that are cooked, dried and cracked into coarse fragments are called bulgur. The tender, chewy texture of bulgur makes it a good alternative to rice, and, at slightly less than one gram of fat per cup, it will reduce the fat substantially when substituted for part of the meat in meatballs and in tomato-and-meat sauces. In addition, bulgur increases the complex carbohydrate and fiber content of a recipe. Look for bulgur in health- or natural-food stores or in the grains section of well-stocked supermarkets.

Old-Fashioned Spaghetti & Meatballs

If you opt for a commercial sauce for this recipe, select one that contains 3 grams of fat or less per ½-cup serving.

- ⅓ cup bulgur
- ¼ pound extra-lean ground beef
- ¼ pound hot Italian sausage (1 link), sausage meat removed from casing
- 1 onion, very finely chopped
- 2 large egg whites, lightly beaten with a fork
- 3 cloves garlic, very finely chopped
- 1 teaspoon dried oregano
- ½ teaspoon salt
- ½ teaspoon freshly ground black pepper
- 1 cup fresh breadcrumbs, preferably whole-wheat
- 4 cups Tomato Sauce (*recipe follows*) *or* commercial tomato sauce
- ½ cup slivered fresh basil leaves
- 1 pound spaghetti
- ½ cup freshly grated Parmesan *or* Romano cheese (1 ounce)

1. In a small bowl, combine bulgur and ½ cup hot water. Let stand until the bulgur has soaked up the liquid and has softened, about 30 minutes.
2. Preheat oven to 350°F. Lightly oil a rack or coat it with nonstick cooking spray, and place it over a baking sheet lined with aluminum foil. Set aside.
3. In a mixing bowl, combine ground beef, sausage,

onions, egg whites, garlic, oregano, salt, pepper and breadcrumbs and the soaked bulgur. Mix well with your hands or a wooden spoon. Form the mixture into 24 meatballs, each about 1 inch in diameter. Place the meatballs on the rack and bake for 15 minutes. Blot the meatballs well with paper towels.

4. In a Dutch oven, bring tomato sauce to a simmer. Add the meatballs and simmer, covered, for 20 minutes. Stir in basil. Taste and adjust seasonings.

5. Meanwhile, in a large pot of boiling salted water, cook spaghetti until al dente, 8 to 10 minutes. Drain and transfer to a serving bowl. Top with sauce and meatballs and serve with grated cheese.

Makes 6 servings.

595 calories per serving: 27 grams protein, 14 grams fat (4.8 grams saturated fat), 93 grams carbohydrate; 530 mg sodium; 35 mg cholesterol, 8 grams fiber.

NUTRITION BONUS: Extending the meat with bulgur boosts the fiber substantially and lowers fat without affecting the taste.

Tomato Sauce

1 tablespoon olive oil
1 onion, finely chopped
6 cloves garlic, finely chopped
7 pounds vine-ripened tomatoes, cut in chunks, *or* four 28-ounce cans plum (Italian-style) tomatoes, drained and coarsely chopped
2 tablespoons tomato paste
2 teaspoons dried oregano
   Salt & freshly ground black pepper to taste

1. In a large heavy pan or Dutch oven, heat oil over medium-low heat. Add onions and cook, stirring often, until softened, about 5 minutes. Add garlic and cook for 30 to 60 seconds. Add tomatoes, tomato paste and oregano; bring to a boil. Simmer, uncovered, over low heat, stirring frequently, until the tomatoes cook down to a thick mass, about 45 minutes.

2. Puree the tomatoes by working them through the medium disc of a food mill or through a coarse sieve into a large saucepan. (Do not use a food processor or blender for this; it grinds up the tomato seeds and makes the sauce bitter.) If the sauce seems too thin, return it to medium-low heat and cook, stirring constantly, until it has the desired consistency. Taste and adjust seasonings with salt and pepper.

Makes about 5 cups.

90 calories per ½ cup: 3 grams protein, 3 grams fat (0.3 gram saturated fat), 18 grams carbohydrate; 30 mg sodium; 0 mg cholesterol; 5 grams fiber.

NUTRITION BONUS: Canned tomato products are rich in lycopene and other cancer-fighting carotenoids.

Spaghetti & Meatballs: An Italian-American tradition enters a new era.

18 Boost flavor with wine and herbs in a makeover of a classic.

Drastic fat reductions often leave a recipe flavorless. Such was the case with *spaghetti alla carbonara.* After cutting out the cream and butter and reducing the number of egg yolks in this Italian peasant dish, the recipe was healthful but bland. The Test Kitchen solved the problem by expanding the seasonings to include a little white wine for acidity and some fresh parsley to bring out the intensity of the primary ingredients.

FAT SAVINGS: At 10 grams of fat per serving, the reconfigured carbonara has one-third the fat of the original version.

Spaghetti alla carbonara

- 1 pound spaghetti
- 2 teaspoons olive oil
- 4 cloves garlic, crushed
- 3 ounces thinly sliced prosciutto, trimmed of fat and diced
- ¼ cup dry white wine
- 1 large egg
- 2 large egg whites
- ⅔ cup freshly grated Parmesan cheese (1½ ounces)
- ¼ cup finely chopped fresh parsley, preferably Italian flat-leaf
  Freshly ground black pepper to taste

1. In a large pot of boiling salted water, cook spaghetti until al dente, 8 to 11 minutes.
2. Meanwhile, in a small nonstick skillet, heat oil over medium heat. Add garlic cloves and cook until they turn golden, 2 to 3 minutes. Remove the garlic and discard. Add prosciutto to the skillet and cook until crisp, 1 to 2 minutes. Pour in wine and simmer 1 minute. Remove from the heat. In a small bowl, whisk egg, egg whites, cheese and parsley. Season with a generous grinding of pepper.
3. Drain the spaghetti and return it to the pot. Add the egg mixture and the cooked prosciutto to the spaghetti. Working quickly with the pot over low heat, toss the pasta until the eggs are creamy, 30 to 40 seconds; do not overcook. Add a generous amount of pepper, toss quickly and serve.

Makes 6 servings.

410 calories per serving: 19 grams protein, 10 grams fat (2.7 grams saturated fat), 58 grams carbohydrate; 475 mg sodium; 44 mg cholesterol; 0.1 gram fiber.

NUTRITION BONUS: Prosciutto, a cured Italian ham, is the perfect stand-in for bacon; it's lower in fat and the flavor is just as wonderful.

Spaghetti alla carbonara is a great last-minute main course.

TECHNIQUE

19 Choose the right ricotta and extend it with breadcrumbs to cut fat in ricotta fillings.

Switching to reduced-fat dairy products is an obvious way to cut fat. But with so many choices, it is hard to know which one to choose. Ricotta comes in fat-free, low-fat, part-skim and whole-milk variations. While the fat numbers on the fat-free and low-fat versions are impressively low, the cheese can be unpleasantly grainy and dry in some dishes. In the EATING WELL Test Kitchen, we have found that 1 cup part-skim ricotta extended with ⅓ cup fine dry breadcrumbs produces a cheesy, rich filling.

F FAT SAVINGS: Switching from full-fat to part-skim ricotta and extending it with breadcrumbs will cut the fat of most filled pastas in half.

Manicotti

This version of manicotti uses crepes—called crespelle *in Italian—to enclose the rich ricotta filling. They are easier to fill than tubular pasta.*

CRESPELLE
- 5 large egg whites
- ½ teaspoon salt
- ½ cup whole-wheat flour
- ½ cup all-purpose white flour

FILLING & SAUCE
- 2 large eggs
- 2 cups part-skim ricotta cheese (20 ounces)
- ⅔ cup fine dry breadcrumbs
- ½ cup chopped fresh parsley, preferably Italian flat-leaf
- ½ teaspoon salt
- ½ cup slivered fresh basil leaves

- 5 cups Tomato Sauce (*page 43*) *or* commercial tomato sauce
- ¼ cup freshly grated Parmesan cheese

TO MAKE CRESPELLE:
1. In a mixing bowl, whisk egg whites until frothy. Add 1⅓ cups water and salt; whisk until blended. Gradually whisk in whole-wheat and all-purpose flours until the batter is smooth. If lumps remain, pour the batter through a strainer set over a bowl.
2. Heat a 6-inch nonstick skillet or seasoned crepe pan over medium-high heat until a drop of water dances on the surface. If the pan is not nonstick, rub it with a paper towel dipped in a little oil before cooking each crepe. Ladle 2 tablespoons batter into the pan and tilt to coat the bottom evenly. (The *crespella* should be thin; if the batter is too thick, stir in 1 to 2 tablespoons more water.) Cook until the underside is light golden, 15 to 30 seconds. Turn over and cook until the second side is golden, about 15 seconds longer. Slide the *crespella* onto a plate. Repeat with the remaining batter, stacking the *crespelle* as they are cooked. (You should have at least 18 *crespelle*.) Cover them loosely with plastic wrap and set aside.

TO MAKE FILLING & ASSEMBLE MANICOTTI:
1. Preheat oven to 350°F. In a mixing bowl, whisk eggs until frothy. Add ricotta, breadcrumbs, parsley and salt and mix well.
2. Stir basil into tomato sauce. Spread about 2 tablespoons of the tomato sauce in each of two 9-by-13-inch or similar large shallow baking dishes. Spread 2 tablespoons of filling down the center of each *crespella*; roll up and arrange in a row in the baking dishes. Spoon the rest of the tomato sauce over the filled *crespelle*.
3. Bake the manicotti for 20 to 25 minutes, or until the sauce is bubbling. Sprinkle with Parmesan and serve.

Makes 18 manicotti, for 6 servings.

435 calories per serving: 25 grams protein, 14 grams fat (6 grams saturated fat), 58 grams carbohydrate; 710 mg sodium; 98 mg cholesterol; 10 grams fiber.

N NUTRITION BONUS: A serving of our manicotti contains about 350 milligrams of calcium. The tomato sauce and whole-wheat flour boost the fiber to 10 grams.

Stuffed Shells

An easy family favorite.

24 jumbo pasta shells (8 ounces)
1½ teaspoons olive oil
2 onions, finely chopped
2 10-ounce packages frozen chopped spinach, thawed and squeezed dry
2 cups part-skim ricotta cheese (20 ounces)
⅔ cup fine dry breadcrumbs
½ cup freshly grated Parmesan cheese
1 large egg white, lightly beaten with a fork
¼ teaspoon freshly grated nutmeg
 Salt & freshly ground black pepper to taste
3 cups Tomato Sauce (*page 43*) *or* commercial tomato sauce

1. Preheat oven to 375°F. In a large pot of boiling salted water, cook shells, stirring often, until al dente, about 15 minutes. Drain and rinse under cold water. Set aside.

2. In a large nonstick skillet, heat oil over medium-high heat. Add onions and sauté until softened, about 3 minutes. Add spinach and toss to mix well. Set aside.

3. In a bowl, combine ricotta, breadcrumbs, ¼ cup of the Parmesan, egg white and nutmeg; mix well. Add the reserved spinach and season with salt and pepper.

4. Stuff each of the reserved shells with a generous 2 tablespoons of the ricotta mixture. Spread 1 cup tomato sauce in the bottom of a 9-by-13-inch baking dish. Arrange the stuffed shells in a single layer. Top with the remaining 2 cups of sauce and sprinkle with the remaining ¼ cup Parmesan. Bake for 30 minutes, or until the top is golden and the shells are heated through. (If the top browns too quickly, tent loosely with aluminum foil.) Let cool for 10 minutes before serving.

Makes 24 stuffed shells, for 8 servings.

365 calories per serving: 21 grams protein, 11 grams fat (5 grams saturated fat), 50 grams carbohydrate; 335 mg sodium; 51 mg cholesterol; 7 grams fiber.

Ⓝ NUTRITION BONUS: Adding frozen spinach to filling is a great way to add valuable folic acid and carotenoids, while at the same time, the spinach extends the filling and lowers the fat in a serving.

TECHNIQUE 20 — Breadcrumbs add body but not fat to pesto.

Oil *and* nuts make pesto a concentrated source of fat and calories. Extending the pesto with a little stock diluted both flavor and consistency. By adding fresh breadcrumbs, we were able to get away with using less oil. The pesto still coats the pasta nicely and its herbal flavor remains intense and vibrant—whether made with basil or parsley.

Ⓕ FAT SAVINGS: Adding fresh breadcrumbs to pesto cuts the fat by about one-third.

Basil Pesto

Pesto means "pounded" in Italian. Great on pasta; also dab on pizza, add to ricotta fillings or use as a dip.

2 slices white bread, crusts trimmed
1 cup loosely packed fresh basil leaves
3 tablespoons pine nuts
1 clove garlic
½ teaspoon salt, plus more to taste
1 tablespoon freshly grated Parmesan cheese
2 tablespoons olive oil, preferably extra-virgin

1. Tear bread into large pieces and pulse in a food processor to fine crumbs. Add basil, pine nuts, garlic and salt and pulse until finely chopped, scraping down the sides of the bowl as needed; continuing processing until a fairly smooth paste forms.

2. Transfer the pesto to a small bowl. Stir in Parmesan, followed by oil. Season with additional salt as desired. (*The pesto can be stored, covered, in the refrigerator for 3 days or for up to 2 months in the freezer.*)

Makes ½ cup, enough for 12 ounces of fresh pasta.

50 calories per tablespoon: 1 gram protein, 6 grams fat (1 gram saturated fat), 4 grams carbohydrate; 180 mg sodium; 1 mg cholesterol; 1 gram fiber.

Bowties with Parsley-Walnut Pesto

2 tablespoons walnuts
2 slices white bread, crusts trimmed
1 cup packed fresh parsley leaves
1 clove garlic, peeled and chopped
2 tablespoons nonfat plain yogurt
2 tablespoons walnut oil *or* extra-virgin olive oil
 Salt & freshly ground black pepper to taste
12 ounces bowtie pasta
2 tablespoons grated Parmesan cheese

1. In a small skillet, toast walnuts over medium heat until fragrant and beginning to brown, 3 to 4 minutes. Transfer to a plate and set aside.

2. Tear bread into large pieces and pulse in a food processor to fine crumbs. Add parsley, garlic and the toasted walnuts and pulse until finely chopped, scraping down the sides of the bowl as needed. Add yogurt and oil; process until smooth. Season with salt and pepper.

3. In a large saucepan of boiling salted water, cook pasta until al dente, 8 to 10 minutes. Drain in a colander and place in a warm large shallow bowl. Toss with pesto until well coated. Sprinkle with Parmesan and serve.

Makes 4 servings.

455 calories per serving: 15 grams protein, 12 grams fat (2 grams saturated fat), 71 grams carbohydrate; 140 mg sodium; 3 mg cholesterol; 1 gram fiber.

 NUTRITION BONUS: Parsley is more than just a garnish—it's a rich source of carotenoids and vitamin C.

Spinach Fettuccine with Pesto

This traditional pasta dish from Italy's Liguria region includes potatoes and green beans with the fresh spinach noodles.

½ pound potatoes (2 small *or* 1 medium), peeled and cut into ¾-inch pieces
¼ pound fresh green beans, trimmed and cut into 1-inch lengths
¾ pound fresh *or* dried spinach fettuccine
⅓ cup Basil Pesto (*page 46*)
¼ cup freshly grated Parmesan cheese

1. In a large pot, bring 4 quarts lightly salted water to a boil. Add potatoes and cook for 3 minutes. Add green beans and pasta and cook until the pasta is al dente, about 1 to 4 minutes for fresh fettuccine or 6 to 8 minutes for dried.

2. Reserving about ½ cup of the cooking water, drain the pasta, green beans and potatoes in a colander and place in a warm large shallow bowl. Add the pesto and the reserved hot cooking water to the bowl and toss well. Sprinkle with Parmesan and serve.

Makes 4 servings.

415 calories per serving: 18 grams protein, 13 grams fat (3.5 grams saturated fat), 64 grams carbohydrate; 390 mg sodium; 80 mg cholesterol; 2 grams fiber.

NUTRITION BONUS: The majority of fat-calories in this dish come from heart-healthy olive oil.

A heady basil-and-garlic mix infuses Spinach Fettuccine with Pesto.

21 Roast eggplant for a fat-free sauce.

When thoroughly cooked, eggplant readily breaks down to a creamy puree that coats pasta quite nicely. The easiest way that we know of to cook the eggplant is to cut it in half lengthwise, set it cut-side down on a baking sheet and broil it until the skin is black. At this point the flesh is soft enough to be scooped out with a spoon.

F FAT SAVINGS: Creamy dressings based on oil, mayonnaise or sour cream will add anywhere from 10 to 20 grams of fat to a serving of an otherwise healthy pasta salad. Roasted eggplant adds creaminess and flavor but not fat.

Soba Noodles Tossed with Roasted Eggplant

Soba noodles add lovely nutty flavor to the dish, but if you cannot find them use linguine.

1	eggplant (1 pound)
2	tablespoons sesame seeds
½	pound soba (Japanese buckwheat) noodles
1	teaspoon plus 1 tablespoon peanut oil
2	cloves garlic, crushed and peeled
½	teaspoon salt
3½	tablespoons rice vinegar
2	tablespoons reduced-sodium soy sauce
2	tablespoons minced fresh ginger
2	tablespoons brown sugar
1½	teaspoons Chinese chile paste
3	cups grated carrots (about 5 carrots)
½	cup chopped fresh cilantro
1	cup diced cucumber

1. Preheat broiler. Cut eggplant in half lengthwise. Place the halves cut-side down on a baking sheet. Broil about 4 inches from the heat until the skin is blackened and the flesh is very soft, 10 to 15 minutes. Set aside to cool.

2. Meanwhile, in a small skillet, stir sesame seeds over medium-low heat until toasted and fragrant, about 2 minutes. Transfer to a small dish to cool.

3. In a large saucepan of boiling salted water, cook noodles until al dente, about 3 minutes. Drain in a colander and rinse under cold water until cool. Press to remove excess water, transfer to a large bowl and toss with 1 teaspoon of the oil to keep them from sticking.

4. With a chef's knife, mash garlic and salt into a paste. Transfer to a small bowl and add vinegar, soy sauce, ginger, brown sugar, chile paste and the remaining 1 tablespoon oil. Whisk until blended and set aside.

5. Peel the skin from the cooled eggplant and discard. Chop the eggplant flesh to a coarse puree. Add it to the noodles, along with carrots, cilantro and the reserved sesame seeds. Add the reserved dressing and toss until well

Soba Noodles Tossed with Roasted Eggplant is a complete meal.

combined. (*The salad can be made ahead and stored, covered, in the refrigerator for up to 1 day. Bring to room temperature before serving.*) Garnish with diced cucumber and serve.

Makes about 8 cups, for 4 servings.

370 calories per serving: 13 grams protein, 8 grams fat (0.4 gram saturated fat), 66 grams carbohydrate; 675 mg sodium; 0 mg cholesterol; 5 grams fiber.

Ⓝ NUTRITION BONUS: Eggplant is a good source of fiber, potassium and trace minerals.

22 Replace meat with mushrooms in tomato sauce.

TECHNIQUE

When making a tomato sauce with meat, first consider whether the meat is really necessary. By omitting 1 pound of lean ground beef from a batch, you will eliminate more than 90 grams of fat. When stirred into a sauce, mushrooms add a depth of flavor and a chewy texture that is just as satisfying as meat.

Ⓕ FAT SAVINGS: Switching to mushrooms from meat will cut about 12 grams of fat from a lasagne serving.

Lasagne al forno

In addition to a lightened tomato sauce, the béchamel sauce for this creamy lasagne is made using low-fat milk and olive oil, not full-fat milk and butter.

1½ tablespoons olive oil
 1 onion, finely chopped
 1 carrot, finely chopped
 1 celery stalk, finely chopped
 ¾ pound mushrooms, chopped (4 cups)
 2 cloves garlic, finely chopped
 ½ cup dry white wine
 1 28-ounce can tomatoes, chopped
 2 sun-dried tomatoes (*not* packed in oil), very finely chopped (2 tablespoons)

 1 teaspoon dried thyme leaves
   Salt & freshly ground black pepper to taste
 ⅓ cup all-purpose white flour
 3 cups low-fat milk
 ¼ teaspoon freshly grated nutmeg
 ½ pound no-boil lasagna noodles, preferably spinach noodles
 8 cups spinach leaves, washed and dried
 1 cup freshly grated Parmesan cheese

1. Heat ½ tablespoon of the oil in a Dutch oven over medium heat. Add onions, carrots and celery and cook, stirring, until the onions have softened, about 5 minutes. Add mushrooms and garlic, and continue to cook until the mushrooms release their liquid, 2 to 3 minutes. Add wine and cook until most of the liquid has evaporated, about 5 minutes.

2. Stir in chopped tomatoes and their liquid, sun-dried tomatoes and thyme; bring to a simmer. Reduce heat to low and simmer, stirring often, until the sauce is thick, about 1 hour. Season with salt and pepper.

3. Heat the remaining 1 tablespoon oil in a heavy saucepan over low heat. Add flour and cook, whisking constantly, until the flour starts to turn a light nutty brown, about 3 minutes. Remove from heat and gradually whisk in milk. Return the pan to medium heat and cook, whisking constantly, until the sauce bubbles and thickens. Season with nutmeg and salt to taste. Remove from heat and set aside.

4. Preheat oven to 375°F. Lightly oil an 8-by-11½-inch baking dish or coat it with nonstick cooking spray. Set aside.

5. To assemble the lasagne, spread ½ cup of the mushroom sauce in the bottom of the prepared pan, arrange a layer of noodles over the sauce and spread with another ½ cup of the mushroom sauce. Arrange a single layer of the spinach leaves over the sauce and drizzle them with ⅓ cup of the béchamel sauce. Sprinkle 2 tablespoons Parmesan over the spinach and top with another layer of noodles. Repeat this layering five more times. Spread the remaining béchamel sauce over the top layer of noodles, covering completely.

6. Cover the lasagne loosely with aluminum foil and bake in the upper part of the oven for 30 minutes. Uncover, sprinkle with the remaining Parmesan, and bake until golden, about 20 minutes longer. Let rest for 10 minutes before serving.

Makes 6 servings.

480 calories per serving: 25 grams protein, 11 grams fat (3.2 grams saturated fat), 68 grams carbohydrate; 553 mg sodium; 80 mg cholesterol; 5 grams fiber.

NUTRITION BONUS: Perhaps even more important than the reduction in total fat is the elimination of more than two-thirds of the saturated fat in this recipe.

Penne with Cremini-Tomato Ragù

Cremini retain their shape and texture when cooked, making them good candidates for a hearty, stewy sauce that suits polenta as well as pasta.

1½ pounds cremini mushrooms, trimmed and cleaned
2 tablespoons olive oil
1 large onion, chopped
2-3 teaspoons minced garlic
1 teaspoon grated orange zest
1 teaspoon kosher salt
1 14- to 16-ounce can whole tomatoes, chopped
1 8-ounce can reduced-sodium tomato sauce
¼ teaspoon red-pepper flakes
3-6 tablespoons chopped fresh mint
1 pound sturdy pasta, such as penne

1. Thinly slice half of the mushrooms. Halve or quarter the remainder. In a large heavy saucepan, heat 1½ tablespoons of the oil over medium heat. Add onions, garlic, orange zest and salt. Toss until the onions are lightly colored, about 5 minutes.
2. Raise the heat to medium-high, add the mushrooms and cook, stirring often, until the juices have nearly evaporated, about 10 minutes. Add tomatoes and their juice, tomato sauce and red-pepper flakes. Cook over low heat, partly covered, for 15 minutes, stirring often. Stir in 2 tablespoons of the mint.
3. Meanwhile, in a large pot of boiling salted water, cook pasta until al dente, 6 to 8 minutes. Drain and transfer to a serving bowl. Toss with the remaining ½ tablespoon olive oil. Top with the sauce and sprinkle with remaining mint to taste.

Makes 4 servings.

585 calories per serving: 21 grams protein, 10 grams fat (1.3 grams saturated fat), 106 grams carbohydrate; 730 mg sodium; 0 mg cholesterol; 2 grams fiber.

NUTRITION BONUS: This is an ideal meatless heart-healthy entrée containing 15 percent of calories from fat.

TECHNIQUE

23 Prebake pizza crusts for maximum crispness.

Because the toppings for healthy pizzas contain little fat, the crusts have a tendency to come out soggy, especially toward the center. To eliminate this problem and create a crispy, flavorful crust just like what you get at the best pizzerias, bake the rolled dough briefly in a very hot oven *without* toppings. Spread the crust with the topping and finish baking until the crust is brown and the topping is bubbling.

1. Roll out dough to a 12-inch circle and transfer to a baking sheet dusted with cornmeal.

2. Bake crusts on the lowest oven rack until golden, about 5 minutes. Remove from the oven and distribute toppings.

(F) FAT SAVINGS: Pizza styles and fat counts vary greatly, but an average slice of cheese pizza contains 10 to 12 grams of fat. The recipe below and the other Eating Well pizzas in this section contain only 1 to 5 grams per slice.

Basic Pizza

Cornmeal for dusting baking sheets
1 pound Quick Pizza Dough (*right*)
1 cup Tomato Sauce (*page 43*) *or* commercial tomato sauce
4 ounces fresh mozzarella cheese, thinly sliced
Salt & freshly ground black pepper to taste
½ cup freshly grated Parmesan cheese
Several fresh basil leaves

1. Set oven rack in lowest position. Preheat oven to 500°F or the highest setting. Sprinkle 2 baking sheets with cornmeal and set aside.
2. Divide pizza dough in half. On a lightly floured surface, roll out one half of the dough to a 12-inch circle. Transfer to a prepared baking sheet. Bake until golden, about 5 minutes. Remove the pan from the oven. Repeat with the second portion of dough.
3. Spread ½ cup of the tomato sauce on one of the crusts. Distribute half of the mozzarella slices on top, season with salt and pepper and sprinkle with ¼ cup of the Parmesan.
4. Bake the pizza until the top is bubbling, about

Quick Pizza Dough

1½ cups all-purpose white flour
½ cup whole-wheat flour
1 package quick-rising yeast
1 teaspoon salt
½ teaspoon sugar
1 teaspoon olive oil

1. In a food processor, combine white and whole-wheat flours, yeast, salt and sugar; pulse to mix.
2. In a small saucepan or in a glass measuring cup in the microwave, heat oil mixed with ¾ cup water to between 125° and 130°F. With the processor on, gradually pour the warm liquid through the feed tube. (If the mixture is too dry, add 1 or 2 tablespoons warm water.) Process until the dough forms a ball, then process for 1 minute to knead.
3. Transfer the dough to a lightly floured surface. Cover with plastic wrap and let rest for 10 to 15 minutes before rolling. (*The dough can be made ahead, enclosed in a plastic bag and stored in the refrigerator overnight. Bring to room temperature before using.*)

Makes 1 pound dough, enough for two 12-inch pizzas.

960 calories per pound: 32 grams protein, 8 grams fat (1.2 grams saturated fat), 192 grams carbohydrate; 2,140 mg sodium; 0 mg cholesterol; 16 grams fiber.

(N) NUTRITION BONUS: Whole-wheat pizza crust has about 2 more grams of fiber per serving than regular crust.

5 minutes. Remove from the oven and immediately garnish with a few basil leaves. Repeat with the remaining crust and toppings.

Makes two 12-inch pizzas, 8 slices each.

50 calories per slice: 3 grams protein, 3 grams fat (1.5 grams saturated fat), 4 grams carbohydrate; 125 mg sodium; 8 mg cholesterol; 2 grams fiber.

(N) NUTRITION BONUS: Frozen pizzas often contain hydrogenated fat in the crust. When you make your own, you control both the amount and *type* of fat.

24 Broil and puree peppers for a low-fat sauce.

Blackening peppers under the broiler imparts a roasted sweetness to the pepper flesh, which is easily pureed with a little garlic to provide a base for a remarkably complex sauce.

F FAT SAVINGS: Roasted peppers have no fat whatsoever yet their richness allows diners not to feel cheated by a pizza without cheese or a sauce without cream.

1. Slice red bell peppers lengthwise into 4 wedges. Trim membranes and remove seeds. Place on a wire rack set over a baking sheet.

2. Broil peppers until skins are blistered and blackened, 12 to 15 minutes, rotating the pan often. Transfer peppers to a bowl and cover.

3. After 10 minutes, peel off pepper skins in large strips with a paring knife.

Fusilli with Smoked Salmon & Red Pepper Sauce

- 4 roasted red peppers, peeled, *or* two 7-ounce jars, drained
- 2 cloves garlic
- 1 teaspoon olive oil, preferably extra-virgin
- 1 small onion, chopped
- 1 tablespoon fresh parsley, finely chopped
- 2 tablespoons red-wine vinegar
- 1 bay leaf
- ¼-½ teaspoon cayenne
- 12 ounces sturdy pasta, such as fusilli
- 4 ounces smoked salmon, lightly flaked, *or* one 6-ounce can solid white tuna in water, drained and flaked
  Salt & freshly ground black pepper to taste
- ½ cup fresh basil leaves, torn

1. In a food processor, combine roasted peppers and garlic. Process to a smooth paste, scraping down the bowl as needed. (*The puree can be stored, covered, in the refrigerator for up to 3 days.*)
2. In a nonstick skillet, heat oil over low heat. Add onions and cook, stirring occasionally, until they are soft and translucent, 3 to 5 minutes. Add parsley, vinegar and bay leaf; cook 1 minute, or until most of liquid has been absorbed. Add the roasted red pepper puree and cayenne and bring to a simmer. Cook over low heat for 20 minutes, stirring occasionally, until

the sauce is thick and the flavors have melded.

3. Meanwhile, cook pasta in a large pot of boiling salted water. Just before the pasta is done, add salmon or tuna to the red pepper sauce, stirring gently; cook just until the fish is heated through. Season with salt and pepper.

4. Drain the pasta. In a large serving bowl, toss the pasta with the sauce and basil. Serve immediately.

Makes 4 servings.

420 calories per serving: 18 grams protein, 6 grams fat (1 gram saturated fat), 74 grams carbohydrate; 235 mg sodium; 7 mg cholesterol; 2 grams fiber.

(N) NUTRITION BONUS: There are 4 grams of fiber in one red pepper.

Tuna, Red Pepper & Onion Pizza

    4   roasted red peppers, peeled, *or* two 7-ounce
        jars, drained
    1   tablespoon tomato paste
    1   clove garlic
    ¼   teaspoon salt, plus more to taste
        Freshly ground black pepper to taste
        Cornmeal for dusting baking sheets
    1   6-ounce can solid white tuna in water,
        drained and flaked
    1   red onion, very thinly sliced
    2   tablespoons capers, drained
    2   tablespoons chopped fresh parsley
    2   tablespoons olive oil, preferably extra-virgin
    1   tablespoon fresh lemon juice
        Salt & freshly ground black pepper to taste
    1   pound Quick Pizza Dough (*page 51*)

1. In a food processor, combine half of the roasted red peppers, tomato paste, garlic and ¼ teaspoon salt; puree until smooth. Taste and adjust seasonings with salt and pepper. Set the sauce aside.

2. Set oven rack in lowest position. Preheat oven to 500°F or the highest setting. Sprinkle 2 baking sheets with cornmeal and set aside.

3. In a bowl, combine tuna, onions, capers, parsley, oil and lemon juice. Slice the remaining roasted peppers and add to the bowl. Season with salt and pepper. Set aside.

4. Divide pizza dough in half. On a lightly floured

surface, roll out one half of the dough to a 12-inch circle. Transfer to a prepared baking sheet. Bake until golden, about 5 minutes. Remove the pan from the oven. Repeat with the second portion of dough.

5. Spread half of the pepper sauce over one of the crusts. Distribute half of the tuna/vegetable mixture on top. Bake until the crust is browned, about 10 minutes. Repeat with the remaining crust and toppings.

Makes two 12-inch pizzas, 8 slices each.

190 calories per slice: 8 grams protein, 5 grams fat (0.7 gram saturated fat), 29 grams carbohydrate; 475 mg sodium; 6 mg cholesterol; 3 grams fiber.

(N) NUTRITION BONUS: This pizza makes a heart-healthy meal with its red-pepper sauce, tuna and mono-unsaturated fat from olive oil.

TECHNIQUE

25 Lightly spritz pizzas with olive oil to keep low-fat toppings from drying out.

Use a spray can of olive oil to lightly mist pizza before it goes into the oven. This allows you to evenly disperse a minimal amount of oil over a wide area with far more control than if you were brushing or drizzling it on.

(F) FAT SAVINGS: A spray of 1 second's duration delivers less than 1 gram of fat: drizzling on 1 teaspoon of oil adds nearly 5 grams of fat.

French Onion Pizza

DOUGH

    2   cups all-purpose white flour
    1   package quick-rising yeast
    1   teaspoon salt
    ½   teaspoon sugar
    1   teaspoon olive oil
    ⅓   cup chopped imported black olives
    ½   tablespoon chopped fresh rosemary
        or ½ teaspoon crumbled dried rosemary
        Cornmeal for dusting baking sheets

TOPPING

- 1   tablespoon olive oil
- 4   cups sliced onions (about 4 medium)
- 1   cup grated part-skim mozzarella cheese (about 4½ ounces)
- ½   cup grated Parmesan cheese (about 1 ounce)

  Freshly ground black pepper to taste
  Olive oil cooking spray

TO MAKE DOUGH:

1. In a food processor, combine flour, yeast, salt and sugar; pulse to mix.

2. In a small saucepan over medium heat, heat oil mixed with ¾ cup water to between 125° and 130°F.

3. With the processor on, gradually pour the warm liquid through the feed tube. (If the mixture is too dry, add 1 or 2 tablespoons warm water.) Process until the dough forms a ball, then process for 30 seconds to knead.

4. Transfer the dough to a lightly floured surface, and knead olives and rosemary into the dough until thoroughly combined. Cover with plastic wrap and let rest for 10 to 15 minutes. (*The dough can be made ahead, enclosed in a plastic bag and stored in the refrigerator overnight. Bring to room temperature before using.*)

TO MAKE TOPPING & ASSEMBLE PIZZA:

1. Set oven rack in lowest position. Preheat oven to 500°F or the highest setting. Sprinkle 2 baking sheets with cornmeal and set aside.

2. In a nonstick skillet, heat oil over medium heat. Add onions and cook, stirring occasionally, until golden brown and very tender, about 10 minutes. Set aside to cool.

3. Divide pizza dough in half. On a lightly floured surface, roll out one half of the dough to a 12-inch circle. Transfer to a prepared baking sheet, and pierce the dough several times with a fork to prevent large air bubbles from forming. Bake until golden, about 5 minutes. Remove the pan from the oven and roll and bake the second portion of dough.

4. Sprinkle ½ cup of the mozzarella and ¼ cup of the Parmesan on one of the crusts. Arrange half of the onions over the cheese, and top with a generous grinding of pepper. Mist lightly with olive oil cooking spray.

5. Bake the pizza until the cheese is melted and the onions are heated through, about 5 minutes. Remove from the oven. Repeat with the remaining crust and toppings.

Makes two 12-inch pizzas, 8 slices each.

125 calories per slice: 6 grams protein, 4 grams fat (1.5 grams saturated fat), 16 grams carbohydrate; 260 mg sodium; 7 mg cholesterol; 1 gram fiber.

N NUTRITION BONUS: It's amazing how easy it is to forget about pepperoni and sausage once you have tasted caramelized onions on your pizza.

Black olives and rosemary flavor the dough for French Onion Pizza.

26

White bean puree makes an unusual and rich-tasting sauce for pizza.

White beans are a Tuscan staple, whether in a salad with tuna and tomatoes or in a garlicky puree for crostini. Making a quick puree from canned beans and spreading it on a pizza is pure EATING WELL. Toppings can be as simple as fresh tomatoes and as savory as sausage and sun-dried tomatoes.

F FAT SAVINGS: At I gram per slice, this pizza provides all the satisfaction of one-with-everything, at half the fat price.

Pizza with White Bean Puree & Fresh Tomatoes

> Cornmeal for dusting baking sheets
> 1 pound Quick Pizza Dough (*page 51*)
> 1 cup White Bean Puree (*recipe follows*)
> 4 tablespoons freshly grated Parmesan cheese
> 6 vine-ripened plum tomatoes
> 2 scallions, thinly sliced
> ½ teaspoon red-pepper flakes
> Olive oil cooking spray

1. Set oven rack in lowest position. Preheat oven to 500°F or the highest setting. Sprinkle 2 large baking sheets with cornmeal; set aside.
2. Divide pizza dough in half. On a lightly floured surface, roll out one half of the dough into a 12-inch circle. Transfer the dough to the prepared pan. Pierce the dough several times with a fork to prevent air bubbles from forming. Prebake the crust for 5 to 6 minutes, or until lightly browned. Repeat with remaining half of dough.
3. Spread the crust with half of the white bean puree. Sprinkle 1 tablespoon Parmesan over the puree. Arrange half of the tomato slices evenly over the pizza; sprinkle with half the scallions, another 1 tablespoon

of the Parmesan and ¼ teaspoon red-pepper flakes.
4. Lightly mist with olive oil cooking spray. Bake the pizza for 5 minutes, or until the bottom and edges of crust are browned. Repeat with remaining toppings on second crust. Slice and serve.

Makes two 12-inch pizzas, 8 slices each.

60 calories per slice: 3 grams protein, I gram fat (0.4 gram saturated fat), 10 grams carbohydrate; 95 mg sodium; I mg cholesterol; I gram fiber.

N NUTRITION BONUS: Beans are a rich source of plant proteins, which researchers believe are more heart-healthy than animal proteins.

White Bean Puree

> 1 clove garlic, cut in half
> 1 15-ounce can cannellini *or* great northern beans, drained and rinsed
> ½ teaspoon olive oil, preferably extra-virgin
> 1 teaspoon finely chopped fresh sage *or* ¼ teaspoon dried rubbed sage
> Salt & freshly ground black pepper

1. Pour ¾ cup water into a saucepan, add garlic and bring to a boil over high heat. Add beans and return to a boil. Drain the beans and garlic, reserving ¼ cup of the cooking liquid.
2. Transfer the beans and garlic to a food processor. Add oil and process, adding just enough of the reserved cooking liquid to make a thick, smooth paste. Stir in sage and season to taste with salt and pepper. (*The puree can be stored, covered, in the refrigerator for up to 2 days.*)

Makes about 1 cup, enough for two 12-inch pizzas.

30 calories per tablespoon: 2 grams protein, 0.2 gram fat (0 grams saturated fat), 6 grams carbohydrate; 30 mg sodium; 0 mg cholesterol; 0 grams fiber.

Fresh Herbs

Are the Healthy Cook's Best Asset

IT'S NOT ENOUGH TO MERELY REDUCE the fat in a dish; today's healthy cook needs to pay attention to flavor. In traditional cooking, butter and oil amplify the flavors of a dish. Quite often in the EATING WELL Test Kitchen, we depend on fresh herbs for that flavor enrichment, and rarely a day goes by without someone chopping up a handful or two or three of herbs. They add a clean freshness of their own while lifting and embellishing the other flavors in the recipe. Use simple herb blends to enliven roast or grilled meats and vegetables.

CHOOSING AND KEEPING FRESH HERBS

Stem ends should look freshly cut, not dried out, wilted or discolored. Don't wash herbs until you are ready to use them. Store sturdy herbs, such as parsley, thyme or oregano, in a perforated plastic bag in the refrigerator. Fragile herbs, such as basil, tarragon, cilantro and chervil, deteriorate quickly when chilled; place them in a glass of water like a bouquet and keep on the counter for a day or two.

SUBSTITUTING DRIED HERBS FOR FRESH

In general you can substitute dried herbs for fresh, with a few exceptions. For most herbs, the ratio of fresh to dried is three-to-one; if a recipe calls for 1 tablespoon chopped fresh thyme, you will need 1 teaspoon dried. Sage becomes quite strong when dried, so use one-fourth the amount of fresh called for in a recipe, and always use dried rubbed sage, not powdered sage, which becomes a bit acrid. Dried parsley and dried basil are close to flavorless and should be avoided.

Fresh Mint Sauce

A natural for grilled lamb or eggplant.

2   teaspoons sugar
½   teaspoon kosher salt
1   tablespoon chopped fresh ginger
1   small serrano *or* jalapeño pepper,
     coarsely chopped
1   clove garlic, crushed and peeled
2   cups lightly packed fresh mint leaves
2   tablespoons rice-wine vinegar
1   teaspoon vegetable oil, preferably canola

Place sugar and salt in a food processor. With the motor running, drop ginger, peppers and garlic through the feed tube; process until very finely chopped. Add mint and pulse until finely chopped. Add vinegar and oil and pulse to mix. Transfer to a small serving bowl; use right away.

Makes about ½ cup, for 4 servings.

25 calories per serving: 0 grams protein, 1 gram fat (0 grams saturated fat), 3 grams carbohydrate; 270 mg sodium; 0 mg cholesterol; 0 grams fiber.

Salsa Verde

Use to garnish grilled or poached fish, roast chicken or grilled vegetables.

3   tablespoons extra-virgin olive oil
3   tablespoons finely chopped fresh parsley,
     preferably Italian flat-leaf
1   tablespoon finely chopped fresh thyme,
     oregano *and/or* rosemary
1   tablespoon capers, rinsed and chopped

1   shallot, finely chopped
1   clove garlic, minced
1   teaspoon fresh lemon juice
1   teaspoon anchovy paste
     Salt & freshly ground black pepper
     to taste

Combine all ingredients in a small bowl.

Makes about ½ cup.

15 calories per teaspoon: 0 grams protein, 1 gram fat (0.3 gram saturated fat), 0 grams carbohydrate; 20 mg sodium; 0 mg cholesterol; 0 grams fiber.

Dukka

Street vendors throughout the Middle East sell little paper cones of dukka, *a blend of herbs, ground nuts and spices. Set out a small bowl of* dukka *for guests to sprinkle on pita bread.*

½   teaspoon black peppercorns
¼   cup fresh thyme leaves *or* 4 teaspoons
     dried thyme leaves mixed with ¼ cup
     chopped fresh parsley
¼   cup chopped hazelnuts
1   teaspoon salt

Crush peppercorns with a heavy pan. Transfer to a blender and add thyme (or dried thyme and parsley), hazelnuts and salt. Using an on-off motion, work the mixture until all ingredients are finely chopped. Transfer to a small bowl.

Makes about ⅔ cup.

5 calories per teaspoon: 0 grams protein, 0.6 gram fat (0 grams saturated fat), 0 grams carbohydrate; 65 mg sodium; 0 mg cholesterol; 0 grams fiber.

Vietnamese Grilled Chicken with Papaya Relish, page 61

THE RECIPES

THE TECHNIQUES

27 Removing the skin from chicken pieces

28 Skinning a whole chicken and cooking it in a clay pot

29 Oven-frying for a crispy coating

30 Browning on the stovetop and finishing in the oven for even cooking

31 Cooking *en papillote* to keep chicken moist and flavorful

32 Glazing to seal in juices

33 Choosing the leanest cut of turkey

34 Reducing the fat in roast turkey, stuffing and gravy

TECHNIQUES 27-34

CHICKEN & Turkey

YOU COULD COOK CHICKEN FOR DINNER EVERY night of the year and never have to repeat a recipe. It's amenable to an infinite combination of seasonings, whether spicy hot or pleasantly herbal, bright citrus or earthy rich. Wonderfully lean chicken has particular appeal for the low-fat cook. A three-ounce portion of cooked chicken breast (without the fatty skin) has a mere three grams of fat and about one-third of that fat is saturated fat. (Take a look at the chart on page 60 for a fat comparison of chicken with and without skin.)

Even leaner than chicken, turkey is muscling its way onto the dinner table—and not only at Thanksgiving. The availability of turkey parts has made turkey an option for quick, healthy weeknight cooking.

27 When sautéing, braising or marinating chicken, first remove the skin.

While poultry meat, particularly breast meat, is quite lean, there is considerable fat in the skin. Even if you don't eat the skin, you want to avoid cooking that fat into the sauce.

F FAT SAVINGS: By removing chicken skin, you save, on average, 4 grams of fat per 3-ounce cooked portion.

1. The skin on chicken breasts lifts away quite easily. Remove any deposits of visible fat with a sharp paring knife.

2. Use a paper towel to grab hold of the skin when pulling it off the legs.

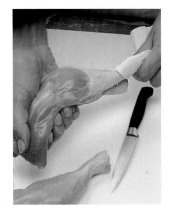

Chicken Marsala Stew

2 tablespoons olive oil
1 pound boneless, skinless chicken breasts, trimmed of fat and cut into 1-inch chunks
   Salt & freshly ground black pepper to taste

? HOW LEAN IS CHICKEN?

It's clear to see that if you leave the skin on the chicken, you will consume twice the amount of fat. As with all meats, we suggest keeping portions to 3 ounces of cooked meat: remember that 4 ounces of raw meat will yield about 3 ounces of cooked meat.

3-ounce cooked portion	Calories	Fat	Saturated Fat
Chicken breast with skin	170	6.6	1.9
Chicken breast without skin	140	3.0	0.8
Chicken leg with skin	200	11.3	3.2
Chicken leg without skin	165	7.2	2.0

1 pound mushrooms, cleaned and sliced
3 onions, chopped
3 tablespoons all-purpose white flour
2 cloves garlic, finely chopped
½ cup dry Marsala wine
1½ cups defatted reduced-sodium chicken broth
1 tablespoon balsamic vinegar

1. In a Dutch oven or large sauté pan with a lid, heat ½ tablespoon of the oil over medium-high heat. Add half of the chicken pieces and season with salt and pepper. Brown the chicken pieces, stirring occasionally, until the meat is no longer pink in the center, about 6 minutes. Transfer to a plate and repeat with another ½ tablespoon of the oil and the remaining chicken. Set aside.
2. Add another ½ tablespoon of the oil to the pot. Add mushrooms and cook, stirring, until they begin to soften and give off liquid, 3 to 5 minutes. Transfer to a bowl and set aside.
3. Add the remaining ½ tablespoon of the oil to the pot. Add onions and cook, stirring, until they soften and start to turn golden, about 10 minutes. Add flour and garlic and cook, stirring, for 1 minute. Pour in Marsala and cook, stirring, for 2 minutes longer. Add chicken broth and the reserved mushrooms. Bring to a simmer, reduce the heat to low and cover

the pan. Cook, stirring often, until the mushrooms are tender, about 15 minutes. Add balsamic vinegar and the reserved chicken. Return to a simmer and season with additional salt and pepper, if needed.

Makes about 5 cups, for 4 servings.

325 calories per serving: 31 grams protein, 9 grams fat (2 grams saturated fat), 22 grams carbohydrate; 320 mg sodium; 66 mg cholesterol; 4 grams fiber.

 NUTRITION BONUS: Serve over wide egg noodles with a green salad and an orange vegetable, for a meal with an ideal balance of nutrients.

Vietnamese Grilled Chicken

Serve with the Papaya Relish at right or other lively, fruity salsa.

¼ cup fresh lime juice (2 limes)
2½ tablespoons fish sauce
4 cloves garlic, minced
2 red "bird" chile *or* jalapeño peppers, seeded and minced
2 tablespoons sugar
1 tablespoon vegetable oil, preferably canola
4 chicken legs (about 2½ pounds total), skin and fat removed, cut in half through the joint

1. In a small bowl, whisk lime juice, fish sauce, garlic, peppers, sugar and oil. Pour about half of this marinade into a shallow glass dish and set the remainder aside. Add chicken pieces to the dish and turn to coat. Cover and marinate in the refrigerator for 20 minutes to 1 hour, turning occasionally.

2. Meanwhile, prepare a charcoal fire or preheat a gas grill.

3. Grill the chicken, covered, turning several times and basting the browned sides with the reserved marinade, until well browned but not charred, and no longer pink inside, 20 to 30 minutes.

Makes 8 chicken pieces, for 4 servings.

275 calories per serving: 25 grams protein, 11 grams fat (2.2 grams saturated fat), 20 grams carbohydrate; 1,165 mg sodium; 80 mg cholesterol; 1 gram fiber.

 NUTRITION BONUS: Canola oil is not quite as high in monounsaturated fat as olive oil, but it is rich in alpha-linolenic acid, which may provide additional protection against heart disease.

? HOW GREAT IS THE SALMONELLA RISK?

The USDA estimates that approximately 25 percent of U.S. poultry is contaminated with salmonella bacteria. Therefore some simple precautions are in order when preparing chicken and turkey.

• Raw poultry should not touch cooked foods or foods that will be served raw. After cutting the raw meat, wash the cutting board and utensils with hot soapy water before using again.

• Remember the 2-hour rule: Raw or cooked, poultry must not be at room temperature for more than 2 hours. In the summer when the temperature goes above 90°F, the time limit drops to 1 hour.

• Thaw frozen chicken and turkey in the refrigerator, never on the kitchen counter.

• The single best protection is to cook chicken and turkey thoroughly. When done, the juices should run clear, and the internal temperature should reach 170°F on an instant-read thermometer for breast meat, 180° for thigh meat.

Papaya Relish

2 cloves garlic, crushed and peeled
½ teaspoon kosher salt
3 tablespoons rice-wine vinegar
2 teaspoons sugar
2 teaspoons hot sauce, such as sambal olek *or* Tabasco
1 firm papaya, peeled, seeded and diced
½ cup finely diced red onion
¼ cup chopped fresh cilantro

With the side of a chef's knife, mash garlic with salt. (*See Technique 9, page 24.*) Transfer to a small bowl and whisk in vinegar, sugar and hot sauce. Add papaya, onions and cilantro; toss gently to mix. (*The relish is at its best served shortly after it is prepared.*)

Makes about 1½ cups, for 4 servings.

35 calories per serving: 1 gram protein, 0 grams fat, 10 grams carbohydrate; 280 mg sodium; 0 mg cholesterol; 1 gram fiber.

Chicken with Artichokes & Olives

*Black olives give a briny kick to
an easy chicken sauté.*

8 chicken thighs (about 2 pounds total), skin
 and fat removed
 Salt & freshly ground black pepper to taste
3 teaspoons olive oil
1 Spanish onion, cut in half lengthwise and
 thinly sliced
2 teaspoons sugar
2 large cloves garlic, very finely chopped
½ cup Kalamata olives (2 ounces), pitted if
 desired
⅔ cup dry white wine
1½ teaspoons dried thyme leaves
1 cup defatted reduced-sodium chicken broth
1 14-ounce can artichoke hearts, drained,
 rinsed and sliced

1. Pat chicken thighs dry and season with salt and
pepper. In a large nonstick skillet, heat 1 teaspoon of
the oil over medium-high heat. Add chicken thighs
and cook, turning occasionally with tongs, until well
browned on all sides, about 8 minutes. Transfer to a
plate lined with paper towels and set aside.

2. Reduce heat to low and add the remaining 2 teaspoons oil. Add onions and sugar; cook, stirring, until the onions are soft and deep golden, about 10
minutes. Add garlic and olives and cook, stirring, for
1 minute. Stir in wine and thyme; cook until wine
has nearly evaporated, about 5 minutes.

3. Add chicken broth, artichoke hearts and the
browned chicken and return to a simmer. Cover and
simmer over low heat until the chicken is tender and
no longer pink inside, about 30 minutes.

4. With tongs, transfer the chicken to a platter and
keep warm. Increase the heat to high and boil the
sauce, uncovered, until slightly thickened, about 5
minutes. Taste and adjust seasonings with salt and
pepper. Spoon the sauce over the chicken and serve.
Makes 4 servings.

355 calories per serving: 28 grams protein, 16 grams fat (3 grams
saturated fat), 22 grams carbohydrate; 282 mg sodium; 80 mg
cholesterol; 2 grams fiber.

ℕ NUTRITION BONUS: Canned artichoke hearts add
flavor to everyday dishes.

TECHNIQUE

28 Skin a chicken and cook it in a clay pot.

Cooking in an enclosed vessel allows you to
prepare a chicken without adding any fat, and
it keeps lean poultry moist, while beautifully
melding and intensifying the flavors.

Ⓕ FAT SAVINGS: At 5 grams of fat per 3-ounce serving,
this is the leanest way to prepare chicken.

1. With a large
sharp knife, cut off
wing tips through
the second joint.

2. With a small
sharp knife, slit the
skin along the
length of the back-
bone. Working on
one side of the bird,
pull the skin away
from the flesh,
using the knife
to free the skin
wherever necessary.

3. As you reach the
legs and wings, turn
the skin inside out
and pull. Continue
to peel the skin
away from the
breast up to the
breast bone. Repeat
with the other side.

Clay-Pot Chicken with a Spice Rub

If you do not have a clay pot, you can cook the chicken in a covered Dutch oven; begin the cooking in a preheated, not a cold, oven.

2   teaspoons chili powder
1   teaspoon cumin seeds
½   teaspoon salt
1   3½-pound chicken, skin and fat removed (*see Steps 1, 2 & 3 at left*)
2   tablespoons fresh lime juice

1. In a small skillet over medium heat, toast chili powder, cumin seeds and salt, stirring constantly, until aromatic, 1 to 2 minutes. Transfer to a plate to cool.
2. Sprinkle chicken with lime juice. Season the surface and cavity with the toasted spice mix. Tie the legs together and tuck the wings under the back. If you like, set in a shallow dish, cover with plastic wrap and refrigerate for 2 to 3 hours to allow the flavors to develop.
3. Soak the bottom and lid of a clay cooker of at least 3-quart capacity in cool water for 15 minutes.
4. Place the chicken in the soaked cooker (*see photograph below*), cover and place in a cold oven. Set the temperature at 350°F and bake for 1 hour, or until

the juices run clear when the thigh is pierced with a fork and a meat thermometer in the thigh registers 180°F.
5. Transfer the chicken to a warm platter. Strain the cooking juices into a small saucepan; place in the freezer for a few minutes to solidify fat. Skim off fat and rewarm the juices before serving with the chicken.

Makes 4 servings.

145 calories per 3-ounce serving: 21 grams protein, 5 grams fat (1 gram saturated fat), 2 grams carbohydrate; 340 mg sodium; 64 mg cholesterol; 0.5 gram fiber.

Ⓝ NUTRITION BONUS: Low in calories as well as fat, the chicken is incredibly flavorful and tender.

29 A buttermilk batter produces crispy *oven*-fried chicken and turkey fingers.

A quick dip in a buttermilk mixture, then a turn in seasoned flour or cornmeal are the only preparation you need to make delicious "faux-fried" chicken or turkey.

Ⓕ FAT SAVINGS: Grandma's fried chicken averaged 20-plus grams of fat per serving. Oven-frying cuts that down to 6 grams.

Oven-Fried Chicken

1   large egg white
½   cup buttermilk
1   teaspoon Tabasco sauce
½   cup all-purpose white flour
1   tablespoon baking powder
2   teaspoons paprika
1   teaspoon dried thyme leaves
1   teaspoon dried oregano
1   teaspoon salt
¼   teaspoon freshly ground black pepper
4   bone-in chicken breasts (about 2½ pounds total), skin and fat removed
    Canola oil in a spray can

1. Preheat oven to 425°F. Set a rack over a baking sheet and spray with nonstick cooking spray.

2. In a shallow bowl, whisk together egg white, buttermilk and Tabasco. Put flour, baking powder, paprika, thyme, oregano, salt and pepper in a large paper bag. Shake the bag to mix well.

3. Dip chicken pieces, one at a time, into the buttermilk mixture, then dredge in the flour mixture by shaking in the bag. Place the chicken on the prepared rack. Spray oil lightly over the chicken.

4. Bake for 35 to 40 minutes, or until browned on the outside and no longer pink inside.

Makes 4 servings.

365 calories per serving: 57 grams protein, 6 grams fat (2 grams saturated fat), 15 grams carbohydrate; 960 mg sodium; 147 mg cholesterol; 0.5 gram fiber.

Ⓝ NUTRITION BONUS: Keep olive oil spray and canola oil spray on hand for oven-frying and oven-roasting—you will use less fat and get a fine, even coating.

Turkey Fingers with Maple-Mustard Sauce

A recipe to please everyone in the family. Children may prefer it plain; adults will go for the sweet-and-spicy mustard sauce.

  1 cup buttermilk
  2 teaspoons grainy mustard
  1 pound turkey tenderloins, center tendons removed, cut into finger-sized strips
  ½ cup yellow cornmeal, preferably stone-ground
  ½ cup all-purpose white flour
  1 teaspoon ground cumin
  1 teaspoon dried thyme leaves
  1 teaspoon salt
  2 tablespoons vegetable oil, preferably canola

MAPLE-MUSTARD SAUCE
  ½ cup grainy mustard
  ¼ cup pure maple syrup

1. Set oven rack at lowest level and preheat oven to 450°F. In a bowl, whisk buttermilk and 2 teaspoons mustard. Add turkey strips and toss to coat. In another bowl, combine cornmeal, flour, cumin, thyme

and salt. Take the turkey strips out of the buttermilk and roll in the cornmeal mixture.

2. Brush the oil on a baking sheet with sides, and place it in the oven for 5 minutes to heat. Using tongs, transfer the turkey strips to the hot baking sheet and return it to the oven. Bake for 10 minutes, or until the undersides of the strips are golden brown. Turn the strips over and bake for another 8 to 10 minutes, or until the turkey is golden brown on the outside and no longer pink in the center.

3. While the turkey is baking, make Maple-Mustard Sauce: In a small bowl, combine ½ cup mustard and maple syrup. Serve the sauce alongside the hot turkey fingers.

Makes 4 servings.

430 calories per serving: 39 grams protein, 12 grams fat (2 grams saturated fat), 41 grams carbohydrate; 770 mg sodium; 80 mg cholesterol; 3 grams fiber.

Ⓝ NUTRITION BONUS: Buttermilk is a valuable ally to the low-fat cook. Despite its name, it is made from either low-fat or skim milk.

TECHNIQUE

30 Start chicken on the stovetop, finish in the oven for a crisp coating and a juicy interior.

An ovenproof skillet is the key to this easy technique. Either an old-fashioned well-seasoned cast-iron skillet or a modern skillet with a nonstick coating and an ovenproof handle works well. Breaded stuffed chicken breasts are browned on one side on the top of the stove, carefully flipped and transferred—still in the pan—to the oven to finish cooking. This guarantees a nice brown crust and an interior that is cooked through yet still moist.

Ⓕ FAT SAVINGS: Even with its cheese stuffing, this chicken has under 10 grams of fat per serving.

Pampered Chicken

4   boneless, skinless chicken breasts
    (about 1 pound total), trimmed of fat
4   slices Monterey Jack cheese
    (2 ounces)
⅓   cup seasoned (Italian-style)
    breadcrumbs
2   tablespoons freshly grated Parmesan
    cheese
2   tablespoons finely chopped fresh
    parsley
½   teaspoon salt
½   teaspoon freshly ground black pepper
2   large egg whites
½   tablespoon olive oil
    Lemon wedges for garnish

1. Preheat oven to 400°F. Place a chicken breast, skinned-side down, on a cutting board. Keeping the blade of a sharp knife parallel to the board, make a horizontal slit along the thinner, long edge of the breast, cutting nearly through to the opposite side. Open the breast so it forms two flaps, hinged at the center. Place a slice of cheese on one flap, leaving a ½-inch border at the edge. Press the other flap down firmly over the cheese and set aside. Repeat with the remaining breasts.

2. In a shallow dish, mix breadcrumbs, Parmesan, parsley, salt and pepper. In another bowl, lightly beat egg whites with a fork. Holding a stuffed breast together firmly, dip in the egg whites and then roll in the breadcrumbs. Repeat with the remaining breasts and set aside.

3. In a large ovenproof skillet, heat oil over high heat until almost smoking. Carefully add the stuffed breasts and cook until browned on one side, about 2 minutes. Turn the breasts over and place the skillet in the oven. Bake until no longer pink inside, about 20 minutes. Serve with lemon wedges.

Makes 4 servings.

250 calories per serving: 34 grams protein, 9 grams fat (4 grams saturated fat), 7 grams carbohydrate; 565 mg sodium; 79 mg cholesterol; 0.5 gram fiber.

Ⓝ NUTRITION BONUS: The richness of this low-fat recipe will make you forget Chicken Kiev forever.

With low-fat breast meat, splurge on cheese for Pampered Chicken.

TECHNIQUE 31 Cook *en papillote* for flavorful, low-fat chicken.

Sealing a chicken breast in a paper wrapping and popping it into the oven is hardly a new trick. The French have done it for centuries. The beauty of this method is that you don't have to add a drop of fat. In the oven, steam rapidly builds up inside the package to cook the contents efficiently. Flavoring agents, such as herbs and leeks, mingle with the juices to create a delicately seasoned dish.

Ⓕ FAT SAVINGS: The only fat in the recipe comes from the chicken itself.

Chicken *en papillote*

4 boneless, skinless chicken breasts (about 1 pound total), trimmed of fat

4 teaspoons grainy mustard

2 leeks, trimmed, cleaned and cut into 2½-inch-long julienne strips

2 carrots, peeled and cut into 2½-inch-long julienne strips

4 teaspoons chopped fresh thyme *or* 1 teaspoon dried thyme leaves
  Salt & freshly ground black pepper to taste

1. Preheat oven to 400°F. Cut 4 pieces of parchment paper or aluminum foil 12 inches by 16 inches. Fold in half to form an 8-by-12-inch rectangle, then cut into a half-heart shape as you would a valentine.

2. Place a chicken breast in the center of one half of each opened paper heart. Spread mustard evenly over chicken breasts. Distribute leeks, carrots and thyme over the chicken. Season with salt and pepper. Seal the packages and place them on a baking sheet.

3. Bake for 10 to 12 minutes, or until the packages are puffed. (Open one package to check that the chicken is no longer pink inside.) Transfer to individual plates and let diners open their own packages.

Makes 4 servings.

190 calories per serving: 28 grams protein, 2 grams fat (0.4 gram saturated fat), 14 grams carbohydrate; 170 mg sodium; 66 mg cholesterol; 1 gram fiber.

 NUTRITION BONUS: Because the steam is contained, none of the nutrients are lost.

Open Chicken *en papillote* to release the herby fragrance.

TECHNIQUE

32 Brush chicken pieces with a glaze to seal in juices during cooking.

When roasted in an oven's dry heat, skinless chicken pieces dry out quickly. When coated with a tasty glaze or coating, the meat stays moist.

 FAT SAVINGS: Skinning the chicken pieces reduces the fat count by about 5 grams of fat per serving.

Spicy Yogurt Chicken

Serve with pita bread, sliced cucumbers and a small bowl of drained yogurt.

2 pinches saffron threads (½ teaspoon)

½ cup nonfat *or* low-fat plain yogurt

1 onion, very finely chopped

3 cloves garlic, very finely chopped

2 tablespoons harissa *or* 2 teaspoons hot sauce *or* ½ teaspoon cayenne

2 tablespoons fresh lemon juice
1 tablespoon honey
1 tablespoon olive oil
½ teaspoon salt
½ teaspoon ground cumin
¼ teaspoon ground cinnamon
8 chicken drumsticks, skin removed

1. In a small bowl, crumble saffron threads over 2 tablespoons hot water. Steep for 5 minutes. In a shallow dish, combine yogurt, onions, garlic, harissa (or hot sauce or cayenne), lemon juice, honey, oil, salt, cumin and cinnamon. Stir in the saffron water. Add drumsticks and coat well. Cover with plastic wrap and marinate in the refrigerator for at least 30 minutes or up to 12 hours.

2. Preheat oven to 450°F. Line a baking sheet with aluminum foil and set an oiled rack on top. Place the drumsticks on the rack and bake until the chicken is golden brown on the outside and no longer pink in the center, about 30 minutes.

Makes 8 drumsticks, for 4 servings.

265 calories per serving: 26 grams protein, 12 grams fat (3 grams saturated fat), 13 grams carbohydrate; 381 mg sodium; 79 mg cholesterol; 1 gram fiber.

NUTRITION BONUS: Yogurt doubles as a tenderizer in the marinade and as a low-fat coating.

Honey-Mustard Chicken

Serve with steamed carrots and couscous tossed with currants and scallion greens.

3 tablespoons honey
3 tablespoons grainy mustard
1 tablespoon vegetable oil, preferably canola
1½ teaspoons curry powder, preferably Madras
½ teaspoon salt
¼ teaspoon freshly ground black pepper
1 3-pound chicken, cut into 8 pieces, skin and fat removed

1. Preheat oven to 400°F. Line a baking sheet with aluminum foil and set an oiled rack on top.

2. In a small bowl, combine honey, mustard, oil, curry powder, salt and pepper. Using a brush, coat chicken pieces all over with the mustard glaze; set the pieces on the rack.

3. Bake, basting occasionally, until the chicken is golden on the outside and no longer pink in the center, 35 to 40 minutes.

Makes 8 pieces, for 4 servings.

295 calories per serving: 32 grams protein, 12 grams fat (2 grams saturated fat), 14 grams carbohydrate; 510 mg sodium; 95 mg cholesterol; 0.5 gram fiber.

NUTRITION BONUS: For greater fat savings, make this recipe with skinless chicken breasts instead of leg pieces.

Browned and glistening, Honey-Mustard Chicken has broad appeal.

33 For very lean meat, choose turkey cutlets.

The mild flavor and tenderness of turkey cutlets make them a fine substitute for veal cutlets, and turkey offers a clear savings in both fat grams and dollar value. In addition, they are a natural convenience food, taking less than 10 minutes to prepare. We suggest lightly pounding cutlets to make them thinner, for quick and even cooking.

F FAT SAVINGS: At 2.8 grams of fat for a cooked 3-ounce portion, turkey cutlets are even leaner than chicken breast.

Turkey Piccata

Lemon segments give the sauce sweetness and body that lemon juice alone would not deliver. Serve the piccata with couscous or rice and sliced tomatoes.

Turkey Piccata makes weeknight cooking a breeze.

1   lemon
4   turkey cutlets (about 1 pound), sliced in half
⅓   cup all-purpose white flour
½   teaspoon salt
½   teaspoon freshly ground black pepper
2   teaspoons olive oil
1   clove garlic, minced
½   cup defatted reduced-sodium chicken broth
1   tablespoon drained capers
½   teaspoon sugar
2   teaspoons butter
1   tablespoon chopped fresh parsley

1. With a sharp knife, remove skin and white pith from lemon and discard. Cut the lemon segments away from their surrounding membranes into a bowl (discard seeds). Chop lemon segments coarsely.

2. Place turkey cutlets between sheets of plastic wrap and pound with the bottom of a heavy skillet to an even ¼-inch thickness. Combine flour, salt and pepper in a plastic bag. Dredge turkey lightly in the flour mixture, shaking off excess.

3. Heat 1 teaspoon of the oil in a large skillet over medium-high heat. Cook half of the turkey for 2 to 3 minutes per side, or until the outside is golden brown and the interior is no longer pink. Transfer to a platter and keep warm. Repeat with remaining oil and turkey. (Do not wash the skillet between batches.)

4. Add garlic and chicken broth to the skillet. Bring to a boil and cook, stirring, for 1 minute, scraping up brown bits. Add lemon, capers and sugar, and cook 30 seconds longer; swirl butter into the skillet until the butter has melted. Spoon the sauce over the turkey. Sprinkle with parsley and grind more pepper over the top.

Makes 4 servings.

245 calories per serving: 36 grams protein, 5 grams fat (2 grams saturated fat), 11 grams carbohydrate; 420 mg sodium; 100 mg cholesterol; 0.5 gram fiber.

N NUTRITION BONUS: Served with a rice or barley pilaf and a vegetable on the side, this quick sauté is a perfect meal for a weight-loss diet.

34 For a healthy holiday, reduce the fat in roast turkey, stuffing and gravy.

A roast stuffed turkey presents three good opportunities for cutting fat. A 4-ounce portion of roast turkey breast meat with the skin on contains 8 grams of fat; a 4-ounce portion of breast meat without the skin contains under 4 grams. Obviously, it makes sense to avoid the skin. It does make sense, however, to leave the skin on while roasting a turkey because it keeps the meat from drying out. Remove the skin before carving and serving the bird.

Another area for fat reduction is the stuffing. You do not need to add a cup of butter to keep stuffing moist. Chicken or turkey stock, wine, fruit juices or a combination thereof do the job quite nicely.

The third opportunity for cutting fat is in making the gravy. Carefully skim off the fat from the pan juices before you begin the gravy and thicken it with cornstarch, not a butter/flour mixture.

F FAT SAVINGS: A serving of turkey breast, stuffing and a spoonful of gravy can have as much as 22 grams of fat. Eating Well's holiday trio has only 12.

Roast Turkey with Madeira Gravy

    Corn Bread & Apple Stuffing (*page 70*)
1 **12- to 14-pound turkey with giblets**
    Salt & freshly ground black pepper to taste
½ **ounce fresh sage leaves (about 6 stems)**
½ **ounce fresh thyme leaves (a bundle about the thickness of your finger)**
½ **cup apple cider *or* apple juice for basting the turkey**

½ **cup Madeira *or* port**
3 **tablespoons cornstarch**
GIBLET STOCK
1 **teaspoon vegetable oil, preferably canola**
1 **onion, chopped**
1 **carrot, chopped**
3½ **cups defatted reduced-sodium chicken broth (two 14-ounce cans)**
2 **cloves garlic, unpeeled**
    A few sprigs fresh parsley
    A few sprigs fresh thyme
6-8 **whole black peppercorns**

1. Make Corn Bread & Apple Stuffing.
2. Preheat oven to 325°F. Place a lightly oiled rack in a large roasting pan. Lightly oil a 2-quart baking dish.
3. Remove the giblets and neck from turkey cavity and reserve for the stock. (Discard the liver.) Remove any visible fat from the turkey. Rinse it inside and out with cold water and pat dry. Season the cavity with salt and pepper.
4. As shown below, separate the turkey skin from the breast meat with your fingers, taking care not to tear the skin or pierce the meat. Place sprigs of sage and thyme between the flesh and the skin on either side of the breastbone.

5. Season the bird with salt and pepper. Spoon about half of the Corn Bread & Apple Stuffing into the turkey and neck cavities, securing the neck cavity with a skewer. Transfer the remaining stuffing to the prepared baking dish, cover with aluminum foil and refrigerate.
6. Tie the drumsticks together. Place the bird, breast-

side up, in the prepared roasting pan. Roast the turkey, basting occasionally with cider and pan juices, until golden brown, about 1½ hours. Cover with aluminum foil, and continue basting from time to time until done. The turkey is done when a meat thermometer inserted into the thickest part of the thigh registers 180°F and registers 165° when inserted into the stuffing.

TO MAKE GIBLET STOCK:

While the turkey is roasting, heat oil over medium-high heat in a medium saucepan. Add the giblets, neck, onions and carrots; cook, stirring occasionally, for 10 to 15 minutes, or until well browned. Add chicken broth, garlic, parsley, thyme, peppercorns and 1 cup water; bring to a boil. Reduce heat to low and simmer for 30 minutes. Strain through a fine sieve (you should have about 2½ cups stock). Chill until ready to use. Skim off fat.

TO MAKE GRAVY:

1. When the turkey is done, transfer it to a carving board. Scoop the stuffing into a serving bowl, cover and keep warm. Place the dish of extra stuffing in the oven to heat. Cover the turkey loosely with aluminum foil and let rest for 20 to 30 minutes before carving.

2. Meanwhile, pour the drippings from the roasting pan through a strainer into a small bowl, then chill in the freezer so that the fat can be skimmed off. Add Madeira or port to the roasting pan and cook, stirring and scraping up any brown bits, for about 1 minute. Strain into a medium saucepan. Add the giblet stock and bring to a simmer. Skim off fat from the chilled pan drippings, then add the drippings to the pan.

3. In a small bowl, dissolve cornstarch in ¼ cup water; slowly add to the simmering gravy, whisking until slightly thickened. Taste and adjust seasonings.

4. Remove string from turkey and carve, discarding skin and herbs. Serve with gravy and stuffing.

Serves 10, with leftovers.

210 calories per serving: 26 grams protein, 5 grams fat (1.5 grams saturated fat), 9 grams carbohydrate; 280 mg sodium; 69 mg cholesterol; 0.5 gram fiber.

Ⓝ NUTRITION BONUS: Turkey meat itself is low-fat and nutritious. The problem with turkey feasts lies in the fatty trimmings and desserts.

Corn Bread & Apple Stuffing

CORN BREAD
- 1 cup yellow cornmeal
- 1 cup all-purpose white flour
- 1½ teaspoon baking powder
- 1 teaspoon salt
- 1 large egg, lightly beaten
- 1 cup skim *or* low-fat milk

STUFFING
- 1 tablespoon olive oil
- 1 onion, chopped (1 cup)
- 1 large stalk celery, diced (½ cup)
- 2 red apples, such as Cortland, cored and diced
- ½ cup golden raisins
- 2 cloves garlic, minced
- 1 tablespoon chopped fresh sage *or* 1 teaspoon dried rubbed sage
- 2 teaspoons chopped fresh thyme
- 1 cup defatted reduced-sodium chicken broth
- ½ cup apple cider *or* apple juice
  Salt & freshly ground black pepper to taste

TO MAKE CORN BREAD:

1. Preheat oven to 350°F. Lightly oil an 8-by-11-inch baking dish or coat it with nonstick cooking spray.

2. In a mixing bowl, combine cornmeal, flour, baking powder and salt. In a separate bowl, whisk together egg and milk. Add to the dry ingredients and stir just until evenly moistened.

3. Turn the batter into the prepared baking dish and bake for 20 to 30 minutes, or until a toothpick inserted in the center comes out clean. Let cool in the pan on a rack. Crumble into large crumbs (you should have about 6 cups crumbs).

4. Spread the corn bread crumbs out on a large baking sheet. Toast in the oven, stirring occasionally, until crisp but not browned, 25 to 30 minutes. Let cool. (*Alternatively, the crumbs can be spread on the baking sheet and left to dry at room temperature overnight.*) (*The crumbs can be made up to 1 week ahead, and kept stored in an airtight container at room temperature.*)

TO MAKE STUFFING:

1. Heat oil in a large nonstick skillet over medium heat. Add onions and celery and cook, stirring, until the onions are softened, about 5 minutes. Add apples, golden raisins, garlic, sage and thyme; cook, stirring, until the apples lose their sharp edges, about 2 minutes. Add ½ cup of the chicken broth and cook until most of the liquid has evaporated. Season with salt and pepper. Transfer to a large bowl.

2. Add the reserved corn bread crumbs and toss to mix. Drizzle apple cider and the remaining ½ cup chicken broth over the bread mixture and toss until evenly moistened.

3. Use as directed in the recipe for Roast Turkey with Madeira Gravy (*page 69*) or transfer the mixture to a 3-quart baking dish and cover with aluminum foil. Bake for 35 to 45 minutes, or until heated through. If you would like a crisp top, remove the foil for the last 15 minutes of baking.

Makes about 8 cups, for 10 servings.

165 calories per serving: 4 grams protein, 3 grams fat (0.5 gram saturated fat), 31 grams carbohydrate; 240 mg sodium; 22 mg cholesterol; 3 grams fiber.

 NUTRITION BONUS: This savory stuffing is one example of a healthy trimming for your turkey feast.

Roast Turkey and Corn Bread & Apple Stuffing prove you don't have to cut back on flavor or tradition when cutting back on fat.

Veal Stew, page 78
Buttermilk Mashed Potatoes, page 116

THE RECIPES

THE TECHNIQUES

35 Starting with lean beef, trimming
the fat *and* controlling portion size

36 Grilling lean steaks to medium-rare
to avoid toughness

37 Cutting the fat in hamburgers

38 Stretching a stew with meaty
vegetables

39 Choosing the leanest cut of pork

40 Blotting the fat from sausages

41 Choosing lean veal chops and
topping with a fat-free flavor accent

42 Deglazing the skillet for flavorful,
low-fat sauces

TECHNIQUES
35-42
MEATS

WHEN GOING OUT TO EAT, TODAY'S
HEALTH-CONSCIOUS DINER PROBABLY
HAS THE GOOD SENSE NOT TO
order the 12-ounce prime rib and
extra sour cream for the baked potato.
But eating well does not imply
abandoning red meats altogether.
Leaner cuts, smaller portions
and rounding out a meaty dish
with vegetables and grains all
mean that beef, pork and lamb can
still be part of your cooking repertoire. To further
reduce fat in these recipes, particularly saturated fat,
we sauté in a bare minimum of vegetable oil and use
no cream, butter or cheese.

35 Start with a lean cut, trim the outside fat and, most important, limit portion size.

Fat grams add up quickly even in lean meats. A healthful serving of meat is no more than 3 ounces of trimmed cooked meat—about the size of a deck of cards.

F FAT SAVINGS: Three ounces of cooked trimmed choice sirloin has 6.6 grams of fat. Compare that to 3 ounces of trimmed and cooked prime T-bone at 8.8 grams or prime rib at 16 grams.

Using a small sharp knife, completely trim the outside fat from meats, here a piece of sirloin.

Spicy Orange Beef & Broccoli Stir-Fry

Hints of orange and a touch of heat dress up a classic combination. Serve with steamed rice.

SAUCE
- ¼ cup fresh orange juice
- 2 tablespoons soy sauce
- 1 tablespoon rice wine *or* dry sherry
- 2 teaspoons sugar
- 1 teaspoon sesame oil
- 1 teaspoon balsamic vinegar

? WHAT ARE THE LEANEST CUTS OF BEEF?

When shopping for lean beef, there are two things to keep in mind. First, choose a cut from the hindquarters of the animal; this includes the top loin, sirloin, tenderloin and round. Buy "Choice" or "Select" grade meat, which is 20 to 35 percent leaner than "prime." Prime indicates a generous marbling of fat throughout the tissue, which is internal fat that cannot be trimmed away before cooking.

Freshly ground black pepper to taste
- ½ cup defatted reduced-sodium chicken broth
- 1 tablespoon cornstarch

MARINADE
- 1 tablespoon peanut oil
- 2 cloves garlic, finely chopped
- 1 teaspoon grated fresh ginger
- ½ teaspoon salt
  Freshly ground black pepper to taste
- ½ tablespoon cornstarch
- 1 pound beef sirloin steak, trimmed of fat and sliced thinly against the grain

STIR-FRY
- 1 tablespoon peanut oil
- 2 small hot dried chile peppers
  Zest of 1 orange, peeled in 1-inch strips
- 1 red bell pepper, julienned
- 1 pound broccoli florets, cut into bite-size pieces and blanched 1 minute in boiling water
- 4 scallions, cut into 1½-inch segments
  Salt to taste

TO PREPARE SAUCE:
In a small bowl, combine orange juice, soy sauce, rice wine or sherry, sugar, sesame oil, vinegar and black pepper; pour 3 tablespoons of this sauce into another bowl to be used in the marinade. Add chicken broth and cornstarch to the first bowl, stirring well to dissolve cornstarch; set aside.

TO PREPARE MARINADE:
To reserved marinade in the large bowl, add peanut

oil, garlic, ginger, salt and black pepper. Sprinkle the cornstarch over beef and rub to coat slices with a thin layer. Add the beef to the marinade, turning to coat slices well. Cover and marinate in the refrigerator for 1 hour.

TO STIR-FRY:

Have all ingredients prepared and within reach. Heat a wok over high heat; drizzle oil down sides of wok. Add chile peppers and orange zest; stir-fry quickly for 10 seconds. Add beef and stir-fry until lightly browned, about 30 seconds. Add bell peppers and stir-fry until slightly softened, 15 to 30 seconds. Add broccoli, scallions and a pinch of salt, and continue stir-frying until the broccoli is heated through, about 30 seconds. Stir the sauce mixture and add to the wok. Bring to a simmer, stirring occasionally. Simmer until thickened, 30 seconds to 1 minute. Serve immediately.

Makes 4 servings.

290 calories per serving: 29 grams protein, 12 grams fat (4 grams saturated fat), 16 grams carbohydrate; 940 mg sodium; 70 mg cholesterol; 4 grams fiber.

Ⓝ NUTRITION BONUS: Pairing a smaller amount of lean beef with broccoli and a delicious sauce is a good way to enjoy the flavor of meat in a healthy meal.

TECHNIQUE 36 When grilling lean beef, cook steaks to medium-rare to avoid tough meat.

Prolonged high heat makes meat tough, and this is particularly apparent with the leaner Choice and Select grades of beef. Don't overcook lean meat: we recommend grilling steaks to medium-rare, 4 to 5 minutes per side. The meat is slightly pink in the center and an instant-read thermometer registers 145°F. Before serving, slice the steak diagonally against the grain.

Ⓕ FAT SAVINGS: Compared to Prime beef, the Choice grade has 20% less fat, the Select grade has 35% less.

Korean Grilled Beef (Bulgogi)

In Korean restaurants, bulgogi *is often cooked with great theatrics at the tables, on a hot brass or iron shield.*

1 tablespoon sesame seeds
Pinch of salt
1 1½-pound boneless sirloin steak (about 1½ inches thick), trimmed of fat
6 scallions, trimmed and thinly sliced
4 cloves garlic, finely chopped
3 tablespoons finely chopped fresh ginger
3 tablespoons reduced-sodium soy sauce
1 tablespoon rice vinegar *or* cider vinegar
1½ teaspoons vegetable oil, preferably canola
1½ teaspoons sugar
Generous grinding of black pepper

1. In a small heavy skillet, toast sesame seeds over medium heat until they begin to brown and have a toasted aroma. Transfer to a mortar, add salt and crush with a pestle. Set aside.

2. Score steak deeply (nearly through to the other side) in a 1-inch crisscross diamond pattern. Turn over and score the other side (do not worry if the meat breaks up into 2 or 3 pieces). Cover with plastic wrap and pound lightly with a mallet or heavy pan to tenderize.

3. In a shallow dish large enough to hold the steak, combine scallions, garlic, ginger, soy sauce, vinegar, oil, sugar, pepper and the ground sesame seeds. Add the steak and turn to coat with the marinade. Cover and marinate in the refrigerator for at least 2 hours or up to 8 hours, turning from time to time.

4. Prepare a charcoal fire or preheat a gas grill. Once the fire is hot, remove the meat from the marinade and grill until medium-rare, about 4 minutes per side. Cut into thin slices against the grain and serve at once.

Makes 6 servings.

225 calories per serving: 35 grams protein, 8 grams fat (2.5 grams saturated fat), 2 grams carbohydrate; 280 mg sodium; 101 mg cholesterol; 0.5 gram fiber.

Ⓝ NUTRITION BONUS: If you're on a strict fat budget, buy Select-grade beef and tenderize by pounding, marinating and cutting into thin strips against the grain.

Grilled Sirloin with a Coffee Bean/Peppercorn Crust

2   cloves garlic

¼   teaspoon kosher salt, plus more to taste

2   tablespoons strong freshly brewed coffee

2   tablespoons balsamic vinegar
    Freshly ground black pepper to taste

2   tablespoons whole coffee beans (*not* flavored beans)

2   teaspoons whole black peppercorns

1   1-pound beef sirloin steak (about 1 inch thick), trimmed of fat

1   teaspoon olive oil

1. Prepare a charcoal fire or preheat a gas grill.

2. Smash and peel 1 of the garlic cloves. Sprinkle with ¼ teaspoon salt and mash into a paste with a chef's knife. (*See Technique 9, page 24.*) Transfer to a small bowl and whisk in brewed coffee and vinegar. Season with ground pepper and set the vinaigrette aside.

3. Place coffee beans and peppercorns on a cutting board; coarsely crush with the bottom of a heavy pan. Mix the crushed coffee beans and peppercorns together and set aside.

4. Cut the remaining clove of garlic in half and rub the cut side over both sides of the steak. Rub oil over the surface and coat with the coffee bean/peppercorn mixture, pressing it into the meat.

5. Salt the steak and grill until it reaches desired doneness, 4 to 5 minutes per side for medium-rare.

6. Transfer the steak to a clean cutting board and let it rest for a few minutes before carving into thin slices against the grain. Fan the meat on plates and drizzle with the reserved vinaigrette.

Makes 4 servings.

180 calories per serving: 26 grams protein, 6 grams fat (2.2 grams saturated fat), 3 grams carbohydrate; 190 mg sodium; 76 mg cholesterol; 0 grams fiber.

NUTRITION BONUS: Serve beef with generous servings of a starchy food, a green vegetable and a yellow/orange vegetable for a wide range of nutrients.

Grilled Sirloin with a Coffee Bean/Peppercorn Crust

TECHNIQUE 37 Ensure the leanest ground beef by choosing ground round, then combine it with beans or bulgur to further lower the proportion of fat in meatloaf and burgers.

Ground beef can be deceiving: even when labeled "extra lean," it might have as much as 14 grams of fat in a 3-ounce cooked portion. Why is it so high? Generally, ground beef comes from the cuts that contain greater amounts of intramuscular fat, which is fat that cannot be trimmed away. To guarantee truly lean ground beef, we suggest buying ground round or buying round steak and having the butcher trim and grind it for you.

To bulk up our burgers and meatloaf, we add bulgur or beans; this adds texture and flavor as well as cutting down on the fat ratio.

F FAT SAVINGS: A big juicy full-fat hamburger might have up to 25 grams of fat. These Eating Well burgers slice that nearly in half.

Meatloaf

Making a free-form loaf means there is more of the tasty crust to enjoy.

- 1 cup dried mushrooms, such as shiitake, porcini *or* chanterelle
- ¾ cup bulgur
- 2 teaspoons olive oil
- 1 small onion, chopped
- 1 stalk celery, chopped
- 2 cloves garlic, minced
- 1 tablespoon Worcestershire sauce
- 1 15-ounce can diced tomatoes, drained (about 1 cup)
- ½ cup evaporated skim milk
- ½ cup catsup
- 1 large egg
- 2 large egg whites
- 1½ pounds lean ground beef, preferably from the round
- 1 cup fine dry breadcrumbs
- ¼ cup chopped fresh parsley
- 2 teaspoons dried thyme leaves
- ½ teaspoon salt

1. In a small bowl, soak mushrooms in 1 cup warm water for 30 minutes. In another small bowl, combine bulgur with 1 cup boiling water and let soak for 30 minutes, or until the bulgur is tender and the water has been absorbed. Remove the mushrooms from the liquid; trim stems and coarsely chop caps.

2. Preheat oven to 350°F. Lightly oil a baking sheet with sides or coat it with nonstick cooking spray.

3. In a small skillet, heat oil over medium-low heat and add onions, celery and garlic. Cook, stirring occasionally, until the vegetables are softened, 5 to 7 minutes. Add Worcestershire and cook for 3 minutes, scraping the pan well as the mixture becomes sticky. Add tomatoes, evaporated milk and catsup; stir to combine. Continue cooking for 3 minutes, or until the mixture is very thick. Remove from the heat and let cool.

4. In a large bowl, whisk egg and egg whites. Add beef, breadcrumbs, the soaked bulgur, the mushrooms and the onion-milk mixture. Stir in parsley, thyme and salt. Mix gently but thoroughly by hand. Mound the meatloaf mixture into a free-form loaf on the prepared baking sheet. Bake for 50 to 60 minutes, or until the internal temperature reaches 160°F. Let cool for 10 minutes before slicing and serving.

Makes one loaf, 10 slices.

190 calories per slice: 15 grams protein, 6 grams fat (1.2 grams saturated fat), 23 grams carbohydrate; 440 mg sodium; 48 mg cholesterol; 3 grams fiber.

 NUTRITION BONUS: Bulgur adds beneficial fiber to the meatloaf; breadcrumbs assist in extending the meat.

Burgers with Bulgur

Meltingly sweet onions top these beef-and-bulgur patties.

- ⅓ cup bulgur
- 2 teaspoons olive oil
- 4 cups sliced onions (4 medium)
- 2 teaspoons sugar
- 2 teaspoons balsamic vinegar
- ¾ pound lean ground beef, preferably from the round
- 2 tablespoons tomato paste
- ¼ cup chopped fresh parsley
- ½ teaspoon salt, plus more to taste
- ¼ teaspoon freshly ground black pepper, plus more to taste
- 4 hamburger buns, split and toasted

1. In a small bowl, combine bulgur with ½ cup warm water and let soak for 30 minutes, or until the bulgur is tender and the water has been absorbed.

2. Meanwhile, in a large nonstick skillet, heat oil over

❓ IS IT OKAY TO EAT A HAMBURGER COOKED RARE OR MEDIUM-RARE?

Grinding meat creates countless minuscule spaces for pathogens to hide and multiply. Unlike whole steaks, ground beef should always be cooked to medium doneness to prevent the risk of food-borne illness. The meat's internal temperature should read 160°F, there should be no trace of pinkness, and the juices should run clear.

low heat. Add onions and sugar; sauté until tender and golden, about 15 minutes. Stir in ¼ cup water and vinegar. Season with a little salt and keep warm.

3. Prepare a grill or preheat the broiler. In a medium bowl, combine the plumped bulgur, beef, tomato paste, parsley, salt and pepper; mix thoroughly but lightly. Shape into four ¾-inch-thick patties.

4. Grill or broil the patties on a lightly oiled rack until browned and cooked through, about 5 minutes per side. Place the patties on buns, top with a spoonful of the caramelized onions.

Makes 4 burgers, for 4 servings.

410 calories per serving: 31 grams protein, 13 grams fat (2.7 grams saturated fat), 47 grams carbohydrate; 580 mg sodium; 66 mg cholesterol; 7 grams fiber.

Ⓝ NUTRITION BONUS: You won't find dietary fiber in a regular hamburger. To up the fiber another notch, serve these burgers on whole-wheat hamburger buns or whole-wheat English muffins.

Chili Burgers

1 slice firm white bread, torn into small pieces
2 tablespoons tomato paste
¾ pound lean ground beef, preferably from the round
⅔ cup canned black beans, drained, rinsed and coarsely chopped
2 tablespoons chopped fresh cilantro *or* parsley
1 teaspoon dried thyme leaves
½ teaspoon salt
½ teaspoon freshly ground black pepper
1 teaspoon vegetable oil, preferably canola
1 small onion, finely chopped
1 clove garlic, finely chopped
1 jalapeño pepper, seeded and finely chopped
2 teaspoons ground cumin
4 onion rolls, split and toasted
    Lettuce for garnish
    Tomato salsa *or* corn salsa for garnish

1. Prepare a grill or preheat the broiler. In a bowl, use a fork to mash bread, tomato paste and 2 tablespoons water to a paste. Add beef, beans, cilantro or parsley, thyme, salt and pepper. Set aside.

2. In a small nonstick skillet, heat oil over medium heat. Add onions and sauté until light golden, about 3 minutes. Add garlic, jalapeños and cumin; sauté until fragrant, about 2 minutes more. (If the mixture becomes too dry, add 1 tablespoon water.) Let cool. Add to the reserved beef mixture and mix thoroughly but lightly. Shape into 4 patties.

3. Grill or broil the patties on a lightly oiled rack until browned and cooked through, about 5 minutes per side. Place the patties on rolls and garnish with lettuce and salsa.

Makes 4 burgers, for 4 servings.

370 calories per serving: 31 grams protein, 13 grams fat (2.7 grams saturated fat), 38 grams carbohydrate; 1,040 mg sodium; 66 mg cholesterol; 6 grams fiber.

Ⓝ NUTRITION BONUS: Black beans and peppers add soluble fiber, the type of fiber that helps lower blood cholesterol and even out the rise in blood-sugar level.

TECHNIQUE

38 Stretch a stew with "meaty" vegetables.

Some vegetables have a chewy, meaty quality—mushrooms, sun-dried tomatoes, peppers and hominy among them—that allows you to get away with using a relatively small quantity of meat and still have diners feel satisfied. In the recipes that follow, the portions have been cut to 1½ or 2 ounces of cooked meat per serving with no loss of satisfaction or flavor.

Ⓕ FAT SAVINGS: Small quantities of lean meat in both of the following recipes mean significant reduction in fat, particularly in saturated fat.

Veal Stew

4 sprigs parsley
1 3-inch sprig fresh rosemary *or* 1 teaspoon dried rosemary, chopped
2 bay leaves
1½ tablespoons olive oil

1½ pounds lean stewing veal (from the leg), trimmed of fat and cut into 1½-inch cubes

1 ounce pancetta, country ham *or* bacon, finely chopped

4 carrots, thickly sliced on the diagonal

1 onion, chopped

2 cloves garlic, finely chopped

2 tablespoons all-purpose white flour

½ cup dry white wine

1 14-ounce can plum tomatoes, drained and chopped

½ cup defatted reduced-sodium chicken broth *or* water

4 cups fresh pearl onions *or* 2 cups frozen pearl onions

1 pound portobello mushrooms, trimmed and cut into large pieces, *or* cremini mushrooms, trimmed and quartered

2 tablespoons chopped fresh parsley
Salt & freshly ground black pepper to taste

1. To make a bouquet garni, tie together parsley sprigs, rosemary and bay leaves with kitchen twine, or place in a cheesecloth bag; set aside.

2. Preheat oven to 325°F. Heat ½ tablespoon of the oil in a large ovenproof pot or Dutch oven over high heat. Add half of the veal and brown well on all sides, about 4 minutes. Transfer to a plate lined with paper towels and repeat with another ½ tablespoon of the oil and the remaining veal. Set aside.

3. Reduce the heat to low, add pancetta, ham or bacon and cook, stirring, until it begins to brown. Add carrots and cook, stirring, until they begin to soften, about 5 minutes. Add chopped onions and cook, stirring, for 2 minutes. Add garlic and flour and stir for 30 seconds. Pour in wine, scraping the solids from the bottom of the pot. Add tomatoes, broth or water, the browned veal and the bouquet garni. Bring the stew to a simmer, cover the pot and transfer to the oven.

4. Bake the stew for about 1½ hours, stirring occasionally, or until the veal is tender when pierced with a fork.

5. Meanwhile, if using fresh pearl onions, bring a large saucepan of water to a boil. Add the onions (unpeeled) and cook for 3 minutes. Drain and rinse under cold water. When they are cool enough to han-

dle, trim the ends and peel off the papery skins. (If using frozen pearl onions, thaw under cool running water and pat dry.)

6. Heat the remaining ½ tablespoon oil in a large nonstick skillet over high heat. Add the pearl onions and sauté until golden, 5 to 7 minutes. Transfer the onions to a bowl and return the pan to the heat. Add mushrooms and sauté until they begin to exude some liquid, about 4 minutes.

7. Stir the pearl onions and mushrooms into the stew during the last 10 minutes of cooking. Just before serving, remove the bouquet garni and stir in chopped parsley. Season with salt and pepper.

Makes 8 servings.

230 calories per serving: 25 grams protein, 8 grams fat (2 grams saturated fat), 16 grams carbohydrate; 235 mg sodium; 80 mg cholesterol; 3 grams fiber.

Ⓝ NUTRITION BONUS: Lycopene in tomatoes is fat-soluble, which means the fat in the dish helps with its absorption by the body.

Beef & Bean Chili

1 tablespoon olive oil

1 pound beef round, trimmed of fat and cut into ½-inch chunks

3 onions, chopped

1 green bell pepper, chopped

12 sun-dried tomatoes (*not* packed in oil), snipped into small pieces

6 cloves garlic, finely chopped

2 jalapeño peppers, seeded and finely chopped

2 tablespoons chili powder

1 tablespoon paprika

2 teaspoons dried oregano

½ teaspoon ground cumin

½ teaspoon cayenne

12 ounces dark beer

1 28-ounce can plum tomatoes, with juice

1 tablespoon grated unsweetened chocolate

1 teaspoon sugar, or to taste

2 19-ounce cans kidney, pinto *or* black beans, drained and rinsed

1 15-ounce can hominy, drained and rinsed

¼ cup chopped fresh cilantro

2 tablespoons fresh lime juice
Salt & freshly ground black pepper to taste

1. Heat ½ tablespoon of the oil in a large heavy pot over high heat. Add beef, in batches if necessary, and sauté until browned on all sides, about 3 minutes. Transfer to a plate lined with paper towels and set aside.

2. Lower heat to medium and add the remaining ½ tablespoon oil. Add onions and green peppers. Cook, stirring, until the onions have softened and are golden brown, 7 to 10 minutes. Add sun-dried tomatoes, garlic and jalapeños. Stir in chili powder, paprika, oregano, cumin and cayenne. Stir until aromatic, about 2 minutes.

3. Pour in beer, bring to a simmer and cook for 10 minutes, scraping up any brown bits clinging to the bottom of the pan. Add canned tomatoes and their juice, chocolate, sugar and the reserved beef. Pour in 2 cups of water and bring to a simmer. Cover the pot and simmer, stirring occasionally, for 1½ to 2 hours, or until the beef is very tender.

4. Add beans and hominy to the pot and cook until the chili is thick, 30 to 45 minutes more. Stir in cilantro and lime juice; season with salt and pepper. (*The chili can be prepared ahead and stored in the refrigerator for up to 2 days or in the freezer for up to 6 weeks.*)

Makes about 10 cups, for 8 servings.

380 calories per serving: 32 grams protein, 7 grams fat (1.5 grams saturated fat), 47 grams carbohydrate; 765 mg sodium; 51 mg cholesterol; 11 grams fiber.

N NUTRITION BONUS: Hominy is a much-overlooked but low-fat, tasty addition to soups and stews.

? ISN'T PORK TOO FATTY FOR A LOW-FAT DIET?

Because of new breeding and feeding techniques, pork is much leaner today than it was 20 years ago. While cuts like the spareribs are still way too high in fat to include in a low-fat diet, there are several cuts left from which to choose. The leanest cuts are the tenderloin and the ham. Sirloin chops, loin roast and loin chops are also lean.

TECHNIQUE

39 Choose very lean pork tenderloin for ease of preparation and tenderness.

The tenderloin is among the most convenient cuts of meat. It is small—averaging around ¾ pound—and has little waste. And at 4 grams of fat in a 3-ounce portion of cooked meat, it is leaner than beef and has just a little more fat than a skinless chicken breast.

F FAT SAVINGS: Grilled pork spareribs have roughly 25 grams of fat in a serving; grilled pork tenderloin has 4 grams.

Using a sharp paring knife, trim visible fat from a pork tenderloin.

Grilled Pork Tenderloin in a Mustard, Rosemary & Apple Marinade

¼ cup frozen apple-juice concentrate, thawed
2 tablespoons plus 1½ teaspoons Dijon mustard
2 tablespoons olive oil
2 tablespoons chopped fresh rosemary

4 cloves garlic, minced
1 teaspoon crushed black peppercorns
2 ¾-pound pork tenderloins, trimmed of fat
3 tablespoons port
2 tablespoons balsamic vinegar
1 small shallot, minced
Salt & freshly ground black pepper to taste
Rosemary sprigs for garnish

1. In a small bowl, whisk apple-juice concentrate, 2 tablespoons of the mustard, 1 tablespoon of the oil, rosemary, garlic and peppercorns. Measure out 3 tablespoons and reserve for basting. Place tenderloins in a shallow glass dish and pour the remaining marinade over them, turning to coat. Cover and marinate in the refrigerator for at least 20 minutes or for up to 2 hours, turning several times.

2. Meanwhile, prepare a charcoal fire or preheat a gas grill.

3. In a small bowl or a jar with a tight-fitting lid, combine port, vinegar, shallots, salt, pepper and the remaining 1½ teaspoons mustard and 1 tablespoon oil; whisk or shake until blended. Set aside.

4. Grill the meat, turning several times and basting the browned sides with the reserved marinade, until the outside is browned and the inside has just a trace of pink, 10 to 15 minutes. (An instant-read thermometer inserted in the center should register 150°F.)

5. Transfer the meat to a clean cutting board and let rest for about 5 minutes before carving into ½-inch-thick slices. Pour any juices that have accumulated on the cutting board into the reserved port vinaigrette. Arrange the pork slices on plates, drizzle with the vinaigrette and garnish with rosemary sprigs.

Makes 6 servings.

220 calories per serving: 25 grams protein, 9 grams fat (2 grams saturated fat), 8 grams carbohydrate; 80 mg sodium; 79 mg cholesterol; 0 grams fiber.

NUTRITION BONUS: Slice grilled meats against the grain into thin slices—it makes the portion size seem generous.

Southern-Style Pork Tenderloin

North Carolina Barbecue Sauce (*page 82*)
2 ¾-pound pork tenderloins, trimmed of fat
1 tablespoon Worcestershire sauce
1 teaspoon freshly ground black pepper

1. Make North Carolina Barbecue Sauce.

2. Brush tenderloins with Worcestershire and sprinkle with pepper. Place in a shallow dish, cover and refrigerate for at least 2 hours or up to 8 hours.

3. Prepare a charcoal fire or preheat a gas grill. Grill the meat over a medium-hot fire, turning once or twice and basting with barbecue sauce, until the outside is browned and the inside has just a trace of pink, 10 to 15 minutes. (An instant-read thermometer should register 150°F.) Let rest 5 minutes before slicing. Pass additional barbecue sauce alongside.

For a delicious supper, serve Grilled Pork Tenderloin in a Mustard, Rosemary & Apple Marinade with orzo and grilled vegetables.

Makes 6 servings.

155 calories per serving: 26 grams protein, 4 grams fat (1.5 grams saturated fat), 2 grams carbohydrate; 355 mg sodium; 83 mg cholesterol; 0 grams fiber.

NUTRITION BONUS: Low in fat *and* calories.

North Carolina Barbecue Sauce

Make the sauce at least 2 days before using.

1   cup distilled white vinegar
4   teaspoons kosher salt
1   tablespoon freshly ground black pepper
1   tablespoon red-pepper flakes
1   teaspoon cayenne

In a jar with a tight-fitting lid, combine all ingredients and shake well. (*The sauce keeps indefinitely at room temperature.*)

Makes 1 cup.

4 calories per tablespoon: 0 grams protein, 0 grams fat, 1 gram carbohydrate; 360 mg sodium; 0 mg cholesterol; 0 grams fiber.

Southern-Style Pork Tenderloin served with Southern-Style Black-Eyed Peas (*page 126*), sweet potatoes and greens.

TECHNIQUE

40 For maximum fat reduction, drain *and* blot fat before adding sausages to stew.

Highly seasoned sausage adds unmatched flavor to hearty stews and gumbos, but a major component of sausage is fat. To take advantage of the robust richness of sausage, you must first sauté the sausage pieces to render much of the fat, and blot the pieces on paper towels to remove even more fat. In the EATING WELL Test Kitchen, we meticulously measured the fat left in the pan and on the paper towels after cooking 1 pound of chorizo sausage. The total amount of fat lost was 85 grams (3 ounces) or nearly 20 percent of the total weight of the sausage!

F FAT SAVINGS: Had we not poured off the fat from the sausage, the fat count would have gone up by 10 to 15 grams per serving. Depending on the type and brand of sausage, draining and blotting takes the fat count down by 10 to 15 grams per serving.

Chorizo & Chickpea Stew

A warming winter dish to serve with crusty bread or rice and a simple salad. Chorizo can be found in the deli section of most large supermarkets.

1   pound chorizo sausage, removed from casing and thinly sliced on the bias
1   tablespoon olive oil
2   large onions, chopped
4   cloves garlic, finely chopped
2   teaspoons dried oregano
1   bay leaf
1   teaspoon paprika
2   green bell peppers *or* 4 Italian frying peppers, diced

1 15-ounce can defatted reduced-sodium chicken broth
3 15-ounce cans chickpeas *or* 3 cups dried chickpeas, cooked (*see box, page 122*)
2 15-ounce cans diced tomatoes, with juice
¼-½ teaspoon red-pepper flakes
1 teaspoon red-wine vinegar
    Salt & freshly ground black pepper to taste
2 tablespoons chopped fresh parsley

1. Place 3 layers of paper towels on a large plate. In a Dutch oven, cook chorizo slices over medium-high heat, stirring frequently, until well browned. Remove with a slotted spoon and transfer to the paper towels. Blot the chorizo with additional paper towels, pressing firmly to remove as much fat as possible. Remove paper towels and set sausage aside.

2. Discard the fat in the pot and wipe it clean with paper towels. Add oil to the pot and heat over medium-low heat; add onions and cook, stirring occasionally, for 10 minutes, or until very soft and golden. Add garlic, oregano, bay leaf and paprika; continue cooking another 5 minutes, or until onions are caramelized and fragrant.

3. Add bell or Italian frying peppers and cook for 3 minutes, or until slightly softened. Add chicken broth, chickpeas, tomatoes and red-pepper flakes. Bring to a boil, then lower heat and simmer for 5 minutes, stirring occasionally. Remove the bay leaf.

4. Add the cooked sausage and simmer for another 5 minutes, stirring carefully to avoid breaking sausage slices. Stir in vinegar, salt and pepper. Just before serving, sprinkle with parsley.

Makes about 10 cups, for 8 servings.

270 calories per serving: 10 grams protein, 10 grams fat (3.1 grams saturated fat), 12 grams carbohydrate; 800 mg sodium; 88 mg cholesterol; 2 grams fiber.

Ⓝ NUTRITION BONUS: By paying attention to portion size (here 1 pound of sausage stretches to serve 8) and pouring off rendered fat, you can still enjoy flavorful sausages.

Variation: For a spicy Southwestern-style stew, use black beans instead of chickpeas; add 2 tablespoons chopped chipotles in adobo sauce when you add the green peppers; and garnish with whole fresh cilantro leaves instead of parsley.

TECHNIQUE 41

Choose lean veal chops and top with a fat-free flavor accent.

Young animals like veal calves have less time to develop fat in their muscles and their meat is therefore leaner. The stovetop-to-oven method is very fast, keeps the meat tender and juicy, and only uses ½ teaspoon of olive oil to cook 4 chops. Just before serving, the meat is sprinkled with gremolata, a fat-free flavor booster borrowed from Italian cuisine: fresh parsley, garlic and grated lemon zest. Gremolata's fat-free elegance is a welcome addition to many meats.

Ⓕ FAT SAVINGS: Veal chops have 40 percent less fat than pork chops.

Roasted Veal Chops with Gremolata

Lamb chops work equally well in this recipe. They need to roast approximately 4 minutes longer. Serve with steamed artichokes or Ratatouille of Roasted Vegetables (page 108).

3 cloves garlic
4 8-ounce bone-in veal chops, about 1 inch thick, trimmed of excess fat
1 teaspoon olive oil
    Salt & freshly ground black pepper to taste
¼ cup minced fresh parsley
1 tablespoon grated lemon zest

1. Preheat oven to 350°F. Cut 1 clove garlic in half lengthwise. Rub veal chops with the garlic, then brush both sides of the chops lightly with olive oil. Season with salt and pepper.

2. Heat 2 cast-iron or other ovenproof heavy skillets over medium-high heat until they are very hot. Place the chops in the pans and cook 2 minutes. Turn over and transfer the skillets to the oven. Roast for 6 to 8 minutes, until the meat is cooked but still slightly pink inside.

3. Meanwhile, mince remaining 2 cloves garlic and combine with parsley and lemon zest. To serve, place the chops on individual serving plates and spoon 1 tablespoon of the parsley mixture on top of each.

Makes 4 servings.

215 calories per serving: 29 grams protein, 10 grams fat (2.5 grams saturated fat), 1 gram carbohydrate; 110 mg sodium; 129 mg cholesterol; 0.2 gram fiber.

NUTRITION BONUS: Fresh parsley is a rich source of vitamin C and carotenoids.

Roasted Veal Chops with Gremolata makes a quick, zesty supper.

TECHNIQUE

42

For a flavorful sauce without added fat, deglaze the skillet after browning meat.

Deglazing is a centuries-old technique that is much used in French cooking. It means to heat wine, stock or other flavorful liquid in the same pan that you have just used to brown meat. The liquid dissolves any caramelized bits that have stuck to the pan, which adds color. Rapidly boiling the liquid concentrates the flavor. Deglazing has much to offer the healthy cook by producing a complex sauce with minimal fat.

A heavy-bottomed, stainless-steel or anodized aluminum skillet or a well-seasoned cast-iron skillet work well for browning and deglazing. A normal smooth-bottom nonstick skillet is not recommended, but a nonstick skillet with a textured bottom and a superdurable coating will allow you to brown and deglaze.

F **FAT SAVINGS:** The only fat in these recipes comes from the meat and the tiny amount of olive oil used for sautéing.

Pork Medallions with a Port-&-Cranberry Pan Sauce

The autumn flavors in this dish go well with any of the roasted vegetables from page 109.

¼   cup dried cranberries
¼   cup port
1   pound pork tenderloin, trimmed of fat
    Salt & freshly ground black pepper to taste
1   teaspoon olive oil

2 cloves garlic, peeled and halved
1 teaspoon balsamic vinegar
2 sage leaves
½ cup defatted reduced-sodium chicken broth

1. In a small bowl, combine cranberries and port. Set aside. Slice tenderloin into medallions 1½ inches thick. Place between 2 layers of plastic wrap, and with the bottom of a saucepan, pound the medallions until they are ½ inch thick. Season both sides with salt and pepper.

2. In a nonstick skillet, heat oil over medium-high heat. Sear medallions on one side until golden brown, 2 to 3 minutes. Turn and sear on the other side for 4 to 5 minutes; turn medallions again and continue cooking until golden brown and no longer pink in the center, 2 to 3 minutes. Remove to a serving platter and cover loosely to keep warm.

3. Return the skillet to medium-high heat. Add garlic and cook, stirring, 1 minute. Add port with cranberries, vinegar and sage leaves; cook for 1 minute, scraping skillet for browned bits. Pour in chicken broth, swirl the skillet and bring to a boil again. Continue cooking until sauce thickens and is reduced by half, about 3 minutes. Remove the garlic and sage. Season the sauce with salt and pepper. Spoon over the pork and serve.

Makes 4 servings.

210 calories per serving: 26 grams protein, 5 grams fat (2 grams saturated fat), 9 grams carbohydrate; 130 mg sodium; 81 mg cholesterol; 0 grams fiber.

Ⓝ NUTRITION BONUS: Dried cranberries boost flavor and add trace minerals.

Lamb Chops with a Balsamic-Vinegar Pan Sauce

Serve with Rösti Potatoes (page 117) and a mixed green salad.

4 6-ounce lamb loin chops *or* eight 4-ounce rib chops, trimmed of visible fat
2 cloves garlic, peeled and halved
1 teaspoon finely chopped fresh rosemary
½ teaspoon salt, plus more to taste
  Freshly ground black pepper to taste
2 teaspoons olive oil
1 tablespoon balsamic vinegar
½ cup defatted reduced-sodium chicken broth
1 sprig fresh rosemary
1 bay leaf

1. Rub lamb well with cut sides of 1 garlic clove; discard garlic. Sprinkle with rosemary, salt and pepper; rub in 1 teaspoon of the oil. Cover and let marinate in refrigerator for at least 1 hour and up to 24 hours.

2. In a large nonstick skillet, heat the remaining 1 teaspoon oil over medium-high heat. Add the second garlic clove and lamb chops. (If using rib chops, it may be necessary to sear them in batches. Do not wipe the pan clean between batches.) Sear lamb on one side until golden brown, 2 to 3 minutes. Turn and sear on the other side for 1 minute; reduce the heat to low and continue cooking until the second side is golden brown and the center is still slightly pink. Transfer the chops to a platter and keep warm.

3. Spoon away any excess fat, leaving the browned bits in the bottom, and return the skillet (with garlic halves) to high heat. Add vinegar and bring to a boil, scraping the skillet for browned bits. Stir in chicken broth, rosemary and bay leaf; boil until the sauce has thickened and reduced by half, 2 to 3 minutes. Remove the garlic, rosemary and bay leaf, then season the sauce with salt and pepper. Spoon over the lamb and serve immediately.

Makes 4 servings.

230 calories per serving: 24 grams protein, 13 grams fat (4 grams saturated fat), 2 grams carbohydrate; 410 mg sodium; 77 mg cholesterol; 0 grams fiber.

Ⓝ NUTRITION BONUS: With a little wine, fruit juice or flavorful vinegar, the possibilities for low-fat pan sauces are endless.

Marinades
Expand Flavor in Grilled Meats

MARINADES AND SPICE RUBS GIVE YOU free access to a world of cuisines—and you don't have to travel any farther than your outdoor grill. These intensely flavored combinations offer much to the low-fat cook who wants vibrant flavors in food without adding fat. The techniques required are minimal, but whenever you are working with raw meat, there are food-safety procedures to keep in mind:

• After mixing up the marinade, set aside a portion to use for basting. Pour the remainder into a stainless-steel or glass dish just big enough to hold the meat or fish. The food need not be completely submerged in the marinade, but it should be turned several times to ensure even flavoring.

• Fish needs only 30 minutes to 1 hour of marinating; chicken can be marinated anywhere from 2 to 8 hours, depending on the intensity of flavor you are looking for; red meat is usually marinated overnight.

• Do not marinate meat for more than 24 hours or it will become mushy.

• Be sure to marinate meat, poultry and seafood in the refrigerator, never at room temperature.

• Drain or blot excess marinade from the food before grilling or broiling, because wet food tends to steam rather than brown.

• Once the surface is seared, you can baste it with the reserved marinade.

• Do not contaminate cooked food with leftover marinade.

• Always place the cooked food on a clean platter or cutting board, not back in the dish that held the marinade.

Moroccan Marinade

This lively blend works well with chicken, swordfish or tuna.

¼	cup nonfat plain yogurt
¼	cup chopped fresh parsley
2	tablespoons chopped fresh cilantro
2	tablespoons lemon juice
1	tablespoon olive oil
3	cloves garlic, finely chopped
1½	teaspoons paprika
1	teaspoon ground cumin
¼	teaspoon salt
¼	teaspoon freshly ground black pepper

In a bowl, stir together all ingredients.

Makes about ½ cup, enough for 1 pound of boneless chicken or fish fillets.

India Spice Marinade

Equally good on chicken or seafood.

2 teaspoons cumin seeds
1 teaspoon mustard seeds
1 tablespoon paprika
½ teaspoon cayenne
½ teaspoon salt
½ teaspoon turmeric
½ cup nonfat plain yogurt
2 tablespoons fresh lime juice
1 small onion, chopped
4 cloves garlic, minced
1 tablespoon finely chopped fresh ginger

1. In a small dry skillet, toast cumin and mustard seeds over medium heat, stirring constantly, until fragrant, about 2 minutes. Transfer to a spice grinder or mortar and pestle and grind to a fine powder. Add paprika, cayenne, salt and turmeric.
2. In a blender or food processor, combine yogurt, lime juice, onions, garlic and ginger. Blend until smooth. Add spices and pulse to combine.

Makes about 1⅓ cups, enough to marinate 2 pounds of boneless chicken or fish fillets.

———

Jamaican Jerk Rub

Habanero or Scotch bonnet chiles are extremely hot. Wash your hands thoroughly after working with them and be careful not to touch your eyes.

¼ cup ground allspice
1 tablespoon ground cinnamon
1 teaspoon freshly grated nutmeg
1 teaspoon dried thyme
1 bunch scallions, thinly sliced
2 cloves garlic, peeled
2 habanero *or* Scotch bonnet chile peppers, seeds and membrane removed
2 tablespoons dark rum
2 tablespoons orange juice

1 teaspoon salt
Freshly ground black pepper to taste

In a small skillet, toast allspice, cinnamon, nutmeg and thyme over medium-low heat, stirring frequently, for 3 to 5 minutes, or until fragrant. Transfer to a blender or food processor. Add scallions, garlic, peppers, rum, orange juice, salt and black pepper; blend to a smooth paste.

Makes about ½ cup rub, for 3 to 4 pounds of bone-in chicken.

———

Greek Lemon-Pepper Marinade

1 tablespoon black peppercorns
½ cup fresh lemon juice
2 tablespoons extra-virgin olive oil
2 tablespoons chopped parsley
4 cloves garlic, lightly crushed
1½ teaspoons salt

Crush peppercorns with a small heavy pan. Transfer to a small bowl and add lemon juice, oil, parsley, garlic and salt, stirring to mix well.

Makes ½ cup marinade, enough for 2 pounds of boneless chicken or pork.

———

Provençal Marinade

½ cup dry white wine
2 tablespoons fresh lemon juice
2 tablespoons extra-virgin olive oil
2 tablespoons Dijon mustard
2 teaspoons finely chopped fresh rosemary
2 cloves garlic, finely chopped
½ teaspoon salt
Freshly ground black pepper to taste

In a small bowl, whisk all ingredients.

Makes about ¾ cup marinade, enough for 2 to 2½ pounds lamb, pork or chicken.

Fish & Chips, page 90

TECHNIQUES 43-46

FISH & Shellfish

FISH WAS ONCE CONSIDERED TO BE "BRAIN FOOD," AND WHILE EATING IT WON'T actually increase your IQ, it certainly is smart to eat fish often. Lean, white-fleshed fish, such as cod or haddock, have about one gram of fat and roughly 125 calories in a four-ounce portion—a boon for dieters. Fattier fish, such as salmon or mackerel, have considerably more fat and calories, but that does not mean they should be avoided. Fish oils are among the heart-healthiest fats around; they contain beneficial omega-3 fatty acids, which have been linked to lower risk of heart attacks.

Shellfish, which are only now shaking the misperception that they raise cholesterol, are quite healthful too. They are rich in trace minerals and, like lean-fleshed fish, generally very low in fat.

43 Fried fish and shellfish— without the deep-fat fryer.

About half of the seafood eaten in America is fried, effectively negating many of its nutritional benefits. But the experience of the hot, crispy coating contrasting with the moist, white interior is hard to forgo altogether. Our technique of dipping fish or shrimp or scallops in batter and breadcrumbs, then baking at high heat, produces the closest thing to fried without actually heating up the fryer.

F FAT SAVINGS: One serving of fried fish has about 12 to 15 grams of fat; the fries add another 10 grams. The oven-frying method produces the same meal for 6 grams. A 4-ounce portion of fried breaded shrimp or scallops contains 12 or more grams of fat. The oven-frying method brings that down to 8 grams or less.

Fish & Chips

1	cup yellow cornmeal, preferably stone-ground
¾	cup all-purpose white flour
1	teaspoon baking powder
¼	teaspoon baking soda
	Freshly ground black pepper to taste
1½	cups fine dry breadcrumbs
1½	teaspoons salt
¾	teaspoon paprika
1½	pounds all-purpose potatoes, preferably Yukon Gold *or* russet (about 4 medium), unpeeled, scrubbed
2	teaspoons olive oil
2	large egg whites
¾	cup buttermilk
1	pound cod fillets, cut into 4-by-5-inch pieces
½	cup malt vinegar *or* cider vinegar

1. Place one oven rack in highest position and another rack in lower third of oven. Preheat oven to 450°F. Spread cornmeal in a thin layer on a large baking sheet; set aside. Lightly oil a second baking sheet or coat it with nonstick cooking spray.

2. In a bowl, whisk flour, baking powder, baking soda and pepper. In a shallow bowl, combine breadcrumbs, 1 teaspoon of the salt, ½ teaspoon of the paprika, and pepper. Set both bowls aside.

3. Cut each potato lengthwise into 8 wedges. In a large bowl, combine oil, the remaining ½ teaspoon salt and ¼ teaspoon paprika, and pepper. Add the potato wedges, toss to coat and spread on the prepared baking sheet. Bake on the upper rack of the oven for 20 minutes.

4. Meanwhile, in a bowl, beat egg whites to soft peaks with an electric mixer. Make a well in the flour mixture and add buttermilk; beat on low speed just until combined. With a rubber spatula, fold in the egg whites. The batter should be light and foamy.

5. Dry fillets well with paper towels. Lightly coat the fish with breadcrumbs; dip into batter, letting excess drip off, and then coat completely with more breadcrumbs. Place the pieces on the prepared baking sheet.

6. Once the chips have been baking for 20 minutes, loosen and turn with a metal spatula. Put the fish on the bottom rack of the oven at this time. Bake fish and chips until golden brown and the fish flakes easily, 12 to 15 minutes. Serve with vinegar.

Makes four 4-ounce servings.

585 calories per serving: 40 grams protein, 6 grams fat (1.2 grams saturated fat), 93 grams carbohydrate; 1,390 mg sodium; 64 mg cholesterol; 6 grams fiber.

N NUTRITION BONUS: Not only are baked potato wedges better for you, they taste better than fried wedges that often come out oily and soggy.

Spicy Peanut Beer-Batter Shrimp

1	pound unpeeled medium shrimp
¼	cup unsalted cocktail peanuts, finely chopped
¾	cup fine dry breadcrumbs
½	teaspoon salt

¼-½   teaspoon cayenne
     Freshly ground black pepper to taste
⅓   cup all-purpose white flour
¼   cup dark beer
1   large egg white
2   tablespoons cornstarch
     Lemon wedges for garnish

1. Preheat oven to 450°F. Lightly oil a wire rack that is large enough to hold shrimp in a single layer or coat it with nonstick cooking spray. Place the rack on a baking sheet and set aside. Peel and devein shrimp, leaving tails intact.

2. In a bowl, combine peanuts, breadcrumbs, ¼ teaspoon of the salt, cayenne and black pepper. Set aside.

3. In another bowl, whisk flour, beer, egg white and the remaining ¼ teaspoon salt until creamy and smooth.

4. Pat shrimp dry with paper towels; rub with cornstarch to coat evenly. Dip shrimp in the seasoned breadcrumbs, then the beer mixture and once again in the breadcrumbs. Place on the prepared rack; the shrimp should not touch. Bake for 12 to 15 minutes, or until coating is golden brown and shrimp are opaque in the center. Serve hot with lemon wedges.

Makes 4 servings.

310 calories per serving: 30 grams protein, 8 grams fat (1.5 grams saturated fat), 29 grams carbohydrate; 565 mg sodium; 174 mg cholesterol; 2 grams fiber.

N NUTRITION BONUS: The old taboo about shrimp on a cholesterol-lowering diet is gone—they're so low in saturated fat that they are now considered heart-healthy.

Lemon-Sesame Scallops

2   tablespoons sesame seeds
½   cup fine dry breadcrumbs
1   tablespoon grated lemon zest
½   teaspoon salt
     Freshly ground black pepper to taste
     Pinch of cayenne
⅓   cup all-purpose white flour
½   cup buttermilk
1   large egg white
1   pound sea scallops *or* large bay scallops
2   tablespoons cornstarch
     Lemon wedges for garnish

1. Preheat oven to 450°F. Spread sesame seeds in a baking pan and toast in the oven as it warms up, stirring often, until golden brown, about 5 to 7 minutes. Lightly oil a wire rack that is large enough to hold scallops in a single layer or coat it with nonstick cooking spray. Place the rack on a baking sheet and set aside.

2. In a bowl, combine the toasted sesame seeds, breadcrumbs, lemon zest, ¼ teaspoon of the salt, black pepper and cayenne. Set aside.

3. In another bowl, whisk flour, buttermilk, egg white and remaining ¼ teaspoon of the salt until creamy and smooth.

4. Rinse scallops under cold running water and pat dry with paper towels. In a shallow bowl, dredge a scallop in cornstarch, and shake to remove excess. Using tongs or 2 forks, dip scallop in the buttermilk mixture, and then in the breadcrumb mixture, shaking to remove excess breading. Place on the prepared rack, and repeat with remaining scallops. Scallops should not touch.

5. Bake the scallops for 12 to 15 minutes, or until the coating is golden brown and the scallops are firm and opaque in the center. Serve hot with lemon wedges.

Makes 4 servings.

240 calories per serving: 24 grams protein, 5 grams fat (1.5 grams saturated fat), 26 grams carbohydrate; 565 mg sodium; 39 mg cholesterol; 2 grams fiber.

N NUTRITION BONUS: Like shrimp, scallops are extremely low in fat. Serve with rice, green beans and carrots for a nutritious low-fat meal.

TECHNIQUE 44

Pan-sear fish in a minimum of oil for maximum flavor.

The trick to cooking lean fish in little oil is to use a heavy-bottomed nonstick skillet or a well-seasoned cast-iron skillet and to disturb the fish as little as possible while it is cooking.

F FAT SAVINGS: Classic American pan-frying recipes call for heating ¼ inch of oil or butter in a skillet: that translates to ¾ cup of fat in a 10-inch skillet! Our recipes ask you to add just 1 tablespoon of oil to the skillet.

Crisp Rockfish Fillets with Mustard Sauce

The fish and sauce are wonderful with mashed potatoes.

 4 rockfish fillets (about 1 pound total), skin on
 ½ cup low-fat milk
 ½ cup all-purpose white flour
  Salt & freshly ground black pepper to taste
 1 tablespoon olive oil, preferably extra-virgin
 2 tablespoons very finely chopped shallots
 ¾ cup dry white wine
 1 teaspoon Dijon mustard
 3 tablespoons chopped fresh parsley
 1 teaspoon butter

1. Dip each fillet in milk, then dredge the skin side in flour seasoned with salt and pepper (the top should not be floured). In a large nonstick skillet, heat oil over medium-high heat. Place the fillets, skin-side down, in the skillet. Cover and cook for 5 minutes, undisturbed. At this point, the fillets should be white on top and crisp on the bottom; if not, cook for another 2 minutes. Transfer the fillets to a platter and cover with foil to keep warm.

2. Return the skillet to medium heat and add shallots. Cook, stirring, until softened, about 1 minute. Add wine and stir, letting it bubble away for 1 minute or

so. Stir in mustard and parsley and cook for 30 seconds. Add butter and stir until the sauce is smooth.

3. Spoon the sauce over the rockfish and serve.

Makes 4 servings.

250 calories per serving: 24 grams protein, 6 grams fat (2 grams saturated fat), 15 grams carbohydrate; 100 mg sodium; 43 mg cholesterol; 1 gram fiber.

N NUTRITION BONUS: A bit of butter goes a long way to flavor this savory sauce and still the saturated fat is kept well within acceptable limits.

Variation: Substitute haddock, ocean perch, red snapper, tilefish or weakfish. Fillets should be under ½ inch thick. Adjust cooking time accordingly.

Pan-Fried Trout

 ⅓ cup buttermilk
 ½ teaspoon salt
 ½ teaspoon freshly ground black pepper
 4 small fresh whole trout (about 1½ pounds total)
 ½ cup yellow cornmeal, preferably stone-ground
 1 tablespoon olive oil
  Lemon wedges

1. In a shallow pan or bowl large enough to hold the fish in a single layer, mix buttermilk and ¼ teaspoon each of salt and black pepper. Add fish and turn to coat evenly, rubbing buttermilk into cavities. Cover and place in refrigerator for 30 minutes.

2. In a shallow pan or on a large plate, combine cornmeal and the remaining ¼ teaspoon each of salt and pepper. Set aside.

3. Remove fish from refrigerator. Heat oil in a 12-inch nonstick pan over medium heat. Shake excess buttermilk off trout, then dredge in cornmeal mixture, turning to coat evenly. Place fish gently in heated pan. (If pan is smaller, cook fish in two batches.) Turn heat to low and cook fish for 10 minutes, or until cornmeal crust is well browned. Turn carefully, using tongs or 2 spatulas if needed; continue cooking on second side for another 10 minutes, or until well browned. Serve immediately with lemon wedges.

Makes 4 servings.

200 calories per serving: 20 grams protein, 7 grams fat (1 gram saturated fat), 15 grams carbohydrate; 310 mg sodium; 50 mg cholesterol; 1 gram fiber.

N NUTRITION BONUS: A cornmeal crust is the only way to have fresh trout. With our method, you can enjoy it without any guilt.

Pan-Grilled Salmon Fillets with Tomato & Tarragon

1-1¼	pounds salmon fillet, skin on (scaling is not necessary), pin bones removed, cut into 4 equal pieces
	Freshly ground black pepper to taste
½	cup dry white wine
⅓	cup very finely chopped fresh chives
3	sprigs fresh tarragon
1	teaspoon butter
2	ripe plum tomatoes, seeded and chopped
	Salt to taste
	Fresh chives for garnish

1. Preheat a 12-inch ovenproof skillet for 3 or 4 minutes over medium-high heat. Preheat the broiler, positioning the top rack about 4 inches from the heat.
2. Place salmon fillets in the skillet, skin-side down, leaving the heat on medium-high. Sprinkle with pepper and cook, undisturbed, for about 6 minutes, or until the salmon flesh begins to turn opaque.
3. Transfer the skillet to the broiler and leave it there for 2 or 3 minutes, just until the salmon browns on top. The salmon should still be moist in the middle.
4. Meanwhile, in a small saucepan, heat wine over medium heat. Let it simmer for about 1 minute. Add chives, tarragon and butter and stir. When the butter has melted, add tomatoes and cook another 30 seconds. Adjust seasonings with salt and pepper. Remove and discard the tarragon. Spoon the sauce over the salmon. Garnish with chives.

Makes 4 servings.

185 calories per serving: 23 grams protein, 8 grams fat (1.7 grams saturated fat), 3 grams carbohydrate; 65 mg sodium; 65 mg cholesterol; 1 gram fiber.

N NUTRITION BONUS: Salmon is one of the fattier fish, but the good news is that it is rich in omega-3 fatty acids, which are believed to help protect against heart attacks.

TECHNIQUE

45 Don't overcook lean swordfish or tuna steaks.

Swordfish and tuna steaks make great summertime eating. They are easy to grill and have a rich flavor and a meaty texture that everyone loves. As with lean beef, you must take care not to overcook these fish or the close-grained flesh will be as dry and tough as that of an overdone top-round roast. To cook, grill swordfish or tuna steaks over a hot fire, turning once. Use a thin-bladed knife to peer into the flesh to check for doneness; when the flesh is no longer translucent, remove from the grill.

F FAT SAVINGS: Swordfish and tuna have about one-third less total fat than lean sirloin. The big savings is in saturated fat—both fish have about half the saturated fat of beef.

Grilled Mesclun-Stuffed Swordfish

¼	cup fresh lime juice
¼	cup dry white wine
2	tablespoons soy sauce
2	teaspoons minced fresh ginger
1	teaspoon Dijon mustard
1	small clove garlic, minced
½	teaspoon sesame oil
½	teaspoon freshly ground black pepper
1¼	pounds swordfish steak, no less than 1¼ inches thick, skin removed
1½	cups mesclun salad greens, washed and dried
1	teaspoon olive oil

1. In a glass measuring cup, whisk lime juice, wine, soy sauce, ginger, mustard, garlic, sesame oil and pepper. Pour all but ¼ cup of the marinade into a shallow dish, add swordfish and turn to coat well. (Set the remaining marinade aside to be used to dress the greens.) Cover and marinate the fish in the refrigerator for 30 minutes to 1 hour.

2. Prepare a charcoal fire or preheat a gas grill. In a bowl, toss salad greens with the reserved marinade and set aside.

3. Place the swordfish on a cutting board. Holding a sharp, thin-bladed knife parallel to the work surface, make a short incision halfway through the thickness of the steak. Insert the knife almost to the opposite edge of the steak, then move it back and forth to create a large pocket. Leave a ½-inch border around the edges, being careful not to cut through the top, bottom or opposite edge of the steak. Stuff the pocket with the greens. Rub the steak with olive oil.

4. Grill over a hot fire until well marked, about 6 minutes per side. Use a thin-bladed knife to peer into the flesh to check for doneness: when the flesh is no longer translucent, remove from the grill. Slice the

Grilled Mesclun-Stuffed Swordfish: The close-grained flesh of swordfish makes it ideal for stuffing.

steak into ½-inch-wide strips and serve.

Makes 4 servings.

210 calories per serving: 29 grams protein, 7 grams fat (1.8 grams saturated fat), 4 grams carbohydrate; 650 mg sodium; 55 mg cholesterol; 0 grams fiber.

Ⓝ NUTRITION BONUS: Mesclun may seem expensive but there is no waste and the variety of baby greens is a nutritional gold mine.

TECHNIQUE

46 Cut the yolks to reduce the fat in crab cakes and salmon cakes.

Classic seafood cakes are bound with whole eggs (and occasionally moistened with heavy cream). The EATING WELL Test Kitchen uses eggs too, but not whole eggs, having found that fat-free whites bind the mixture nicely. And instead of pan-frying the cakes in a half-inch of sputtering butter or oil, we brown the cakes in a teaspoon or two of oil. This step cuts the fat by another 10 or 12 grams.

Ⓕ FAT SAVINGS: Full-fat crab cakes tip the scales at 12 to 15 grams of fat per serving. Eating Well crab cakes weigh in at 5 grams per serving.

Crab Cakes

1   pound fresh lump crabmeat (2 cups), picked over, drained and squeezed dry
1   cup fresh breadcrumbs (about 4 slices fresh *or* day-old bread)
3   tablespoons reduced-fat mayonnaise
1   tablespoon Dijon mustard
1   large egg white, lightly beaten with a fork
2   scallions, trimmed and finely chopped
¼   cup finely diced red *or* green bell pepper
1   tablespoon chopped fresh parsley
1   teaspoon Old Bay seafood seasoning
¼   teaspoon freshly ground black pepper

¼-½ teaspoon Tabasco sauce
½ cup fine dry breadcrumbs
1 tablespoon vegetable oil, preferably canola
Lemon wedges for garnish

1. Place a baking sheet in the oven and preheat oven to 450°F. In a large bowl, combine crabmeat, fresh breadcrumbs, mayonnaise, mustard, egg white, scallions, bell peppers, parsley, Old Bay seasoning, black pepper and Tabasco.

2. Put the dry breadcrumbs in a shallow dish. Form the crab mixture into six ½-inch-thick cakes. (The mixture will be very soft.) Dredge the cakes in the dry breadcrumbs, reshaping as necessary.

3. Brush ½ tablespoon of the oil evenly over the bottom of a large skillet. Heat the skillet over medium-high heat. Add half of the crab cakes and cook until the undersides are golden, 1 to 2 minutes. Carefully turn the crab cakes over with a spatula, and cook the second side until golden, 1 to 2 minutes. Transfer to the baking sheet in the oven. Add the remaining ½ tablespoon of the oil to the skillet, and repeat the process with the remaining crab cakes. Bake until heated through, 5 to 7 minutes. Serve with lemon wedges.

Makes 6 cakes, for 6 servings.

140 calories per cake: 16 grams protein, 5 grams fat (1 gram saturated fat), 12 grams carbohydrate; 385 mg sodium; 45 mg cholesterol; 1 gram fiber.

Ⓝ NUTRITION BONUS: At 2 grams of fat in 4 ounces, crabmeat is very low in total fat and has negligible saturated fat.

───────

Salmon Cakes

1½ cups frozen hash brown potatoes, thawed
1 7-ounce can salmon, drained, picked over and flaked
1 large egg white
1 tablespoon reduced-fat mayonnaise
2 teaspoons drained capers, coarsely chopped
1 scallion, trimmed and thinly sliced
Salt & freshly ground black pepper to taste
1 teaspoon olive oil, preferably extra-virgin

1. Preheat oven to 450°F. In a bowl, partially mash potatoes with a fork until they begin to hold together. Add salmon, egg white, mayonnaise, capers, scallions, salt and pepper. Shape into 4 cakes, each about ½ inch thick.

2. In an ovenproof nonstick skillet, heat oil over medium heat. Add the salmon cakes and cook until browned on the underside, 4 to 5 minutes. Carefully turn the cakes over with a spatula and transfer the skillet to the oven. Bake until heated through and golden brown on the second side, 5 to 7 minutes.

Makes 4 cakes, for 2 servings.

120 calories per cake: 13 grams protein, 5 grams fat (1 gram saturated fat), 8 grams carbohydrate; 410 mg sodium; 30 mg cholesterol; 1 gram fiber.

Ⓝ NUTRITION BONUS: Canned salmon is high in calcium.

───────

Tartar Sauce

½ cup Amazing Mayonnaise (*page 22*) *or* commercial reduced-fat mayonnaise
2 teaspoons fresh lemon juice
1 cornichon *or* sour gherkin, chopped
1 anchovy fillet, minced
1 teaspoon capers, rinsed and chopped
1 teaspoon dried tarragon
1 teaspoon minced fresh parsley

In a small bowl, blend all ingredients.

Makes ⅔ cup.

4 calories per tablespoon: 0 grams protein, 2 grams fat (0 grams saturated fat), 2 grams carbohydrate; 145 mg sodium; 1 mg cholesterol; 0 grams fiber.

Feta & Spinach Soufflé, page 98

THE TECHNIQUES

47 Eliminating egg yolks to cut fat in scrambled eggs and soufflé

48 Lowering the fat in deviled eggs and egg salad

49 Substituting polenta for eggs in a hearty brunch dish

50 Using evaporated skim milk to enrich a quiche

51 Boosting flavor with full-fat cheeses

52 Making your own nonfat yogurt cheese

TECHNIQUES 47-52

EGGS & Cheese

THESE TWO FOODS ARE FUNDAMENTAL COMPONENTS OF MUCH OF WHAT WE EAT. AMERICAN breakfast would look rather sorry without eggs, and lunch or dinner without cheese to flavor, enrich, fill or top our favorite dishes would be less enjoyable. As with many foods that taste good, eggs and cheese are high in fat. But that doesn't mean they have to be banished from the refrigerator or your table. Cutting back on egg yolks, relying on smaller amounts of more flavorful cheeses and using low-fat cooking methods are all part of keeping eggs and cheese on a healthy menu.

47 To cut the fat, increase the proportion of whites to yolks in a recipe.

There are 5 grams of fat in an egg yolk; there is no fat in an egg white. As a first step in cutting the fat in egg-rich dishes, the EATING WELL Test Kitchen reduces the number of egg yolks and increases the number of egg whites. We have discovered that almost all savory egg dishes can take the elimination of some of the yolks without any adverse effect.

F FAT SAVINGS: Doubling the whites in proportion to the yolks effectively cuts the amount of fat in scrambled eggs in half.

Scrambled Eggs with Smoked Salmon

- 4 large eggs
- 4 large egg whites
  Freshly ground black pepper to taste
- 1 teaspoon vegetable oil, preferably canola
- 2 scallions, green tops only, thinly sliced
- 1 ounce smoked salmon, thinly sliced

1. Combine eggs, egg whites and pepper in a small bowl. Stir briskly with a fork until well blended.
2. In a nonstick skillet, heat oil over medium-low heat. Add scallions and cook, stirring, until softened, about 30 seconds.
3. Pour the eggs into the skillet and cook until they just begin to set, about 10 seconds; stir in salmon. Cook, stirring gently from time to time, until the eggs have thickened into soft, creamy curds, 3 to 5 minutes. Serve immediately.

Makes 4 servings.

110 calories per serving: 11 grams protein, 7 grams fat (2.1 grams saturated fat), 1 gram carbohydrate; 170 mg sodium; 214 mg cholesterol; 0 grams fiber.

N NUTRITION BONUS: Smoked salmon is a good source of omega-3 fatty acids.

 AREN'T EGGS TERRIBLY HIGH IN CHOLESTEROL?

Yes, at 213 milligrams (all contained in the yolk), the cholesterol content of an egg is quite high. But the cholesterol found in eggs is *dietary* cholesterol, which is not the same as *blood* cholesterol. Curiously enough, in most people, eating dietary cholesterol does not make blood cholesterol rise. Saturated fat in the diet is the main culprit that raises blood cholesterol.

Feta & Spinach Soufflé

Inspired by Greek spinach pie, spanakopita, *this soufflé is light but satisfying.*

- 2 tablespoons fine dry breadcrumbs
- ½ pound fresh spinach, stemmed and washed (8 cups)
- 1½ teaspoons olive oil
- 1 onion, finely chopped
- 1 clove garlic, minced
- 1½ cups low-fat milk
- ⅓ cup cornstarch
- 2 large egg yolks
- ½ cup crumbled feta cheese (2 ounces)
- 2 tablespoons chopped fresh mint *or* dill
- 1 teaspoon salt
- ½ teaspoon freshly ground black pepper
- 6 large egg whites

1. Position rack in the lower third of the oven; preheat to 375°F. Lightly oil a 2-quart soufflé dish or coat it with nonstick cooking spray. Sprinkle with breadcrumbs, tapping out the excess.
2. Put spinach, with the water still clinging to the leaves, in a pot. Cover and cook over medium heat just until wilted. Transfer to a colander to drain. Squeeze out the excess liquid and chop.
3. In a nonstick skillet, heat oil over medium heat. Add onions and garlic; cook, stirring, until softened, about 5 minutes. Add the chopped spinach and cook, stirring, until heated through and quite dry, about 2 minutes. Set aside.

4. In a heavy saucepan, heat 1 cup of the milk until steaming. In a small bowl, stir cornstarch into the remaining ½ cup cold milk; add to the hot milk and cook, whisking constantly, until thickened and smooth, 2 to 3 minutes. Remove from the heat and let cool slightly. Add egg yolks, one at a time, whisking until incorporated. Stir in the reserved spinach mixture, feta, mint or dill, ½ teaspoon salt and pepper.

5. In a large mixing bowl, beat egg whites with an electric mixer on medium speed until foamy and opaque. Add the remaining ½ teaspoon salt; gradually increase the speed to high and beat until stiff (but not dry) peaks form.

6. Whisk about one-third of the beaten egg whites into the spinach mixture to lighten it. Using a rubber spatula, fold the spinach mixture back into the remaining whites. Transfer to the prepared soufflé dish and smooth the top with the spatula.

7. Bake until puffed and the top feels firm to the touch, about 35 minutes. Serve immediately.

Makes 4 servings.

240 calories per serving: 15 grams protein, 9 grams fat (4.5 grams saturated fat), 25 grams carbohydrate; 895 mg sodium; 125 mg cholesterol; 2.5 grams fiber.

(N) NUTRITION BONUS: This soufflé is a rich source of trace minerals and a good source of folic acid and calcium.

TECHNIQUE 48 Cut back on the yolks to lower the fat in egg salad and deviled eggs.

Crowd-pleasers like a stack of freshly made egg salad sandwiches or a platter of stuffed hard-boiled eggs don't have to be eliminated because of fat concerns. Just don't use all the yolks (remember every yolk you omit cuts 5 grams of fat) and bind the fillings with reduced-fat, not full-fat, mayonnaise.

(F) FAT SAVINGS: An Eating Well deviled egg has 3 grams of fat; a full-fat version has 6. The fat reduction for egg salad sandwiches is even more dramatic: 7 grams vs. 18.

(?) WHAT'S THE BEST WAY TO HARD-BOIL EGGS?

The EATING WELL Test Kitchen has a favorite technique for boiling eggs:

Prior to cooking, lightly tap each egg with the back of a spoon to make a hairline crack. Place eggs in a large saucepan, cover with cold water and bring water to a simmer. Simmer gently for 9 minutes.

Drain immediately and set the pan and eggs under cold running water for 1 minute. Because a cooked egg white begins to stick to the shell as it cools, remove the shells right away, starting at the larger end. If the shell sticks, finish removing it under cold running water.

Egg Salad Sandwiches with Watercress

Watercress adds a zesty note to this enlightened version of an American classic.

8   hard-boiled eggs, peeled
¼   cup Amazing Mayonnaise (*page 22*) *or* commercial reduced-fat mayonnaise
1   tablespoon grainy mustard
4   scallions, trimmed and chopped
    Salt & freshly ground black pepper to taste
¾   cup washed and stemmed watercress
8   slices whole-grain, rye *or* pumpernickel bread

1. Scoop out egg yolks. Place 2 yolks in a small bowl and discard the rest. Chop egg whites and reserve. Mash the yolks with a fork and stir in mayonnaise and mustard. Add chopped egg whites and scallions and season with salt and pepper.

2. Arrange watercress on 4 bread slices. Top with the egg salad and cover with the remaining bread slices.

Makes 4 sandwiches, for 4 servings.

230 calories per serving: 15 grams protein, 7 grams fat (0.8 gram saturated fat), 34 grams carbohydrate; 620 mg sodium; 106 mg cholesterol; 4 grams fiber.

(N) NUTRITION BONUS: Despite their bad rap, eggs are low in saturated fat and rich in minerals and vitamins, particularly vitamin E.

Deviled Eggs

12 hard-boiled eggs, peeled
½ cup Amazing Mayonnaise (*page 22*)
  or commercial reduced-fat mayonnaise
2 tablespoons chopped chives
2 teaspoons Dijon mustard
  Salt & freshly ground black pepper to taste
  Paprika for garnish

1. Slice eggs in half lengthwise. Scoop out the yolks, discarding half and putting the rest in a small bowl.
2. Thoroughly mash the yolks with a fork. Stir in mayonnaise, chives and mustard. Season with salt and pepper.
3. Spoon the mixture into the hollows in the egg whites and sprinkle with paprika. Arrange on a platter.

Makes 24 deviled eggs.

45 calories per deviled egg: 3 grams protein, 3 grams fat (0.9 gram saturated fat), 1 gram carbohydrate; 60 mg sodium; 111 mg cholesterol; 0 grams fiber.

N NUTRITION BONUS: Dijon mustard is a great fat-free flavor booster; it also helps to naturally color the filling.

TECHNIQUE

49 Substitute commercial cooked polenta for eggs in a brunch dish.

It started out as a sautéed polenta dish, but when the tasters walked into the Test Kitchen at EATING WELL and commented on how great the scrambled eggs looked, Test Kitchen Director Patsy Jamieson knew she was on to something. For this recipe, cooked polenta (you will find it on the refrigerated shelves at the supermarket, often next to the cheese) is diced and sautéed with sausage and peppers. The result is a creamy, satisfying brunch dish that looks like eggs but isn't.

F FAT SAVINGS: Using cooked polenta instead of eggs cuts the fat by 5 grams per serving.

Scrambled Polenta, Sausage & Peppers

Prepared polenta packaged in a plastic casing is one of the most convenient products to turn up in supermarkets lately. Thick, cold homemade polenta can be used as well.

¼ pound sweet Italian sausage
  (about 2 small links)
1 pound prepared polenta
3 teaspoons olive oil
2 onions, chopped
2 red bell peppers, seeded and
  chopped
  **Salt & freshly ground black
  pepper to taste**
¾ cup grated part-skim mozzarella
  cheese (3 ounces)
2 tablespoons chopped fresh
  parsley

Scrambled Polenta, Sausage & Peppers provides much flavor with little fat.

1. Pierce sausages with a fork and place in a sauce-pan. Cover with water and simmer over low heat for 10 minutes. Transfer the sausages to a cutting board. Let cool slightly, then cut into thin rounds; set aside.

2. Meanwhile, pat polenta dry and cut into ½-inch-thick slices. Stack slices, 4 or 5 at a time, and cut into quarters. Pat slices dry and set aside.

3. In a 12-inch heavy nonstick or cast-iron skillet, cook the sausage slices, stirring, over medium-high heat, until browned, 3 to 5 minutes. Transfer to a plate lined with paper towels, blot fat and set aside.

4. Add 1 teaspoon of the oil to the skillet. Add onions and cook, stirring, until soft, 2 to 3 minutes. Add peppers, season with salt and pepper and cook, stirring, until tender, about 3 minutes longer. Transfer the vegetables to a plate and set aside.

5. Wipe out the skillet and add the remaining 2 teaspoons oil. Add the reserved polenta and sauté until nicely browned, 3 to 5 minutes.

6. Add the reserved vegetables and sausages and shake the skillet over the heat until everything is heated through. Taste and adjust seasonings with salt and pepper. Remove from the heat, sprinkle with cheese and garnish with parsley. Serve right away.

Makes 6 servings.

200 calories per serving: 9 grams protein, 9 grams fat (3.5 grams saturated fat), 18 grams carbohydrate; 375 mg sodium; 23 mg cholesterol; 3 grams fiber.

Ⓝ NUTRITION BONUS: Polenta stands in for eggs and extends the flavors of sausage and peppers.

TECHNIQUE 50 — Use evaporated skim milk to enrich an egg-reduced custard.

Evaporated skim milk is made by evaporating nearly half of the water from fresh skim milk. The canned milk product is fat-free, yet it adds a creamy richness to custards.

Ⓕ FAT SAVINGS: Quiches made with heavy cream and whole eggs in the custard have two or even three times the fat contained in Eating Well's quiche.

Leek & Gruyère Quiche

CRUST

- 1 tablespoon butter
- 3 tablespoons canola oil
- 1 cup all-purpose white flour
- ¼ teaspoon salt

FILLING

- 2 teaspoons olive oil
- ½ pound leeks, white and light green part only, washed thoroughly and thinly sliced (about 2 cups)
- 2 large eggs
- 4 large egg whites
- ¾ cup evaporated skim milk
- ¾ cup skim *or* low-fat milk
- ¼ teaspoon salt
- ¼ teaspoon freshly ground black pepper
- ¼ teaspoon freshly grated nutmeg
  Pinch of cayenne
- 1 teaspoon Dijon mustard
- 1 tablespoon fine dry breadcrumbs
- ¾ cup grated Gruyère cheese (about 3 ounces)
- 1 tablespoon freshly grated Parmesan cheese

TO MAKE CRUST:

1. Position rack in the lower third of the oven; pre-heat to 425°F. In a small saucepan, melt butter over low heat. Swirling the pan, cook butter for about 30 seconds, or until it is a light nutty brown. (*See Technique 81, page 154.*) Pour into a small bowl and let cool. Stir in canola oil.

2. In a medium bowl, whisk flour and salt. Using a fork, slowly stir the butter-oil mixture into the flour mixture until it is crumbly. Gradually stir in enough ice water (1 to 2 tablespoons) for the dough to hold together. (*See Technique 85, page 166.*) Gather the dough into a ball.

3. Place the dough between two sheets of plastic wrap and flatten into a disk. Roll to a 12-inch circle. Remove the top plastic sheet and invert dough into a 9-inch pie pan. Remove the remaining plastic. Fold edges under at the rim and crimp.

4. Line the dough with a piece of foil or parchment paper large enough to lift out easily; fill evenly with pie weights or dried beans. Bake for 7 minutes. Remove paper and weights and bake for 3 to 5 minutes longer, or just until lightly browned. (The crust will not be fully baked.) Cool on a wire rack. Reduce oven temperature to 350°F.

TO MAKE FILLING:

1. Meanwhile, in a nonstick skillet, heat olive oil over low heat. Add leeks and cook, stirring occasionally, for 15 minutes, or until leeks are soft and wilted. Set aside to cool.

2. In a large bowl, whisk eggs and egg whites. Stirring gently to avoid creating bubbles, add evaporated milk, skim or low-fat milk, salt, pepper, nutmeg and cayenne.

TO ASSEMBLE & BAKE QUICHE:

Spread mustard over the bottom of the prebaked crust; sprinkle evenly with breadcrumbs. Top with Gruyère, then the cooked leeks. Carefully pour in the egg mixture. Sprinkle with Parmesan. Bake for 25 to 30 minutes, or until just set and a knife inserted in the center comes out clean. Transfer to a wire rack and let cool for at least 10 minutes before slicing.

Makes one 9-inch quiche, for 8 servings.

250 calories per serving: 12 grams protein, 13 grams fat (4 grams saturated fat), 21 grams carbohydrate; 295 mg sodium; 71 mg cholesterol; 1 gram fiber.

Ⓝ NUTRITION BONUS: Cutting back on the egg yolks in the custard helps to further reduce the fat in this recipe.

TECHNIQUE 51 — To boost flavor, choose full-fat cheeses, and use them judiciously.

Hard cheeses, such as Cheddar or Monterey Jack, have about 9 grams of fat in every ounce. And it's not only the quantity of fat in cheese that is a concern, it's the fact that nearly two-thirds of it is saturated fat. It would seem that a simple switch to reduced-fat cheese would be the best way to cut fat in recipes calling for cheese. But reduced-fat cheeses just don't offer the same flavor.

After countless tests and retests in the EATING WELL kitchen, we concluded that to maintain the rich flavor, it's best to stick with a full-fat cheese but to pick the most flavorful variety and use a smaller amount. If a recipe calls for Cheddar, use the sharpest Cheddar you can find. If it calls for Parmesan, make it authentic Parmigiano-Reggiano, not grated Parmesan in a can.

Ⓕ FAT SAVINGS: The originals of each of the following recipes weighed in at about 35 grams of fat per serving. These reduced-fat versions maintain a cheesy, rich flavor at one-third to one-fourth the fat.

Macaroni & Cheese

½ pound elbow macaroni
1½ cups low-fat (1%) cottage cheese
1 cup skim *or* low-fat milk
1 tablespoon all-purpose white flour
1 cup grated sharp Cheddar cheese (4 ounces)
¼ teaspoon freshly grated nutmeg
⅛ teaspoon cayenne
Salt & freshly ground black pepper to taste
2 tablespoons freshly grated Parmesan cheese
2 tablespoons fine dry breadcrumbs

1. Preheat oven to 375°F. Lightly oil a shallow 2-quart baking dish or coat it with nonstick cooking spray.

2. In a large pot of boiling salted water, cook macaroni until al dente, 8 to 10 minutes. Drain in a colander and rinse with cold water; set aside.

3. Puree cottage cheese in a food processor or blender until smooth; set aside.

4. In a large heavy saucepan, heat ¾ cup of the milk over medium heat until steaming. In a small bowl, whisk flour and the remaining ¼ cup milk until smooth. Stir into the hot milk and cook, whisking, until the sauce is smooth and thick, about 2 minutes. Remove from the heat and stir in Cheddar, pureed cottage cheese, nutmeg, cayenne, salt and pepper. Stir in the cooked macaroni and spoon into the prepared baking dish. Sprinkle with Parmesan and breadcrumbs. Bake until bubbling and brown, about 35 minutes.

Makes 4 servings.

455 calories per serving: 30 grams protein, 13 grams fat (8 grams saturated fat), 53 grams carbohydrate; 635 mg sodium; 40 mg cholesterol; 0.2 gram fiber.

 NUTRITION BONUS: Our macaroni and cheese provides about 395 milligrams of calcium.

Crustless Crab Quiche

2	teaspoons olive oil
1	onion, chopped
1	red bell pepper, seeded and chopped
¾	pound mushrooms, sliced (about 4½ cups)
2	large eggs
2	large egg whites
1½	cups low-fat (1%) cottage cheese
½	cup nonfat plain yogurt
¼	cup all-purpose white flour
¼	cup freshly grated Parmesan cheese
¼	teaspoon cayenne
¼	teaspoon salt
¼	teaspoon freshly ground black pepper
½	pound cooked lump crabmeat (fresh *or* frozen and thawed), drained and picked over (about 1 cup)
½	cup grated sharp Cheddar cheese (2 ounces)
¼	cup chopped scallions

1. Preheat oven to 350°F. Lightly oil a 10-inch pie pan or porcelain quiche dish, or coat it with nonstick cooking spray.

2. In large nonstick skillet, heat 1 teaspoon of the oil over medium-high heat. Add onions and peppers and cook, stirring, until softened, about 5 minutes; transfer to a mixing bowl.

3. Add the remaining 1 teaspoon oil to the skillet and heat over high heat. Add mushrooms and cook, stirring, until they have softened and most of the liquid has evaporated, 5 to 7 minutes. Add to the onion mixture.

4. In a food processor or blender, blend eggs, egg whites, cottage cheese, yogurt, flour, Parmesan, cayenne, salt and pepper until smooth; add to the bowl with the vegetables. With a rubber spatula, fold in crab, Cheddar and scallions. Transfer to the prepared pie pan or quiche dish.

5. Bake for 40 to 50 minutes, or until a knife inserted into the center comes out clean. Let stand for 5 minutes before serving.

Makes one 10-inch quiche, for 6 servings.

230 calories per serving: 24 grams protein, 9 grams fat (4 grams saturated fat), 13 grams carbohydrate; 390 mg sodium; 125 mg cholesterol; 1.7 grams fiber.

 NUTRITION BONUS: Traditional quiches derive much of their saturated fat from the crust.

Crustless Crab Quiche makes a hearty, wholesome brunch dish.

52 Make yogurt cheese from nonfat yogurt to add rich dairy flavor to cheese fillings.

Yogurt cheese is a valuable tool for cutting fat. Made by draining the whey from yogurt, this fresh cheese is a great substitute for sour cream or cream cheese in fillings. When making yogurt cheese, begin with nonfat plain yogurt; check the label to make sure that it does not contain starch, gums or gelatin. Estimate that you will finish with about one-third of the original volume of yogurt: the final yield will vary somewhat depending on the brand of yogurt used and the time allowed for draining. (Extra yogurt cheese is delicious on bagels or baked potatoes.) Yogurt cheese can be stored, covered, in the refrigerator for up to 1 week.

F FAT SAVINGS: Yogurt cheese made from nonfat yogurt is fat-free; compare that to 1 ounce of full-fat cream cheese at 9.8 grams of fat or 1 ounce of sour cream at 5.9 grams of fat.

Set a fine-mesh stainless-steel sieve over a bowl. Spoon in yogurt, cover with plastic wrap and refrigerate for at least 8 hours or overnight. Discard the liquid.

Herbed Yogurt Cheese

Remember to start draining the yogurt the day before blending the cheese.

- 2 cups yogurt cheese, made from 6 cups nonfat plain yogurt (*see photograph at left*)
- 3 tablespoons snipped chives *or* chopped scallion greens
- 2 tablespoons chopped fresh parsley
- 1 tablespoon chopped fresh basil
- 1 clove garlic, minced
- ½ teaspoon salt
- ¼ teaspoon freshly ground black pepper

In a bowl, blend together yogurt cheese, chives or scallion greens, parsley, basil, garlic, salt and pepper with a wooden spoon. (*The cheese may be prepared ahead and stored, covered, in the refrigerator for up to 2 days.*) Serve on crostini (French bread toasts), crackers or Pita Crisps (*page 125*).

Makes 2 cups.

25 calories per tablespoon: 3 grams protein, 0 grams fat, 3 grams carbohydrate; 65 mg sodium; 1 mg cholesterol; 0 grams fiber.

N NUTRITION BONUS: Cream cheese contains about 60 times more fat per cup than yogurt cheese.

Cheese Triangles

- ¾ cup nonfat yogurt cheese, made from 2½ cups nonfat plain yogurt (*see photograph at left*)
- ½ cup crumbled feta cheese, preferably imported (2 ounces)
- 1 large egg white, lightly beaten with a fork
- ¼ cup chopped fresh parsley
- 2 tablespoons freshly grated Parmesan cheese
- 1 tablespoon fine dry breadcrumbs
  Pinch of cayenne
- 8 sheets phyllo dough (14x18 inches), thawed if frozen
- 2 tablespoons olive oil, preferably extra-virgin

1. Position rack in the upper third of the oven; pre-heat to 350°F. Lightly oil a baking sheet or coat it with nonstick cooking spray; set aside.

2. In a bowl, stir together yogurt cheese, feta, egg white, parsley, Parmesan, breadcrumbs and cayenne.

3. Set the stack of phyllo sheets to one side of the work surface; keep covered with a damp towel as you work. Working with one sheet at a time and with a long edge toward you, brush the first sheet of phyllo lightly with some of the olive oil. Top with a second sheet of phyllo and brush lightly with olive oil. Cut the phyllo vertically into 6 equal strips.

4. Place a heaping teaspoon of the cheese filling at the bottom of each phyllo strip. Fold one corner of the strip up and over the filling, then continue to fold the strip loosely (as you would fold a flag) to form a neat triangle. Place the triangles on the prepared baking sheet. Repeat 3 more times with the remaining sheets of phyllo and filling. Brush the tops of the triangles lightly with the remaining oil. With a sharp paring knife, make a small slit in the top of each triangle to allow steam to escape. *(If you like, the triangles can be prepared up to this point and frozen. Freeze them in a single layer, then enclose in a plastic bag or airtight container and store in the freezer for up to 2 months. Do not thaw before baking.)*

5. Bake the triangles until they are golden brown, 25 to 30 minutes. Let cool for 5 minutes before serving warm.

Makes 24 triangles.

35 calories per triangle: 2 grams protein, 2 grams fat (1 gram saturated fat), 2 grams carbohydrate; 65 mg sodium; 3 mg cholesterol; 0 grams fiber.

NUTRITION BONUS: A lower-fat appetizer is much appreciated by guests who are trying to watch fat and don't want to offend their host.

Impress your guests with Cheese Triangles—they look harder to make than they actually are, thanks to our phyllo technique, and are lower in fat than the usual can't-stop-eating-them party appetizer.

Ratatouille of Roasted Vegetables, page 108

TECHNIQUES
53-63

Vegetables

THE NEXT TIME YOU'RE AT THE SUPERMARKET, take stock of the wealth of fruits and vegetables in the produce aisle. There are a dozen varieties of pepper where once there was only standard bell. Today's "greens" come in a rainbow of colors, and tomatoes even have flavor. This abundance is great news not only in terms of menu options but also for your health. It's a fact: eating vegetables will reduce your risk of cancer and heart disease.

Vegetables by nature are very low in fat, and as long as they are not bathed in butter or smothered in cheese sauce, they stay low in fat. The challenge is to make them irresistible. The combination of innovative cooking methods and exciting flavor boosters should leave you without any vegetable leftovers.

53 Roast vegetables in the oven to enhance their natural sweetness.

The oven's high heat not only cooks vegetables, it transforms them into sweet irresistible flavor nuggets by sealing in juices and caramelizing the sugars. Nutrient retention improves when juices are sealed in rather than leached out (as happens in boiling). To prepare, you need to coat most vegetables with a little oil—we use heart-healthy olive or canola oil—to prevent them from drying out in the oven. Check the simple instructions opposite for cooking times for individual vegetables or use the mixed-vegetable recipes on the following pages.

F FAT SAVINGS: When cooked by the roasting method, vegetables don't need that pat of butter or cheese sauce to dress them up.

Ratatouille of Roasted Vegetables

1	large head garlic
12	ripe plum tomatoes, halved and seeded
1	eggplant (1-1¼ pounds), cut lengthwise into ½-inch-thick slices
2	small zucchini, cut in half lengthwise
2	small summer squash, cut in half lengthwise
1	Spanish onion, cut into ½-inch-thick slices
1	large red bell pepper, cut in half lengthwise and seeded
1	large yellow bell pepper, cut in half lengthwise and seeded
¼	cup chopped fresh basil
2	tablespoons olive oil
1	tablespoon chopped fresh thyme
1	teaspoon dried oregano
2	bay leaves
½	teaspoon salt
¼	teaspoon freshly ground black pepper

1. Position oven racks at the two lowest levels; preheat to 400°F. Roast garlic as illustrated on page 25.

2. Meanwhile, lightly oil 2 baking sheets or coat them with nonstick cooking spray. Arrange tomatoes, eggplant slices, zucchini, summer squash, onions, red bell peppers and yellow bell peppers on the prepared baking sheets. Roast for 20 minutes, turning once, until just tender and browned. Let cool slightly. Reduce oven temperature to 350°F.

3. Squeeze the soft garlic pulp into a Dutch oven or covered casserole. Slip skins from the tomatoes and peppers. Cut all the vegetables into pieces and add to the garlic. Stir in basil, oil, thyme, oregano, bay leaves, salt and pepper. Cover and bake, stirring occasionally, for 30 minutes, or until heated through and thickened. Remove bay leaves. Taste and adjust seasonings. Serve hot or at room temperature.

Makes about 5 cups, for 4 servings.

180 calories per serving: 5 grams protein, 8 grams fat (1 gram saturated fat), 26 grams carbohydrate; 475 mg sodium; 0 mg cholesterol; 7 grams fiber.

N NUTRITION BONUS: Served with rice or noodles, the ratatouille is hearty enough to eat as a main course.

Roasted Vegetable Sandwiches

These hearty sandwiches may be assembled ahead of time and are perfect for a summer picnic.

1	small eggplant, thinly sliced into rounds
1	zucchini, thinly sliced
1	summer squash, thinly sliced
1	red bell pepper, seeded and thinly sliced
2	teaspoons olive oil
2	cloves garlic, finely chopped
	Salt & freshly ground black pepper to taste
¼	cup nonfat sour cream *or* nonfat plain yogurt
2	tablespoons reduced-fat mayonnaise
1	tablespoon chopped fresh basil
1	teaspoon fresh lemon juice
1	16-inch-long French baguette
1	bunch watercress, washed, large stems removed (about 2 cups)

1. Preheat oven to 450°F. In a large roasting pan, toss eggplant, zucchini, summer squash and red pepper

ROASTED VEGETABLES PLAIN & SIMPLE

Position the rack in the bottom third of the oven; preheat to 450°F. Total fat content ranges from 1.1 to 2.2 grams per serving with no or negligible saturated fat; the calorie range is 35 to 130 per serving.

BEETS Scrub but do not peel 2 pounds trimmed medium beets. Roast on a lightly oiled baking sheet for 1 to 1½ hours, or until tender when pierced with a sharp knife. When cool enough to handle, peel and cut into ¼-inch-thick sticks. Toss with 1 tablespoon Dijon mustard and 1 teaspoon olive oil. Season with salt and pepper. Makes 4 servings.

BUTTERCUP SQUASH Cut in half 1 medium squash (1½ pounds), peel and seed. Cut into 1-inch chunks. Spread on a lightly oiled baking sheet, cover with foil and roast for 8 to 12 minutes, or until tender. Toss with 2 teaspoons lime juice mixed with 1 teaspoon chili powder, 1 teaspoon canola oil and ¼ teaspoon salt. Makes 3 servings.

CARROTS Peel 1 pound carrots and cut into ½-inch-thick sticks. Toss with 2 teaspoons brown sugar mixed with 2 teaspoons balsamic or cider vinegar and 1 teaspoon olive oil. Roast on a lightly oiled baking sheet for 15 to 20 minutes, stirring every 5 minutes, or until browned and tender. Season with salt and pepper. Makes 3 servings.

GREEN BEANS & RED PEPPERS Trim ¾ pound green beans and cut 1 large red bell pepper into strips. Toss with 1 teaspoon olive oil; roast on a lightly oiled baking sheet for 12 minutes, stirring midway, or until wrinkled, browned and tender. Season with salt and pepper. Makes 4 servings.

RED ONIONS Cut 2 unpeeled medium red onions in half lengthwise. Place cut-side down in a lightly oiled baking pan. Cover with foil and roast for 20 to 30 minutes, or until very tender. Turn onion halves over and drizzle each with ¼ teaspoon olive oil. Season with salt and pepper. Makes 4 servings.

SWEET POTATOES & APPLES Peel and halve 2 medium sweet potatoes and 2 apples; cut into ¼-inch slices. Toss with 2 tablespoons maple syrup, 2 teaspoons lemon juice, 1 teaspoon canola oil, ¼ teaspoon ground ginger and ¼ teaspoon salt. Spread on a lightly oiled baking sheet. Cover with foil. Roast for 15 minutes. Uncover and roast for 10 to 15 minutes more, or until tender and browned. Makes 4 servings.

---

slices with oil and garlic. Season with salt and pepper. Roast the vegetables, stirring occasionally, until tender and starting to brown, 30 to 35 minutes. Let cool.

2. Meanwhile, in a small bowl, whisk sour cream or yogurt, mayonnaise, basil and lemon juice. Season with salt and pepper; reserve in the refrigerator.

3. Split baguette lengthwise and spread both halves with the mayonnaise mixture. Place watercress on the bottom layer, top with the vegetable mixture and the bread tops. Slice into 4 sandwiches.

Makes 4 sandwiches, for 4 servings.

405 calories per sandwich: 14 grams protein, 8 grams fat (1 gram saturated fat), 73 grams carbohydrate; 710 mg sodium; 0 mg cholesterol; 7 grams fiber.

Ⓝ NUTRITION BONUS: A deli sandwich this size packed with lunch meat instead of vegetables can have 20 to 25 grams of fat.

Roasted Vegetable & Linguine Salad

- ¾ pound linguine
- 1 teaspoon plus 2 tablespoons olive oil, preferably extra-virgin
- 1½ pounds asparagus, trimmed and peeled
- 3 bunches scallions, trimmed
- 2 large red, green *and/or* yellow bell peppers, seeded
- 1 teaspoon salt
- 1 teaspoon freshly ground black pepper
- ½ cup freshly grated Parmesan cheese
- ¼ cup balsamic vinegar
- 2 tablespoons chopped fresh parsley, preferably Italian flat-leaf (optional)

1. Position oven racks in the lower third and middle of the oven; preheat to 450°F.

2. Break linguine into pieces about 3 inches long. In a large pot of boiling salted water, cook the broken linguine until al dente, 6 to 8 minutes. Drain in a colander and rinse under cold water until cool. Press to remove excess water. Transfer to a large bowl, toss with 1 teaspoon of the oil and set aside.

3. Cut asparagus and scallions into pieces about 3 inches long. Slice bell peppers into thin strips. In a large bowl, toss the vegetables with the remaining 2 tablespoons oil, salt and pepper. Divide the vegetables between 2 large baking sheets, spreading them in an even layer.

4. Roast for about 10 minutes, then stir the vegetables and switch the positions of the baking sheets. Continue roasting, stirring occasionally, until the vegetables are tender and well browned, 10 to 15 more minutes.

5. Add the vegetables to the linguine and toss to combine. Add Parmesan, vinegar and parsley and toss again. (*The salad can be prepared ahead and stored,*

Balsamic vinegar mellows this quick Roasted Vegetable & Linguine Salad.

covered, in the refrigerator for up to 1 day. Bring to room temperature before serving.)

Makes about 8 cups, for 4 servings.

520 calories per serving: 21 grams protein, 14 grams fat (3.8 grams saturated fat), 79 grams carbohydrate; 785 mg sodium; 10 mg cholesterol; 4 grams fiber.

Ⓝ NUTRITION BONUS: The bright reds and greens of this salad hint at its richness in folic acid and carotenoids.

TECHNIQUE 54 Develop complex flavors through low-fat braising.

Braising involves cooking foods in a closed container with a small amount of liquid and aromatic herbs. Usually reserved for the slow-cooking of tough meats, braising works magic on sturdy vegetables like carrots, fennel or endive.

Ⓕ FAT SAVINGS: This method is not usually associated with vegetables, but it results in rich, satisfying, stewy dishes that don't need meat to accompany them.

Braised Fennel with Orange & Olives

Pernod intensifies the slightly licorice flavor of fennel, but it can be omitted and additional orange juice substituted. Serve as an antipasto or with fish.

- 2 teaspoons olive oil
- 1 fennel bulb, trimmed, cored and sliced
- 1 small red onion, sliced
- ¼ cup fresh orange juice
- 1 tablespoon licorice-flavored liqueur, such as Pernod
- 1 tablespoon slivered pitted black olives, preferably Niçoise
  Salt & freshly ground black pepper to taste

In a nonstick skillet, heat oil over medium heat. Add fennel and onions and sauté for about 1 minute. Stir in orange juice and liqueur. Reduce heat to low and cover tightly. Simmer until the fennel is tender, 7 to 10 minutes. Stir in olives and season with salt and pepper. Serve hot or cold.

Makes 4 servings.

55 calories per serving: 2 grams protein, 3 grams fat (0.4 gram saturated fat), 8 grams carbohydrate; 100 mg sodium; 0 mg cholesterol; 1 gram fiber.

Ⓝ NUTRITION BONUS: Fennel is a fair source of calcium.

Belgian Endive Braised in Cider

A lightened version of traditional butter-braised Belgian endive. If large endives are not available, use 8 small ones and leave them whole.

- 4 very large Belgian endives, halved lengthwise
- 1 tablespoon vegetable oil, preferably canola
- 2 onions, chopped
- 1 carrot, chopped
- 2 ounces lean baked ham *or* Canadian bacon, chopped (½ cup)
- ½ teaspoon juniper berries, finely chopped, *or* a pinch of ground allspice
- ¾ cup apple cider
- 1 tablespoon fresh lemon juice
- ½ teaspoon salt, preferably kosher
- ¼ teaspoon finely ground white pepper
- 1½ teaspoons cornstarch

1. Preheat oven to 325°F. Choose a shallow baking dish that will hold the endive halves tightly in a single layer. Lightly oil or coat it with nonstick cooking spray. Arrange endive halves in the prepared baking dish; set aside.

2. Heat oil in a nonstick skillet over medium heat. Add onions, carrots, ham and juniper berries and cook, stirring often, until just barely colored but not browned, 5 to 7 minutes. In a measuring cup, combine cider, lemon juice, salt and pepper; gradually stir in the cornstarch. Add to the pan all at once and bring to a boil, stirring. Spoon evenly over the endives. Place a sheet of oiled parchment paper or aluminum foil on the vegetables to fit closely inside the rim of the baking dish.

3. Bake for 1 hour, basting once or twice. Continue baking, without basting, until very tender, about 30 minutes. Serve hot. (*The recipe can be prepared ahead. Cool, cover and refrigerate for up to 2 days. Reheat in the oven at 350°F for about 30 minutes.*)

Makes 4 servings.

125 calories per serving: 5 grams protein, 5 grams fat (0.6 gram saturated fat), 17 grams carbohydrate; 460 mg sodium; 8 mg cholesterol; 2 grams fiber.

Ⓝ NUTRITION BONUS: Canadian bacon has about half the fat of cooked regular bacon.

Braised Winter Vegetables

If you cannot find parsnips, use turnips or more carrots.

- 2 teaspoons olive oil
- 4 shallots, peeled and quartered
- 2 leeks, white part only, cleaned, halved lengthwise and cut into ½-inch pieces
- 2 carrots, peeled and sliced
- 2 parsnips, peeled, cut into quarters lengthwise and cut into sticks
- 1 stalk celery, cut in half lengthwise and sliced diagonally
- 1 tablespoon chopped fresh thyme *or* 1 teaspoon dried thyme leaves
- ¼ cup dry white wine
- ¼ cup defatted reduced-sodium chicken broth Salt & freshly ground black pepper to taste

1. In a large nonstick skillet, heat oil over medium heat. Add shallots and sauté for 2 minutes, or until softened. Add leeks, carrots, parsnips and celery and sauté for 1 minute.

2. Sprinkle with thyme, then stir in wine and broth. Reduce heat to low, cover the pan tightly and simmer until the vegetables are tender, 7 to 10 minutes. Season with salt and pepper and serve.

Makes 4 servings.

130 calories per serving: 2 grams protein, 3 grams fat (0.4 gram saturated fat), 24 grams carbohydrate; 70 mg sodium; 0 mg cholesterol; 5 grams fiber.

Ⓝ NUTRITION BONUS: As evidenced by their pale color, parsnips do not contain the carotenoids of carrots.

TECHNIQUE 55

Grill vegetables for a robust and satisfying meal.

Instead of depending on steaks or hamburgers for an easy summer supper, try grilling vegetables. They need little preparation; just trimming or slicing and a bare coating of oil. Grill vegetables over a medium-hot fire, not a scorching one, and remove with tongs as they are done. Dense vegetables like fennel or onions take longer than peppers or zucchini. Potatoes are best if boiled first.

F FAT SAVINGS: A meat-free meal one or two nights a week is a good way to cut down on the saturated fat in your diet.

Grilled Vegetable Salad

- 2 plum tomatoes, cored and halved lengthwise
- 1 red bell pepper, quartered lengthwise and seeded
- 1 medium Vidalia *or* other sweet onion, cut into ½-inch-thick slices
- 1 small eggplant, cut into ½-inch-thick rounds
- 5 small red potatoes, boiled
- 1 tablespoon olive oil, preferably extra-virgin
  Salt & freshly ground black pepper to taste
- ⅓ cup pitted and chopped Kalamata *or* other briny black olives
- ⅔ cup Basil Vinaigrette (*page 18*)
- 8 cups torn romaine lettuce leaves
- 2 cups Garlic Croutons (*page 26*)

1. Prepare a charcoal fire or preheat a gas grill.
2. Put tomatoes, peppers, onions, eggplant and boiled potatoes in a large bowl. Add oil, salt and pepper and toss gently. With tongs, transfer the vegetables one by one to the grill. Grill until softened and browned, about 5 minutes per side, removing them to a dish as they are done. When cool enough to handle, cut into bite-sized pieces.

3. In a bowl, toss the vegetables and olives with half of the Basil Vinaigrette. On a platter, toss romaine with the remaining vinaigrette. Mound the vegetables in the center and top with the Garlic Croutons.
Makes 6 servings.

210 calories per serving: 6 grams protein, 6 grams fat (0.8 gram saturated fat), 35 grams carbohydrate; 270 mg sodium; 0 mg cholesterol; 6 grams fiber.

N NUTRITION BONUS: This colorful mix of vegetables is rich in carotenoids.

TECHNIQUE 56

Stir-fry vegetables with a minimum of fat.

The rapid action of stir-frying cooks vegetables quickly, preserving nutrients and flavor. The key is to first heat a well-seasoned wok or skillet over medium-high heat, then add the oil, pouring it around the rim and swirling the pan for even distribution. For cooking 1 pound of vegetables, you should only need 1 tablespoon of oil.

F FAT SAVINGS: Most traditional recipes call for stir-frying in two or three times the amount of oil called for here.

Shiitake & Asparagus Stir-Fry

Plenty of flavor, texture and drama for little labor.

- 6 ounces fresh shiitake mushrooms
- 1½ teaspoons soy sauce
- 1 teaspoon fresh lemon juice
- 1 teaspoon honey
  Generous pinch of finely ground white pepper
- 1 tablespoon corn oil *or* peanut oil
- ½ pound asparagus, trimmed and cut on the diagonal into ¾-inch lengths
- 3 scallions, white and green parts separated, thinly sliced

1. Reserve shiitake stems for another use. Clean caps with a soft brush. Tear or slice the caps into halves or quarters.

2. In a small dish, blend together soy sauce, lemon juice, honey and white pepper; set aside.

3. Heat a wok or large skillet over medium-high heat; pour oil around the rim and swirl to distribute. Add the shiitake, asparagus and white part of scallions; stir-fry until barely tender, 3 to 4 minutes. Add scallion greens and the reserved soy mixture. Toss briefly and serve.

Makes 4 servings.

50 calories per serving: 2 grams protein, 4 grams fat (0.5 gram saturated fat), 4 grams carbohydrate; 115 mg sodium; 0 mg cholesterol; 1 gram fiber.

Ⓝ NUTRITION BONUS: Asparagus is a good source of folic acid.

Swiss Chard & Sweet Pepper Stir-Fry

1	tablespoon corn oil *or* peanut oil
1	onion, cut in half and thinly sliced
1	large red bell pepper, seeded and thinly sliced
3	tablespoons vegetable broth *or* water
1½	teaspoons hoisin sauce
1	pound Swiss chard, washed, stems diced, leaves shredded (6 cups)
	Salt to taste

1. Heat a wok or large skillet over medium-high heat; pour oil around the rim and swirl to distribute. Add onions and stir-fry until they are translucent and slightly soft, about 2 minutes.

2. Add peppers, broth or water and hoisin sauce; bring to a boil. Reduce heat to medium-low and simmer, covered, for 2 to 3 minutes. Add chard stems and leaves, tossing to combine. Cook, covered, just until the chard is tender, 3 to 5 minutes. Season with salt and serve.

Makes 4 servings.

75 calories per serving: 3 grams protein, 4 grams fat (0.4 gram saturated fat), 10 grams carbohydrate; 305 mg sodium; 0 mg cholesterol; 3 grams fiber.

Ⓝ NUTRITION BONUS: Chard is a good source of vitamin C and beta carotene.

TECHNIQUE

57 Bake—don't fry—eggplant for a great low-fat eggplant Parmesan.

Old-fashioned recipes for this Italian classic call for sautéing or frying the eggplant slices in oil before assembling the dish. Anyone who has ever done this knows that eggplant is an insatiable sponge when it comes to oil. Our technique of lightly breading the eggplant slices and baking them in a hot oven dramatically slashes the total fat from the recipe, yet leaves the eggplant mellow and meaty.

Ⓕ FAT SAVINGS: A serving of eggplant Parmesan can have upwards of 40 grams of fat: the Eating Well version has 7 grams per serving.

Eggplant Parmesan

2	eggplants (about 2 pounds total)
3	egg whites
1	cup fine dry breadcrumbs
½	cup freshly grated Parmesan cheese (1 ounce)
½	teaspoon salt
½	teaspoon freshly ground black pepper
¼	cup slivered fresh basil leaves
2½	cups Tomato Sauce (*page 43*) *or* commercial tomato sauce
¾	cup grated part-skim mozzarella cheese (3 ounces)

1. Preheat oven to 400°F. Lightly oil 2 baking sheets or coat them with nonstick cooking spray. Also oil an 8-by-11½-inch baking dish or coat it with nonstick cooking spray. Set aside.

2. Cut eggplants crosswise into ¼-inch-thick slices. In a shallow dish, whisk egg whites with 3 tablespoons water until frothy. In another shallow dish, combine breadcrumbs, ¼ cup of the Parmesan, salt and pepper. Dip the eggplant slices into the egg-white mixture, then coat with the breadcrumb mixture. (Discard any leftover breadcrumbs and egg white.) Arrange the eggplant slices in a single layer on the prepared baking sheets. Bake for 15 minutes, turn the eggplant slices over, and bake for about 15 minutes longer, or until crisp and golden.

3. Stir basil into tomato sauce. Spread about ½ cup of the sauce in the bottom of the prepared baking dish. Arrange half of the eggplant slices over the sauce, overlapping slightly. Spoon 1 cup of the remaining sauce over the eggplant and sprinkle with half of the mozzarella cheese. Add a layer of the remaining eggplant slices and top with the remaining sauce, mozzarella and Parmesan. Bake, uncovered, until the sauce bubbles and the top is golden, 15 to 20 minutes.

Makes 6 servings.

250 calories per serving: 13 grams protein, 7 grams fat (3 grams saturated fat), 38 grams carbohydrate; 515 mg sodium; 12 mg cholesterol; 9 grams fiber.

(N) NUTRITION BONUS: When fried, eggplant soaks up oil like a sponge; baking eliminates this problem.

---

58 Mushrooms take the place of meat in a sandwich and a burger.

Mushrooms have what the Japanese call *umami*, or meaty taste, and that meatiness stands out in two types of mushrooms commonly available today—portobello and cremini. (These cultivated mushrooms are actually the same variety—the portobellos are in fact cremini that have been allowed to mature and open up.) We have found that the big, broad and flat portobello caps grill wonderfully well, and the pudgy, sturdy cremini have a rich-flavored flesh that holds its shape when cooked.

(F) FAT SAVINGS: Switching from meat to mushrooms cuts the total fat in a sandwich by at least half and reduces the saturated fat to nearly nothing.

The PBT (Portobello, Basil & Tomato Sandwich)

A new take on the BLT. Grilled portobellos add a smoky richness to this meatless sandwich.

- 2 tablespoons reduced-fat mayonnaise
- 2 tablespoons nonfat sour cream *or* nonfat plain yogurt
- 1 teaspoon fresh lemon juice
- 1 tablespoon olive oil
- 2 4-ounce portobello mushrooms, stems removed, caps wiped clean and sliced ⅜ inch thick
  Salt & freshly ground black pepper to taste
- 8 slices sourdough bread
- 1 clove garlic, halved
- 1 cup loosely packed basil leaves, washed, dried and torn into shreds (if large)
- 2 vine-ripened tomatoes, cored and sliced

1. Prepare a grill or preheat the broiler. In a small bowl, combine mayonnaise, sour cream or yogurt, and lemon juice; set aside.

The PBT (Portobello, Basil & Tomato Sandwich) vs. the BLT.

2. Brush oil over the cut sides of the mushrooms. Grill or broil the mushroom slices until tender and golden, 2 to 3 minutes per side. Season with salt and pepper. Meanwhile, toast bread on the grill or under the broiler. Rub both sides of the bread with garlic clove.

3. Spread half of the mayonnaise mixture over 4 toasted bread slices and arrange basil on top. Top with the grilled mushroom slices, followed by tomato slices and salt and pepper. Finish with a dollop of the remaining mayonnaise mixture and cover with the remaining pieces of toast. Cut sandwiches in half and serve.

Makes 4 sandwiches, for 4 servings.

190 calories per sandwich: 6 grams protein, 7 grams fat (1 gram saturated fat), 31 grams carbohydrate; 310 mg sodium; 0 mg cholesterol; 3 grams fiber.

Ⓝ NUTRITION BONUS: An old-fashioned BLT weighs in at about 23 grams of fat and 350 calories; the Eating Well PBT is a far healthier choice.

Mushroom & Pecan Burgers

Meaty mushrooms and crunchy pecans make this a satisfying burger.

- 1 tablespoon olive oil
- 1 onion, chopped
- 3 cloves garlic, finely chopped (1 tablespoon)
- ½ pound cremini mushrooms, trimmed and sliced
- ½ cup toasted pecan halves (2 ounces)
- 1 cup cooked rice, preferably brown basmati
- 1 cup grated carrots
- 1 cup fresh breadcrumbs (3 slices bread)
  Salt & freshly ground black pepper to taste
  Cayenne to taste
- 1 large egg, lightly beaten

1. Preheat the broiler. Lightly oil a baking sheet or coat it with nonstick cooking spray and set aside.

2. Heat oil in a nonstick skillet over medium-high heat until hot. Add onions and garlic and sauté until the onions are soft, about 3 minutes. Add mushrooms and sauté until they are slightly soft, about 3 more minutes. Remove the pan from the heat.

3. In a food processor (not a blender) coarsely chop pecans. Add rice, carrots and the sautéed onion mixture. Pulse a few times until the mixture has a mealy consistency, and transfer it to a large bowl. Add breadcrumbs and mix well. Season with salt, pepper and cayenne. Stir in egg.

4. Shape the mixture into 6 patties. Place the patties on the prepared baking sheet. Broil, about 6 inches from the heat, until lightly browned, 5 to 7 minutes per side.

Makes 6 burgers, for 6 servings.

210 calories per burger: 5 grams protein, 10 grams fat (1.2 grams saturated fat), 26 grams carbohydrate; 60 mg sodium; 35 mg cholesterol; 2 grams fiber.

Ⓝ NUTRITION BONUS: You won't find dietary fiber in an all-beef hamburger.

TECHNIQUE

59 Microwave sliced potatoes for low-fat chips.

Just as good (some say better) as the fried version, homemade low-fat chips are quite fun to make. Just slice waxy potatoes into thin rounds, toss with a little olive oil and salt, then pop them in the microwave oven.

Ⓕ FAT SAVINGS: One ounce of fried potato chips has 10 grams of fat; one ounce of Eating Well's potato chips has 2 grams.

Potato Chips

Use a plastic mandoline or a vegetable peeler to slice potatoes. The recipe also works well with ¼-inch hand-sliced rounds—hefty chips but still crunchy.

- 1 pound baby red potatoes (about 6)
- 1½ teaspoons olive oil
- ½ teaspoon salt

1. Slice potatoes into thin (⅛-inch) rounds. Place slices in a large bowl and cover with cold water. Let soak for 30 minutes.

2. Drain the potatoes and dry thoroughly with paper towels. In a medium bowl, combine the potatoes, oil and salt; toss to coat evenly.

3. Lightly oil a microwave-proof plate or coat it with nonstick cooking spray. Arrange some of the potato slices in a single layer on the plate. Microwave on high for 3 minutes. Turn slices over; continue to microwave for another 3 to 4 minutes. Check frequently and re-arrange slices as needed to prevent scorching. Transfer to another plate and allow to cool completely. (They will crisp up even more as they cool.) Meanwhile, repeat the process with the remaining potato slices. (*Store in an airtight container for up to 3 days.*)

Makes 2 cups chips, for 4 servings.

130 calories per serving: 2 grams protein, 2 grams fat (0.3 gram saturated fat), 26 grams carbohydrate; 275 mg sodium; 0 mg cholesterol; 0 grams fiber.

(N) NUTRITION BONUS: Potatoes are an excellent source of potassium.

TECHNIQUE 60 — To cut the fat but not the flavor, use buttermilk and Yukon Gold potatoes for the best mashed potatoes.

Grandma probably made her mashed potatoes with butter and a little milk or cream. While it's unlikely she measured precisely, on the average she added about 1 tablespoon of whole milk and ½ tablespoon of butter per serving, then dotted the top with a melting pat or two for good measure. We find that buttermilk, which is most often made from skim milk, adds a dairy richness without adding fat. In addition, the creamy-yellow-fleshed Yukon Gold potatoes give the illusion both in color and in taste that they are richer than they really are.

(F) FAT SAVINGS: Grandma's potatoes had 8 to 10 grams of fat per serving. Yours will have 2 grams of fat per serving.

Buttermilk Mashed Potatoes

Garlic cloves, cooked along with the potatoes, give this puree extra body.

2   **pounds all-purpose potatoes, preferably Yukon Gold (about 6 medium potatoes), peeled and cut into chunks**
6   **cloves garlic, peeled**
    Salt to taste
2   **teaspoons butter**
1   **cup buttermilk**
    Freshly ground white *or* black pepper to taste

1. Place potatoes and garlic in a large heavy saucepan. Add water to cover and season with salt. Bring to a boil. Reduce heat to medium, cover, and cook for 10 to 15 minutes, or until potatoes are very tender.

2. Meanwhile, in a small saucepan, melt butter over low heat and cook, swirling, until it turns a nutty brown, about 1 minute. Stir in buttermilk and heat until just warm. (Do not overheat or it will curdle.)

3. When potatoes are done, drain in a colander and return to the pan. Place pan over low heat and shake for about 1 minute to dry potatoes.

4. Mash the potatoes and garlic with a potato masher, an electric hand-held mixer or by working through a ricer. Add enough of the buttermilk mixture to make a smooth puree. Season with salt and pepper and serve.

Makes 6 servings.

145 calories per serving: 4 grams protein, 2 grams fat (0.9 gram saturated fat), 30 grams carbohydrate; 60 mg sodium; 4 mg cholesterol; 2 grams fiber.

Variations: For **Chèvre Mashed Potatoes,** cut 3 ounces goat cheese (chèvre) into small pieces and stir into the potatoes after mashing.

For **Herbed Mashed Potatoes,** substitute 2 teaspoons olive oil for the butter, and stir in 1 tablespoon minced fresh parsley, 1 tablespoon minced fresh chives and 1 teaspoon minced fresh thyme along with the salt and pepper.

(N) NUTRITION BONUS: Though the *exact* health benefits of garlic are controversial, there's no doubt that it contains potent disease-fighting phytochemicals.

For more recipes using buttermilk, see pages 21, 22, 136, 154, 157 and 180.

61 Start on the stove-top, finish in the oven for a crispy, low-fat potato cake.

Rösti, a Swiss specialty, is a large potato cake that is fried in butter until golden. At least that is how EATING WELL's Test Kitchen Director Patsy Jamieson learned to make rösti during a stay in Switzerland. Determined to recreate the crispy cake without the requisite 3 ounces of butter, she employed one of her favorite techniques—browning the food in a small amount of oil in a skillet on the stovetop and finishing it off in a hot oven—and found it was most successful.

F FAT SAVINGS: The stovetop-to-oven method cuts out about 12 grams of fat per serving.

Rösti Potatoes

 2   **pounds russet potatoes (about 4), peeled and cut into 2-inch chunks**
 ½   **teaspoon salt, plus more to taste**
 1   **tablespoon Dijon mustard**
 ½   **teaspoon freshly ground black pepper**
 ½   **cup chopped scallions**
 2   **teaspoons olive oil *or* vegetable oil**
 1   **teaspoon butter**

1. Preheat oven to 425°F. Cut out a 10-inch circle of parchment paper or aluminum foil and spray one side with nonstick cooking spray.

2. Place potatoes in a large saucepan, cover with cold water and add salt to taste. Cover and bring to a full boil. Drain the potatoes and refresh under cold water. (They will not be fully cooked.) Pat dry.

3. Grate the potatoes (a food processor fitted with a grating disc works well) and place in a large bowl. Add mustard, ½ teaspoon salt and pepper; toss to combine. Gently mix in scallions.

4. In a 10-inch cast-iron or other ovenproof skillet, heat oil and butter over medium heat. Use a pastry brush to spread the mixture evenly over the bottom and about 1 inch up the sides of the skillet. Add the potato mixture and press firmly into a large pancake. Place the paper or foil circle, sprayed-side down, directly on top of the potatoes. Transfer the skillet to the oven and bake for about 30 minutes, or until the potatoes are golden on the bottom.

5. Remove the paper or foil circle and use a thin metal spatula to loosen bottom and sides of the rösti. Invert a serving plate over the skillet. Grasping the skillet and plate (protect hands with oven mitts), invert and unmold the rösti. Cut into wedges and serve.

Makes 6 servings.

170 calories per serving: 4 grams protein, 3 grams fat (1.4 grams saturated fat), 32 grams carbohydrate; 240 mg sodium; 5 mg cholesterol; 2 grams fiber.

N NUTRITION BONUS: Potatoes don't have to be just a side dish; accompanied by vegetables, they can be the center of the meal.

Rösti Potatoes are wonderfully crispy without all the butter.

62 Pick a cheese with lots of flavor for the tastiest low-fat gratins.

Traditionally the potatoes in a gratin slowly baked in a rich blend of cream, butter and lots of cheese—a virtual bath of saturated fat. By making a white sauce with low-fat milk and a little olive oil, we cut most of the fat. To maintain the complex, cheesy flavor, we left in the cheese and just used less of it. Be sure to choose a robust cheese like Gruyère or sharp Cheddar to get the most flavor from a small amount.

F FAT SAVINGS: Either of these gratins has one-fourth to one-third the fat of classic French gratins.

Potato Gratin

This classic potato gratin is great with roasted meat and poultry.

1   tablespoon olive oil
1½   tablespoons all-purpose white flour
2   cups low-fat milk
1   teaspoon salt
¼   teaspoon freshly ground black pepper
¼   teaspoon freshly grated nutmeg
2   pounds russet potatoes, peeled
2   cloves garlic, peeled and slivered
¼   cup grated Gruyère cheese

1. Preheat oven to 400°F. Lightly oil a 1½-quart gratin dish or other shallow baking dish, or coat it with nonstick cooking spray.
2. In a heavy saucepan, preferably nonstick, heat oil over medium heat. Add flour and cook, stirring constantly, until the flour begins to turn golden, 2 to 3 minutes. Gradually whisk in milk. Increase heat to medium-high and cook, stirring constantly, until the mixture just begins to boil, about 5 minutes. (The

sauce may seem thin.) Remove from the heat and season with salt, pepper and nutmeg. Place a piece of wax paper directly on the surface to prevent a skin from forming, and set aside.
3. Cut potatoes into ¼-inch-thick slices (a food processor does the job nicely); toss with garlic and spread evenly in the prepared dish. Pour the sauce over the potatoes and bake, uncovered, for 40 to 45 minutes, or until the potatoes are very tender. Sprinkle cheese over the top and bake for 10 to 12 minutes longer, or until the top is golden.

Makes 6 servings.

225 calories per serving: 7 grams protein, 5 grams fat (1.8 grams saturated fat), 38 grams carbohydrate; 420 mg sodium; 9 mg cholesterol; 4 grams fiber.

N NUTRITION BONUS: Use smaller amounts of full-flavored cheeses, such as Gruyère, rather than larger amounts of fat-reduced cheeses, which have less flavor.

Kohlrabi & Ham Gratin

3   pounds kohlrabi (about 14 small), trimmed, peeled and thinly sliced
1⅓   cups low-fat milk
3   tablespoons all-purpose white flour
2   ounces smoked ham, cut into thin slivers
¼   cup grated sharp Cheddar cheese
½   teaspoon salt
¼   teaspoon freshly ground black *or* white pepper
       Pinch of freshly grated nutmeg
⅓   cup fresh breadcrumbs

1. Preheat oven to 400°F. Lightly oil a 1½-quart gratin dish or other shallow baking dish, or coat it with nonstick cooking spray.
2. Cook kohlrabi in a large pot of boiling salted water until very tender, about 20 minutes. Drain and set aside.
3. In a small saucepan, heat 1 cup of the milk over medium heat until steaming. In a small bowl, combine flour and the remaining ⅓ cup milk to make a smooth paste; stir into the hot milk and cook, whisking constantly, until the sauce bubbles and thickens, 2 to 3 minutes. Remove from the heat and stir in ham and cheese. Season with salt, pepper and nutmeg.

4. Distribute the cooked kohlrabi in the prepared dish. Pour the cheese sauce over the top, spreading evenly. Sprinkle with breadcrumbs. (*The gratin can be prepared ahead to this point and stored, covered, in the refrigerator to be baked the following day.*) Bake for 30 to 40 minutes, or until bubbling and golden.

Makes 6 servings.

140 calories per serving: 10 grams protein, 3 grams fat (1.6 grams saturated fat), 21 grams carbohydrate; 420 mg sodium; 12 mg cholesterol; 4 grams fiber.

NUTRITION BONUS: Kohlrabi, a member of the cancer-fighting cabbage family, is an excellent source of vitamin C and potassium.

TECHNICAL

63 Make crispy fries in the oven.

Frying in hot oil was always a chore; it was messy and smelly long before we took notice of just how much fat it added to foods. But if you're still hungry for some fries, slice potatoes (or sweet potatoes for a real treat) into long thin wedges and toss in the smallest amount of oil, along with salt and pepper. Spread the wedges on a baking sheet and pop into a hot oven where they crisp to perfection.

FAT SAVINGS: Fast-food fries have about 12 grams of fat per serving (and that's for a small order). Eating Well fries weigh in at 2 grams of fat per serving.

Oven Fries

1½ pounds scrubbed all-purpose potatoes (preferably Yukon Gold) *or* scrubbed sweet potatoes
2 teaspoons olive oil
½ teaspoon salt
¼ teaspoon paprika
Freshly ground black pepper to taste

1. Position oven rack in the upper third of the oven; preheat to 450°F. Coat a baking sheet lightly with nonstick cooking spray. Cut each potato or sweet potato lengthwise into 8 wedges.

2. In a large bowl, combine oil, salt, paprika and pepper. Add potato or sweet potato wedges and toss to coat. Spread on the prepared baking sheet and roast for 20 minutes. Loosen and turn; roast for 10 to 15 minutes longer, or until golden brown. Serve immediately.

Makes 4 servings.

205 calories per serving of **potatoes**: 4 grams protein, 2 grams fat (0.4 gram saturated fat), 43 grams carbohydrate; 280 mg sodium; 0 mg cholesterol; 4 grams fiber.

195 calories per serving of **sweet potatoes**: 3 grams protein, 3 grams fat (0.4 gram saturated fat), 41 grams carbohydrate; 285 mg sodium; 0 mg cholesterol; 5 grams fiber.

NUTRITION BONUS: If you use sweet potatoes, your oven fries will be rich in carotenoids.

Oven-fried potatoes and sweet potatoes are just as irresistible as the full-fat version.

Braised Cabbage with Cranberry Beans & Rice, page 122

TECHNIQUES

64-69

BEANS & RICE

IN A GLOBAL CONTEST FOR MOST POPULAR FOOD, RICE WOULD BEAT ALL OTHERS (even wheat), just as it would have for the past 2,000 or 3,000 years. Over half the world's population eats rice every day. Leguminous beans (a.k.a. poor man's meat) are up there in the charts as well. Yet you won't find a lot of techniques for taking the fat out of bean or rice dishes. Why not? By nature they are some of the leanest, most nutritious foods you can eat. However, a few classic preparations, such as cheese-rich risotto or old-fashioned pork and beans, depend on high-fat ingredients for their flavor. By eliminating needless fat or by choosing flavor components that mimic high-fat ingredients, you can keep beans and grains at their low-fat best.

? WHAT IS THE BEST WAY TO COOK DRIED BEANS?

First pick through the beans to find any small stones, then rinse well. Soak overnight in about three times their volume of water. (*Alternatively, put them in a saucepan and add cold water to cover generously. Bring to a simmer and cook for 2 minutes. Remove from the heat and let stand, covered, for 1 hour.*) Drain the soaked or simmered beans and rinse. Place in a saucepan and cover generously with fresh water. Simmer over medium-low heat until tender—the time varies greatly depending on the type of bean and their freshness. Always add salt toward the end of cooking, when the beans are nearly tender; adding salt at the start makes the skins tough.

Cooked beans can be kept in the refrigerator for 3 or 4 days. One cup of dried beans yields about 2 cups cooked beans. One 16-ounce can of beans contains 2 cups of cooked beans.

TECHNIQUE 64

Combine beans and grains for healthy meatless meals.

A simple step toward a healthier diet is to eat at least one meatless meal per week. You need not worry about getting enough protein; the bean-and-rice recipe here, for instance, meets almost 40 percent of the average woman's daily protein needs. Beans are not only extremely low in fat and rich in protein, the plant proteins and other substances in beans are believed to protect against cancer. Grains provide much-needed complex carbohydrates.

F FAT SAVINGS: The greatest benefit from choosing a bean or grain dish over meat is in saturated fat. With beans and grains, the saturated fat is negligible; with meat, saturated fat runs between 35% and 38% of the total fat.

Braised Cabbage with Cranberry Beans & Rice

- 1 tablespoon olive oil
- ½ cup chopped onions
- ½ head of a large green cabbage, thinly shredded (8-9 cups)
- 2 14-ounce cans defatted reduced-sodium beef, chicken *or* vegetable broth (3½ cups) Pinch of salt, plus more to taste
- 2 cups cooked cranberry, Roman *or* red kidney beans (*see box at left*)
- 1 cup medium-grain rice, preferably arborio Freshly ground black pepper to taste

1. In a large saucepan, heat oil over low heat. Add onions and cook, stirring occasionally, until tender and translucent, about 5 minutes. (If the onions begin to stick, add 1 to 2 tablespoons of water.)
2. Stir in shredded cabbage, 1 cup of the broth and a pinch of salt. Cover the saucepan and cook over medium-low heat for 20 minutes.
3. Stir in beans and the remaining 2½ cups broth; bring to a simmer. Add rice and salt to taste. Reduce the heat to low, cover and cook until the rice is tender and most of the broth has been absorbed, 15 to 20 minutes. (Add a little more water or broth if needed.) Sprinkle with pepper before serving.

Makes about 6 cups, for 4 servings.

395 calories per serving: 16 grams protein, 6 grams fat (1.1 grams saturated fat), 73 grams carbohydrate; 605 mg sodium; 4 mg cholesterol; 4 grams fiber.

N NUTRITION BONUS: Cabbage contains cancer-fighting phytochemicals called indoles.

Gingered Couscous with Chickpeas

For an easy vegetarian supper, bake halves of small winter squash and fill them with this couscous; serve with a green salad and warm pita bread.

- 2 teaspoons olive oil
- 1 teaspoon cumin seeds
- 2 tablespoons freshly grated ginger
- 1½ tablespoons curry powder, preferably Madras

? WHAT IS THE MEDITERRANEAN DIET AND WHY IS IT SO HEALTHY?

For centuries and centuries, people living around the Mediterranean have eaten a diet rich in plant foods. In the 1970s, researchers found that the people who continue to follow the traditional eating patterns of the region enjoy very low rates of heart disease, similar to those of Asian peoples who eat very low-fat diets (*see page 129*). But surprisingly, the amount of fat in the Mediterranean diet is as high or higher than it is in the United States, approximately 35 to 40 percent of calories from fat. The key difference is the type of fat consumed. In Naples, Italy, it is heart-healthy monounsaturated fat in the form of olive oil; in Naples, Florida, it is more likely to be cholesterol-raising saturated and hydrogenated fats from processed foods, meat and dairy products.

Most Mediterranean meals feature a grain, such as rice or pasta or bread, accompanied by vegetables cooked in—or seasoned with—olive oil. Legumes provide a significant source of protein. Fish and cheese are eaten when available, and meat is used more as a flavoring than a main course. The high intake of plant foods, particularly vegetables, is thought to be an important protecting factor because vegetables are a source of antioxidants and other natural disease-preventing chemicals. (Recipes like Braised Cabbage with Cranberry Beans & Rice, *at left*, or Spinach Fettuccine with Pesto, *page 47*, are excellent examples of this heart-healthy cooking style.)

Wine with meals is another Mediterranean custom that protects against heart disease. Alcohol raises HDL ("good") cholesterol, and reduces the formation of blood clots that can precipitate a heart attack. Some researchers believe *red* wine has an enhanced protective effect because of its antioxidant flavonoids.

---

1   15-ounce can chickpeas, drained
1   14-ounce can chopped tomatoes, with juice
1   tablespoon honey
¼   teaspoon salt, plus more to taste
¼   teaspoon freshly ground black pepper
1½   cups plain couscous
⅓   cup chopped fresh cilantro

In a large saucepan, heat oil over medium-high heat. Add cumin seeds and stir until the seeds begin to pop, about 1 minute. Add ginger and stir until fragrant, about 30 seconds. Add curry powder and stir until it is toasted, about 30 seconds longer. Add chickpeas, tomatoes, honey, ¼ teaspoon salt, pepper and 1¾ cups water; bring to a boil. Stir in couscous, remove from the heat and cover. Let stand until the liquid has been absorbed, about 5 minutes. With a fork, fluff the couscous and stir in cilantro. Season with salt.

Makes 6 servings.

300 calories per serving: 11 grams protein, 4 grams fat (0 grams saturated fat), 57 grams carbohydrate; 485 mg sodium; 0 mg cholesterol; 6 grams fiber.

Ⓝ NUTRITION BONUS: To increase the fiber content further, use whole-wheat couscous.

Gingered Couscous with Chickpeas is great for lunch too.

Hoppin' John

The first printed recipe for this old Low Country Carolina dish called for a pound of bacon.

4   cups fresh *or* thawed frozen black-eyed peas
2   teaspoons vegetable oil
1   onion, chopped
2   red *or* green bell peppers, seeded and chopped
1   14-ounce can tomatoes, drained and chopped
6   cloves garlic, minced
1   cup long-grain white rice
2   cups defatted reduced-sodium chicken broth
¼   pound smoked ham, diced (¾ cup)
1   teaspoon salt, plus more to taste
    Pinch of cayenne
¾   cup chopped scallions (3-4 scallions)
½   cup chopped fresh parsley,
    Freshly ground black pepper to taste

1. If using fresh black-eyed peas, pick them over, removing any debris, and rinse in a colander. Place black-eyed peas in a large saucepan and add enough water to cover them by 1 inch. Bring to a boil, reduce the heat to low and simmer, uncovered, for 20 minutes. Drain and set aside. (Peas will still be tough.)
2. Meanwhile, in a Dutch oven or large wide saucepan, heat oil over medium heat. Add onions and peppers; sauté until softened, about 5 minutes. Add tomatoes and garlic and cook, stirring, for 5 minutes. Add rice and stir for 1 minute to coat the grains. Pour in chicken broth and bring to a simmer. Add ham, salt, cayenne and the partially cooked fresh (or thawed frozen) black-eyed peas. Cover and simmer over low heat for 20 minutes, or until the rice and black-eyed peas are tender and the liquid has been absorbed. Stir in scallions and parsley. Season with salt and pepper and serve.

Makes 6 servings.

355 calories per serving: 18 grams protein, 4 grams fat (1 gram saturated fat), 60 grams carbohydrate; 970 mg sodium; 13 mg cholesterol; 9 grams fiber.

N NUTRITION BONUS: A small amount of flavorful smoked ham adds only 2 grams of fat per serving.

Hoppin' John is a healthful Southern tradition.

TECHNIQUE 65 Substitute sun-dried tomatoes for salt pork in baked beans.

Puritan housewives and generations thereafter have added a hefty chunk of salt pork to the bean pot for flavor. We discovered that sun-dried tomatoes provide a similar mellowed richness.

F FAT SAVINGS: Old-fashioned baked beans have 4 or 5 grams of fat per serving; our baked beans have 1 gram of fat per serving.

Boston Baked Beans

Slow-cooked baked beans are a must at summer cookouts.

1   pound dried pea beans *or* great northern beans (2½ cups), rinsed and picked over
1   onion, chopped
1   14-ounce can stewed tomatoes, with juice
½   cup molasses
6   sun-dried tomatoes (*not* oil-packed), chopped
2   teaspoons salt, or to taste
    Freshly ground black pepper to taste

1. Soak beans (*see box, page 122*). Drain and rinse the beans; place in a large pot and cover with fresh water. Bring to a simmer and cook over low heat until almost tender, about 45 minutes.

2. Meanwhile, preheat oven to 300°F. Transfer beans and cooking liquid to a 2-quart casserole or bean pot. Add onions, stewed tomatoes, molasses and dried tomatoes. Cover and bake for 2 to 3 hours, or until the beans are very tender and the sauce has thickened. (Add more water as needed to keep the beans barely covered.) Season with salt and pepper and serve.

Makes about 6 cups, for 8 servings.

140 calories per serving: 5 grams protein, 1 gram fat (0 grams saturated fat), 30 grams carbohydrate; 685 mg sodium; 0 mg cholesterol; 5 grams fiber.

Ⓝ NUTRITION BONUS: It's hard to beat our baked beans' low-fat, high-fiber profile, especially with tomatoes' contribution of cancer-fighting carotenoids.

TECHNIQUE 66 Make low-fat spreads with beans as a base.

When cooked to complete tenderness, beans can be mashed or pureed to create spreads that have the unctuousness of high-fat spreads without the fat and calories.

Ⓕ FAT SAVINGS: Spread a tablespoon of softened cream cheese on a little toast for 3 grams of fat; spread a tablespoon of bean puree for 1 gram.

Hummus

1   head garlic, roasted (*see Technique 10, page 25*) and peeled
1   16-ounce can chickpeas, drained and rinsed, *or* 2 cups cooked chickpeas (*see box, page 122*)
2   tablespoons fresh lemon juice
1   tablespoon reduced-sodium soy sauce
1   tablespoon tahini (sesame paste)
2   tablespoons chopped fresh parsley
    Salt to taste
    Paprika for garnish

In a food processor, puree roasted garlic, chickpeas, lemon juice, soy sauce, tahini and about 2 tablespoons water (enough to make a fairly firm dip). Transfer to a bowl, stir in parsley and season with salt. (*The hummus will keep, covered, in the refrigerator for up to 2 days.*) Garnish with a sprinkle of paprika.

Makes about 1⅔ cups.

25 calories per tablespoon: 1 gram protein, 1 gram fat (0.1 gram saturated fat), 4 grams carbohydrate; 105 mg sodium; 0 mg cholesterol; 1 gram fiber.

Ⓝ NUTRITION BONUS: Rinsing canned chickpeas removes much of the excess salt.

Pita Crisps

Pita crisps are the perfect scoop for dips and spreads. To make them, preheat oven to 425°F. Cut 4 pita breads (about 6-inch diameter) into 8 triangles. Separate each triangle into 2 halves at the fold and arrange, rough-side up, on a baking sheet. Bake for about 8 minutes, or until golden and crisp. (*The pita crisps may be stored in a closed container at room temperature for up to 1 week.*)

Makes 64 crisps.

10 calories per crisp: 0 grams protein, 0 grams fat, 2 grams carbohydrate; 20 mg sodium; 0 mg cholesterol; 0 grams fiber.

Ⓝ NUTRITION BONUS: A serving of commercial crackers, such as Wheat Thins, has 4 grams of fat. Homemade crisps are fat-free.

Crostini with Cannellini Beans

2-3 cloves garlic, peeled
1 tablespoon olive oil, preferably extra-virgin
2 cups cooked cannellini, cranberry *or* Roman beans (*see box, page 122*), or one 16-ounce can cannellini beans, drained and rinsed
Salt & freshly ground black pepper to taste
12 ½-inch-thick slices Italian bread
1 cup stemmed and chopped arugula *or* watercress
2 vine-ripened tomatoes, seeded and chopped

1. Mince 1 of the garlic cloves. Combine it with oil in a medium saucepan. Stir over low heat until golden, about 2 minutes. Add beans, ½ cup water and salt and pepper. Bring to a simmer over low heat and cook, stirring often, until the mixture has thickened, 8 to 10 minutes. Mash the beans with a fork.
2. Toast or grill bread slices. Rub one side of each with the remaining garlic cloves and top with some beans, followed by arugula or watercress and tomatoes.

Makes 12 crostini.

145 calories per crostini: 6 grams protein, 1 gram fat (0.2 gram saturated fat), 26 grams carbohydrate; 200 mg sodium; 0 mg cholesterol; 2 grams fiber.

(N) NUTRITION BONUS: This is an appetizer a nutritionist can love, with more fiber than fat and packed with vitamins and minerals.

TECHNIQUE 67 For full flavor, cook black-eyed peas in a ham-scented broth.

Simmering a piece of ham in broth for an hour effectively transfers the ham's flavor to the broth. Chilling the broth solidifies any fat on the surface, making it easy to remove. The fat-free ham-scented broth then infuses black-eyed peas with authentic, Southern-style flavor.

(F) FAT SAVINGS: Traditional black-eyed peas seasoned with pork have up to 12 grams of fat per cup; this tasty revision has 1 gram per cup.

Southern-Style Black-Eyed Peas

For a Southern meal, serve with Southern-Style Pork Tenderloin (page 81) and North Carolina Barbecue Sauce (page 82) and Buttermilk Biscuits (page 136).

1½ quarts defatted reduced-sodium chicken broth
½ pound country ham, cubed, *or* smoked ham hock
1 Spanish onion, chopped
2 teaspoons black peppercorns
3 cups fresh *or* frozen black-eyed peas *or* field peas
Salt & freshly ground black pepper to taste

1. In a soup pot, combine chicken broth, ham, onions, peppercorns and 2 cups water. Bring to a boil, reduce heat and simmer, covered, for 1 hour. Let cool. Strain and refrigerate the broth until cold; skim the fat from the surface.
2. In a saucepan, combine peas and the broth. Simmer over medium heat until very tender, about 45 minutes. Add salt and pepper. Transfer the peas to a serving bowl along with some of the broth.

Makes about 6 cups, for 8 servings.

130 calories per serving: 5 grams protein, 2 grams fat (0.5 gram saturated fat), 24 grams carbohydrate; 490 mg sodium; 5 mg cholesterol; 8 grams fiber.

(N) NUTRITION BONUS: A little ham goes a long way to make this dish flavorful and satisfying.

TECHNIQUE 68 Cut back on fat in rice dishes.

Most pilaf and risotto recipes call for 2 tablespoons of butter or oil to 1 cup of raw rice for the initial sautéing of the grains. We have found that half the amount is plenty; if you have a good nonstick pan, 2 teaspoons is sufficient. And, as always, heart-healthy olive oil is the oil of choice.

(F) FAT SAVINGS: Reducing the oil cuts the fat by approximately 3.5 grams per serving in pilaf and risotto.

Risotto with Spring Vegetables

We have opted for frozen artichokes here because fresh ones take a long time to trim.

5½-6½	cups defatted reduced-sodium vegetable *or* chicken broth
16	baby carrots (6 ounces), trimmed, peeled and cut in half lengthwise
16	thin stalks *or* 8 medium-sized stalks asparagus (6 ounces), trimmed and cut into 2-inch lengths
1	cup (4 ounces) sugar snap peas *or* thin green beans (haricots verts), trimmed
1	9-ounce package frozen artichoke hearts
2	teaspoons olive oil
1	onion, chopped
1	clove garlic, minced
1½	cups arborio rice
½	cup dry white wine
1½	tablespoons chopped fresh thyme *or* 1½ teaspoons dried thyme leaves
¾	cup freshly grated Parmesan cheese Salt & freshly ground black pepper to taste

1. In a saucepan, bring vegetable or chicken broth to a boil over medium heat. Add carrots and cook for 3 to 5 minutes, until almost tender. Add asparagus and peas or beans and cook for 1 minute longer. With a slotted spoon, remove the vegetables to a bowl to cool. Reduce heat to maintain the broth at a gentle simmer. Place artichoke hearts in a sieve and thaw under warm water; set aside.

2. In a Dutch oven or large wide saucepan, heat oil over medium-low heat. Add onions and garlic and cook, stirring, until softened, 3 to 5 minutes. Add rice and stir to coat grains. Pour in wine and cook, stirring frequently, until most of the liquid has been absorbed, 2 to 3 minutes.

3. Add ½ cup of the simmering broth to the rice and cook, stirring frequently, until most of the liquid has been absorbed, 2 to 3 minutes more. Continue adding broth ½ cup at a time, stirring frequently, until the rice begins to soften, about 15 minutes. Stir in the reserved artichoke hearts and thyme, adding more broth as needed, until the mixture is creamy, about 5 minutes more. Stir in the reserved vegetables

and Parmesan. Season with salt and pepper.

Makes 4 servings.

520 calories per serving: 20 grams protein, 9 grams fat (1 gram saturated fat), 86 grams carbohydrate; 460 mg sodium; 16 mg cholesterol; 4 grams fiber.

N NUTRITION BONUS: It's hard to believe this creamy, rich, meat-free entrée is not loaded with saturated fat.

Risotto with Spring Vegetables: A satisfying meatless entrée.

Skillet Rice with Shrimp

Shrimp and vegetables make this a one-pot meal; if you like, omit the shrimp for a colorful side dish.

1	tablespoon olive oil
1	onion, peeled and chopped
1	green *or* red bell pepper, seeded and chopped
2	cloves garlic, minced
1	cup raw long-grain white rice
½	cup dry white wine
1	14-ounce can recipe-ready tomatoes
1	14-ounce can defatted reduced-sodium chicken broth
1	tablespoon Worcestershire sauce
1½	teaspoons chopped fresh thyme *or* ½ teaspoon dried thyme leaves
¼	teaspoon salt
1	pound large peeled cooked shrimp, thawed if frozen
1	cup frozen peas, thawed
¼	cup chopped fresh parsley, preferably Italian flat-leaf

1. In a Dutch oven or a deep skillet with a lid, heat oil over medium heat. Add onions, peppers and garlic; cook, stirring with a wooden spoon, until the onions are soft, 3 to 5 minutes. Add rice to the pan and cook, stirring constantly, for 1 minute. Pour in wine and cook rapidly until almost all the liquid has evaporated.

2. Stir in tomatoes and their juices, chicken broth, Worcestershire, thyme and salt. Once the mixture begins to bubble and simmer, reduce the heat to low and cover the pan. Cook until the rice is tender and most of the liquid has been absorbed, about 20 minutes.

3. Gently stir in shrimp, peas and parsley. Cover and cook until the shrimp are warmed through, 3 to 5 minutes.

Makes about 7 cups, for 4 servings.

390 calories per serving: 31 grams protein, 5 grams fat (1 gram saturated fat), 52 grams carbohydrate; 885 mg sodium; 220 mg cholesterol; 4 grams fiber.

N NUTRITION BONUS: Shrimp is a practically fat-free high-protein food.

69 Make fried rice with one-third the fat.

TECHNIQUE

Like pilafs, most recipes for fried rice call for more fat than you actually need, often 2 or 3 tablespoons for a recipe serving 4. As long as your wok is well-seasoned (or you are using a good nonstick skillet) and you heat it before adding the oil, you can get away with 2 or 3 teaspoons of oil for a dish. Eliminating one of the egg yolks in the scrambled egg garnish will cut the total fat by another 1.25 grams per serving.

F FAT SAVINGS: Our recipe has half the fat of traditional fried rice.

Cinnamon Fried Rice

The key to good fried rice is to allow the cooked rice to cool completely before stir-frying.

2	cinnamon sticks
1	cup long-grain fragrant rice, such as jasmine *or* Texmati
3	teaspoons peanut oil *or* canola oil
1	large egg, lightly beaten
1	large egg white, lightly beaten
1	leek, thinly sliced (1 cup)
6	cloves garlic, minced
1½	tablespoons curry powder, preferably Madras
2	carrots, peeled and cut into ¼-inch dice (1 cup)
2	small turnips, peeled and cut into ¼-inch dice (1 cup)
4	tablespoons Chinese rice wine *or* sake
2	teaspoons sugar
1	cup frozen peas, thawed
3	tablespoons reduced-sodium soy sauce
½	teaspoon freshly ground black pepper

1. In a heavy saucepan, bring 3 cups water and cinnamon sticks to a boil. Reduce heat to low, cover and simmer for 30 minutes. The cinnamon water should

WHAT IS THE ASIAN DIET AND WHY IS IT SO HEALTHY?

Throughout much of Asia, heart disease, cancer and other diet-related diseases are far less common than they are in the United States. This is not to say that the foods we eat are inferior to foods eaten in Asia—it is more a matter of proportions. For example, in China, the diet is higher in carbohydrates and lower in fat, and although the average calorie intake is actually higher than in the United States, obesity is rare. The Chinese have blood-cholesterol values that are about half what they are here.

But when Asians emigrate to this country and adopt our diet and more sedentary lifestyle, their protection against disease disappears. Experts say that the following characteristics of the Asian diet have protective effects, and that we would all be better off adopting some of these habits.

High in complex carbohydrates: Wheat noodles or rice are consumed in generous quantities at every meal, along with native fruits, leafy greens and a wide variety of vegetables. Cabbage, squash, sweet potatoes, corn, cucumbers, radishes, onions, pea pods and mushrooms are among the most popular.

Because of the generous amounts of complex carbohydrates, the typical Asian diet contains about three times the amount of dietary fiber as the typical American diet, and far more disease-fighting plant chemicals.

Low in fat and animal products: The average American eats at least twice the amount of fat as the average Asian, and much higher levels of saturated fat from animal products. The total amount of meat, fish or eggs in most traditional Asian dishes is very small by Western standards, whereas soy products, such as tofu, are the important source of protein. Researchers say the low amount of saturated fat is the main reason the Asian diet does not promote heart disease, and some believe that eating protein from plant sources is also protective.

Tea drinking: Green tea is the most common beverage consumed with meals in Asia, and researchers now have evidence that the antioxidants and other natural chemicals in tea have a cancer-fighting effect. Tea may be at least partly responsible for the lower cancer rates in Asian countries.

---

reduce to 2 cups; measure it, adding more water if needed. Return water and cinnamon sticks to the saucepan.

2. Rinse the rice in a strainer under cold water until the water runs clear, about 3 minutes. Add the rice to the cinnamon water and bring to a boil. Reduce heat to low, cover and simmer until craters appear on the surface and the water has been absorbed, about 20 minutes. Remove from the heat and fluff with a fork. Cover and let sit for 15 minutes, then uncover and cool in the pan for 1 hour. Remove the cinnamon sticks. Using a fork, spread the rice out on a baking sheet to cool completely. (*The rice can be cooked ahead of time and refrigerated for up to 3 days.*)

3. Heat a wok or large skillet over medium heat. Add 1½ teaspoons oil and heat until hot. Add egg and egg white and scramble for about 30 seconds. Transfer the eggs to a plate and set aside.

4. Return the wok to the burner and heat the re-

maining 1½ teaspoons oil over medium heat. Add leeks and garlic and stir-fry until the leeks are translucent, about 3 minutes. Add curry powder and stir-fry until fragrant, about 10 seconds. Add carrots, turnips, 2 tablespoons of the rice wine or sake, sugar and ½ cup water. Return to a boil. Cover and cook until the vegetables are tender, about 8 minutes.

5. Add the reserved rice, breaking it up with a spatula. Stir in peas, soy sauce, pepper, the remaining 2 tablespoons rice wine or sake and the reserved scrambled eggs. Toss lightly until the rice and vegetables are heated through, about 2 minutes. Transfer to a serving dish and serve hot.

Makes 6 cups. Serves 6 as a side dish, 3 as an entrée.

230 calories per cup: 7 grams protein, 4 grams fat (0.5 gram saturated fat), 40 grams carbohydrate; 335 mg sodium; 35 mg cholesterol; 4 grams fiber.

 NUTRITION BONUS: Turnips are part of the crucifer family, which is rich in cancer-fighting phytochemicals.

Zucchini-Oatmeal Muffins, page 132

TECHNIQUES
70-74
QUICK BREADS

HOMEY QUICK BREADS (AND THEIR MUFFIN, BISCUIT AND COFFEE-CAKE COUSINS) HAVE INSTANT APPEAL. WHO can resist a basket of homemade scones, a slice of hot-from-the-oven coffee cake or a truly luscious doughnut? The beauty of these irresistible treats has always been that you don't have to be a certified pastry chef to bake them. The drawback has been that quick breads and the like tend to be high in fat, particularly saturated fat. In the EATING WELL Test Kitchen, we have found the genre to be very adaptable. Fruit purees, buttermilk, low-fat dairy products and even a special pan stepped in to help cut the fat from over a dozen favorite recipes.

TECHNIQUE 70

Use fruit purees to replace three-fourths of the fat in quick-bread recipes.

You don't have to be a nutritionist to know that your old coffee-cake and quick-bread recipes are too high in fat for a healthy diet. But when taking the fat out of unhealthy recipes, it's important to understand why it is there in the first place.

One purpose of fat in quick-bread recipes is to waterproof or coat the starchy flour particles. Without this step, gluten—a toughening agent—forms when the flour is moistened and stirred. But fat isn't the only thing that will coat flour particles. Fruit purees do the job nearly as well—with a couple of caveats. After much experimentation in the EATING WELL Test Kitchen, we have learned a thing or two about working with fruit purees.

When we first took all the butter or oil out of a recipe, we ended up with tender baked goods that became increasingly gummy over time. We learned to keep some fat—about 25 percent of the original amount—in the recipe to maintain crisp edges and to prevent gumminess.

We have used prune puree (available commercially in cans as prune pie filling or Lekvar), apple butter and mashed bananas to successfully replace much of the fat in the following recipes. We have also had excellent results with the commercial fruit puree fat replacements now available in supermarkets; generally, the purees are made from prunes and apples.

F FAT SAVINGS: Switching to fruit puree, which contains no fat, can reduce the fat in traditional baked goods by up to 75%.

Zucchini-Oatmeal Muffins

½ cup plus 1 tablespoon rolled oats
¼ cup pecan pieces
1½ cups all-purpose white flour
1 cup whole-wheat pastry flour
1½ cups sugar
1 tablespoon baking powder
1½ teaspoons ground cinnamon
1 teaspoon salt
2 large eggs
3 large egg whites
½ cup fruit puree fat replacement *or* apple butter
¼ cup canola oil
2 cups grated zucchini (1 medium)

1. Preheat oven to 375°F. Lightly oil 16 muffin cups or coat with nonstick cooking spray.
2. Spread rolled oats and pecans on separate areas of a baking sheet and bake for 5 to 10 minutes, or until lightly toasted. Let cool. Chop the pecans.
3. In a large bowl, stir together flours, sugar, baking powder, cinnamon, salt, ½ cup oats and pecans.
4. In a mixing bowl, whisk together eggs, egg whites, fruit puree fat replacement or apple butter, and oil. Stir in zucchini. Add the dry ingredients and stir just until moistened.
5. Spoon the batter into the prepared muffin cups, filling them about three-fourths full. Sprinkle the remaining 1 tablespoon oats over the tops. Bake for 20 to 25 minutes, or until the tops are golden and spring back when touched lightly. Cool on a wire rack.

Makes 16 muffins.

225 calories per muffin: 4 grams protein, 6 grams fat (0.6 gram saturated fat), 40 grams carbohydrate; 215 mg sodium; 27 mg cholesterol; 1 gram fiber.

N NUTRITION BONUS: Commercial whole-grain muffins may sound healthy, but you should check the fat count; many contain 10 to 15 grams of fat per muffin.

Banana & Carrot Muffins

1½ cups raisins
1½ cups all-purpose white flour
1 cup oat bran
½ cup toasted wheat germ

2 teaspoons baking powder
1 teaspoon baking soda
2 teaspoons ground cinnamon
¼ teaspoon ground allspice
¼ teaspoon salt
4 large egg whites
1 cup packed brown sugar
1 cup mashed bananas (2 medium bananas)
½ cup low-fat milk
¼ cup canola oil
1 teaspoon pure vanilla extract
2 cups grated carrots (4 medium carrots)
⅓ cup chopped walnuts

1. Preheat oven to 400°F. Lightly oil 18 muffin cups or coat with nonstick cooking spray.

2. In a small bowl, cover raisins with hot water; let soak for 5 minutes. Drain and set aside.

3. In a large mixing bowl, whisk flour, oat bran, wheat germ, baking powder, baking soda, cinnamon, allspice and salt; set aside.

4. In a medium bowl, whisk egg whites until frothy. Add brown sugar and whisk until it has dissolved. Mix in bananas, milk, oil and vanilla.

5. Make a well in the center of the dry ingredients. Add the wet ingredients; stir with a rubber spatula just to moisten the dry ingredients. Gently stir in carrots and the drained raisins.

6. Spoon the batter into the prepared muffin cups and sprinkle with nuts. Bake for 15 to 20 minutes, or until the tops spring back when touched lightly. Cool on a wire rack.

Makes 1½ dozen muffins.

210 calories per muffin: 5 grams protein, 5 grams fat (0.5 gram saturated fat), 40 grams carbohydrate; 140 mg sodium; 0 mg cholesterol; 3 grams fiber.

(N) NUTRITION BONUS: Packed with fruit and fiber, these are great muffins for a healthy breakfast. Use whole-wheat pastry flour to boost fiber even more.

Apple Spice Cake

2 cups plus 2 tablespoons all-purpose white flour
2 teaspoons baking soda
2 teaspoons ground cinnamon

WHY DO EATING WELL RECIPES SPECIFY CANOLA OIL FOR BAKED GOODS?

Pressed from rapeseed, canola oil is a neutral-flavored oil that is extremely low in saturated fats and quite high in heart-healthy monoun-saturated fats. Canola oil is also high in linolenic acid, the plant version of omega-3 fatty acids, which is generally low in the American diet. New research suggests that a higher proportion of plant omega-3s may help lower the risk of several chronic diseases. If you don't have canola oil, safflower, corn or other vegetable oils will certainly work in these recipes—they just don't have quite as healthy a nutrition profile.

2 teaspoons ground ginger
1 teaspoon ground allspice
¼ teaspoon salt
1 tablespoon butter
1 large egg
1 cup apple butter *or* fruit puree fat replacement
¾ cup packed light brown sugar
3 tablespoons canola oil
½ cup raisins
½ cup buttermilk
2 teaspoons pure vanilla extract

1. Preheat oven to 350°F. Lightly oil an 8-inch square baking pan or coat it with nonstick cooking spray; set aside.

2. In a bowl, whisk flour, baking soda, cinnamon, ginger, allspice and salt; set aside.

3. In a small saucepan, melt butter over medium heat; swirl the pan until the butter turns a nutty brown, about 60 seconds. (*See Technique 81, page 154.*) Pour into a mixing bowl. Add egg, apple butter or fruit puree fat replacement, brown sugar (breaking up any lumps) and oil and whisk until smooth. Add raisins, buttermilk and vanilla; mix well. Add the reserved dry ingredients and stir just until they are moistened.

4. Turn the batter out into the prepared pan and bake for 35 to 40 minutes, or until a knife inserted in the center comes out clean. Let cool in the pan on a wire rack for 10 minutes. Cut into squares and serve warm.

Makes 9 servings.

340 calories per serving: 5 grams protein, 7 grams fat (1.5 grams saturated fat), 65 grams carbohydrate; 285 mg sodium; 28 mg cholesterol; 1 gram fiber.

(N) NUTRITION BONUS: One ounce of raisins contains 2 grams of fiber.

Gingery Coffee Cake

½ cup nonfat plain yogurt
⅓ cup unsulfured molasses
2 tablespoons canola oil
1½ cups cake flour
1 tablespoon ground ginger
1 tablespoon ground cinnamon
1 teaspoon baking powder
¼ teaspoon baking soda
½ cup light brown sugar
½ cup fruit puree fat replacement *or* prune pie filling (Lekvar)
1 large egg
1 large egg white
¼ cup crystallized ginger, finely chopped
   Confectioners' sugar for dusting

1. Preheat oven to 350°F. Lightly oil an 8-inch square baking pan or coat it with nonstick cooking spray; set aside.

2. In a small bowl, mix yogurt, molasses and oil. Into a mixing bowl, sift flour, ground ginger, cinnamon, baking powder and baking soda. Set bowls aside.

3. In a large bowl, beat brown sugar and fruit puree fat replacement or prune pie filling with an electric mixer until well combined. Add egg and beat 2 minutes, or until thick and bubbly. Add egg white and continue beating another 2 minutes. With a rubber spatula, fold in half of the dry ingredients just until blended. Fold in half of the yogurt mixture. Repeat with remaining dry ingredients and yogurt mixture. Fold in crystallized ginger.

4. Pour the batter into the prepared baking pan. With the spatula, spread evenly and push the batter up the sides of the pan ¼ inch to encourage level rising. Bake for 30 to 35 minutes, or until a skewer

inserted in the center comes out clean. Let cool in the pan on a wire rack. Dust with confectioners' sugar just before serving.

Makes 9 servings.

220 calories per serving: 3 grams protein, 4 grams fat (0.5 gram saturated fat), 47 grams carbohydrate; 100 mg sodium; 24 mg cholesterol; 1 gram fiber.

(N) NUTRITION BONUS: Fruit puree fat replacements are made from dried plums and dried apples, so they are rich in pectin and other soluble fibers.

Cranberry Coffee Cake

STREUSEL
½ cup packed brown sugar
⅔ cup all-purpose white flour
½ teaspoon ground cinnamon
2 tablespoons frozen apple-juice concentrate, thawed
1 tablespoon canola oil
CAKE
1 tablespoon butter
½ cup fruit puree fat replacement
1 cup sugar
1 large egg
1 large egg white
1 cup nonfat plain yogurt
1 tablespoon canola oil
1 tablespoon pure vanilla extract
2¼ cups cake flour, unsifted
1 teaspoon baking powder
1 teaspoon baking soda
½ teaspoon salt
1 12-ounce package fresh cranberries (3 cups)

TO MAKE STREUSEL:

In a bowl, stir together brown sugar, flour and cinnamon. Sprinkle in apple-juice concentrate and oil. Blend with a fork or your fingers until crumbly. (*See Technique 88, page 173.*) Set aside.

TO MAKE CAKE:

1. Preheat oven to 350°F. Lightly oil a 9-by-13-inch baking dish or coat it with nonstick cooking spray; set aside.

2. In a small saucepan, melt butter over medium heat. Cook, swirling the pan, until the butter turns a light nutty brown, about 60 seconds. (*See Technique 81, page 154.*) Pour into a mixing bowl and add fruit puree fat replacement, sugar, egg, egg white, yogurt, oil and vanilla, whisking until smooth.

3. Place flour, baking powder, baking soda and salt in a sifter over the mixing bowl; sift into the wet ingredients and fold in with a rubber spatula just until the dry ingredients are moistened.

4. Spread half of the batter in the prepared pan. Top with cranberries, then with the remaining batter. Sprinkle the streusel over the top. Bake for 40 to 45 minutes, or until a skewer inserted in the center comes out clean. Serve warm.

Makes 12 servings.

305 calories per serving: 4 grams protein, 4 grams fat (1 gram saturated fat), 64 grams carbohydrate; 225 mg sodium; 20 mg cholesterol; 0.5 gram fiber.

NUTRITION BONUS: As if being low-fat, moist and delicious weren't enough, this coffee cake contains calcium and trace minerals.

TECHNIQUE

71 To keep quick breads moist and low in fat, add nonfat yogurt.

The fat in quick-bread recipes not only tenderizes, it keeps the bread from becoming unpleasantly dry. Nonfat yogurt keeps baked goods moist; this is particularly useful in a quick bread that contains dried fruits, which tend to draw moisture from the batter during baking.

FAT SAVINGS: Switching from sour cream to nonfat plain yogurt in baked goods will save you 48 grams of fat per cup.

Apricot-Nut Bread

½ cup coarsely chopped hazelnuts *or* walnuts
1½ cups coarsely chopped dried apricots
¼ cup apricot nectar *or* apple juice

2½ cups all-purpose white flour
1 tablespoon baking powder
1 teaspoon baking soda
½ teaspoon salt
1 large egg
2 large egg whites
½ cup sugar
⅔ cup nonfat plain yogurt
3 tablespoons hazelnut oil *or* canola oil
1 tablespoon grated lemon zest
1 teaspoon pure vanilla extract
¾ cup golden raisins

1. Preheat oven to 350°F. Lightly oil a 9-by-5-inch loaf pan or coat it with nonstick cooking spray; set aside. In a shallow pan, toast hazelnuts or walnuts in the oven for 3 to 5 minutes, or until golden brown and fragrant. Set aside to cool.

2. In a small saucepan, combine ½ cup of the apricots and nectar or juice. Bring to a simmer, remove from heat and let stand for 10 minutes. Transfer the apricots and their liquid to a food processor and process until a chunky puree forms; set aside. (You should have about ½ cup puree.)

3. In a large bowl, whisk flour, baking powder, baking soda and salt. In another large bowl, whisk egg, egg whites, sugar, yogurt, oil, lemon zest, vanilla and

Adding yogurt ensures a moist Apricot-Nut Bread.

the apricot puree. Stir the apricot mixture into the dry ingredients just until combined. Fold in raisins, hazelnuts and the remaining 1 cup chopped apricots. (The batter will be thick.) Turn the batter out into the prepared pan, smoothing the top.

4. Bake for 50 to 60 minutes, or until the top is golden brown and a skewer inserted in the center comes out clean. Let cool in the pan for 10 minutes. Loosen the edges and invert the loaf onto a wire rack to cool.

Makes 1 loaf, 16 slices.

165 calories per slice: 4 grams protein, 6 grams fat (0.5 gram saturated fat), 25 grams carbohydrate; 200 mg sodium; 14 mg cholesterol; 2 grams fiber.

(N) NUTRITION BONUS: Dried apricots are a good source of carotenoids, potassium and trace minerals.

TECHNIQUE 72 — For tender biscuits and scones, depend on buttermilk.

For generations, Southern cooks have known that buttermilk along with lard or butter makes biscuits tender. In the EATING WELL Test Kitchen, we found that the tenderizing action of buttermilk is quite effective even when you use less fat. (It works for fat-busting in scones as well).

(F) FAT SAVINGS: Typical homemade buttermilk biscuits have 5 grams of fat (and your average refrigerated biscuit has 4 grams). Eating Well's biscuit has only 3 grams.

Buttermilk Biscuits

- ¾ cup buttermilk
- 1 tablespoon canola oil
- 1 cup all-purpose white flour
- 1 cup unsifted cake flour
- 1 tablespoon sugar
- 1½ teaspoons baking powder
- ½ teaspoon baking soda
- ½ teaspoon salt
- 1½ tablespoons cold butter, cut into small pieces
- 1 tablespoon low-fat milk for brushing

1. Preheat oven to 425°F. Lightly oil a baking sheet or coat it with nonstick cooking spray; set aside.

2. Combine buttermilk and oil and set aside. In a large bowl, whisk flours, sugar, baking powder, baking soda and salt. Using your fingertips or 2 knives, cut butter into the dry ingredients until crumbly. Make a well in the center and gradually pour in the reserved buttermilk/oil mixture, stirring with a fork just until combined.

3. Transfer the dough to a floured surface and sprinkle with a little flour. Lightly knead the dough 8 times, then pat or roll out to an even ¾-inch thickness. Cut into 2-inch rounds and transfer to the prepared baking sheet. Gather any scraps of dough and cut more rounds.

4. Brush the tops with milk. Bake for 12 to 16 minutes, or until golden brown. Transfer to a wire rack and let cool slightly before serving.

Makes 1 dozen biscuits.

105 calories per biscuit: 2 grams protein, 3 grams fat (1 gram saturated fat), 17 grams carbohydrate; 195 mg sodium; 4 mg cholesterol; 1 gram fiber.

(N) NUTRITION BONUS: Buttermilk adds moistness and boosts flavor in place of fat.

Currant Scones

Save your favorite jam for these teatime treats.

- 2 cups all-purpose white flour
- ¼ cup light brown sugar
- 1 teaspoon baking powder
- 1 teaspoon cream of tartar
- ½ teaspoon salt
- ¾ cup buttermilk
- ⅔ cup currants
- 1 tablespoon canola oil
- 1 tablespoon low-fat milk for brushing

1. Preheat oven to 350°F. Lightly oil a baking sheet or coat it with nonstick cooking spray.

2. In a large bowl, whisk flour, brown sugar, baking powder, cream of tartar and salt. In another bowl, stir together buttermilk, currants and oil. Make a well in the center of the dry ingredients and gradually stir in the buttermilk mixture.

3. On a lightly floured surface, pat or roll the dough into a round about ½ inch thick. With a long knife, cut the round into 12 wedges and transfer to the prepared baking sheet. Brush the tops with milk. Bake for 15 to 20 minutes, or until golden brown. Serve warm.

Makes 1 dozen scones.

130 calories per scone: 3 grams protein, 1 gram fat (0.2 gram saturated fat), 27 grams carbohydrate; 175 mg sodium; 1 mg cholesterol; 1 gram fiber.

 NUTRITION BONUS: Traditional scones contain large amounts of butter. We cut the butter out completely and use canola oil.

Strawberry Shortcakes

FILLING
   2   **pints fresh strawberries, hulled**
  ½   **cup sugar**
   1   **cup nonfat vanilla yogurt**
  ½   **cup nonfat sour cream**
SHORTCAKES
      Buttermilk Biscuits (page 136)
   1   **tablespoon sugar**

TO MAKE FILLING:
If strawberries are large, slice them. Put the strawberries in a bowl, sprinkle with sugar and refrigerate while you bake shortcakes. In a small bowl, blend yogurt and sour cream; set aside in the refrigerator.

TO MAKE SHORTCAKES:
Mix as for Buttermilk Biscuits and use a 2½-inch round or star cookie cutter to cut out 8 shortcakes. Transfer them to the prepared baking sheet. After brushing with milk, sprinkle with 1 tablespoon sugar.

TO BAKE & ASSEMBLE SHORTCAKES:
1. Preheat oven to 425°F. Bake the shortcakes for 12 to 16 minutes, or until golden. Transfer to a wire rack and let cool slightly.

2. Using a serrated knife, split the shortcakes. Set the bottoms on dessert plates, spread with some of the yogurt cream, spoon on the strawberries and juices and crown with the shortcake lids. Top with a dollop of yogurt cream and serve.

Makes 8 servings.

250 calories per serving: 5 grams protein, 6 grams fat (2.2 grams saturated fat), 36 grams carbohydrate; 420 mg sodium; 9 mg cholesterol; 1 gram fiber.

 NUTRITION BONUS: By replacing the traditional whipped cream with a nonfat topping, you save about 10 grams of fat per serving.

The vanilla yogurt cream for Strawberry Shortcakes is fat-free.

TECHNIQUE 73 — Enrich an easy stollen with low-fat (1%) cottage cheese.

Stollen, a traditional German Christmas bread, is often made with a sweetened yeast dough containing much butter and many eggs. We make a quick-bread version of the loaf that uses low-fat (1%) cottage cheese instead of butter. It's just as good and a lot faster to make.

F FAT SAVINGS: Traditional recipes vary, but stollen can have as much as 10 grams of fat in a slice. Ours has 5 grams per slice.

Stollen is scented with spice and studded with fruit.

Stollen

⅓ cup slivered almonds
2½ cups all-purpose white flour
¼ cup diced glacé orange *or* lemon peel
4 teaspoons baking powder
½ teaspoon salt
¼ teaspoon freshly grated nutmeg
½ cup golden raisins
½ cup currants
1½ cups low-fat (1%) cottage cheese
¾ cup sugar
1 large egg
2 tablespoons plus 1 teaspoon canola oil
1 tablespoon cold butter, cut into small pieces
2 teaspoons pure vanilla extract
¼ teaspoon pure almond extract
1½ teaspoons coarse *or* pearl sugar for sprinkling

1. Preheat oven to 350°F. Lightly oil a baking sheet or coat it with nonstick cooking spray. Spread almonds in a pie pan and bake, stirring occasionally, until lightly toasted, 4 to 6 minutes. Let cool and chop coarsely.
2. Place flour, citrus peel, baking powder, salt and nutmeg in a food processor; process until the peel is finely ground. Transfer to a large mixing bowl. Stir in raisins, currants and the toasted almonds; set aside.
3. Puree cottage cheese in the food processor until smooth. Add sugar, egg, 2 tablespoons of the oil, butter, vanilla and almond extracts; process until very smooth.
4. Make a well in the center of the dry ingredients. Pour in the cottage-cheese mixture and stir with a wooden spoon until the dry ingredients are moistened. Turn the dough out onto a lightly floured surface, dust with flour and knead several times to make a smooth dough.
5. Pat the dough into an oval about 10 inches by 8½ inches. With the side of your hand, press a line into the dough just above the imaginary 10-inch line that bisects the dough horizontally. Using a wide metal spatula, lift and fold the smaller section over the larger section. Carefully transfer the stollen to the prepared baking sheet.
6. Brush 1 teaspoon oil over the top. Sprinkle with

coarse or pearl sugar. Bake for 45 to 55 minutes, or until golden brown and a skewer inserted in the center comes out clean. Transfer to a wire rack and let cool slightly. Slice and serve warm.

Makes 1 loaf, 16 slices.

200 calories per slice: 6 grams protein, 5 grams fat (1 gram saturated fat), 35 grams carbohydrate; 255 mg sodium; 16 mg cholesterol; 1 gram fiber.

Ⓝ NUTRITION BONUS: The cottage cheese, currants and raisins all contribute calcium.

74 Use a special pan to make low-fat doughnuts.

TECHNIQUE

The secret to EATING WELL's low-fat doughnuts lies in the pan, a mini-Bundt pan. The roughly 9-by-13-inch pan comprises six fluted molds, each with a hole in the center, just like a large Bundt pan. If you don't have a mini-Bundt pan, use a muffin tin—you just won't be able to call them doughnuts.

Ⓕ FAT SAVINGS: One plain cake doughnut from your local doughnut shop has 18 grams of fat, three and a half times as much fat as in the doughnuts here.

To duplicate the crispy outside of a good fried doughnut, thoroughly coat molds of a mini-Bundt pan with nonstick cooking spray or oil and dust with sugar before spooning in batter.

Apple Cider Doughnuts

Like a trip to Vermont during apple-picking season.

- 3 tablespoons granulated sugar (approximately) for preparing pans
- 2 cups all-purpose white flour
- 1½ teaspoons baking powder
- 1½ teaspoons baking soda
- ½ teaspoon salt
- 2 teaspoons ground cinnamon
- 1 large egg, lightly beaten
- ⅔ cup packed brown sugar
- ½ cup apple butter
  or fruit puree fat replacement
- ⅓ cup pure maple syrup
- ⅓ cup apple cider
- ⅓ cup nonfat plain yogurt
- 3 tablespoons canola oil

MAPLE GLAZE
- 1¼ cups confectioners' sugar
- 1 teaspoon pure vanilla extract
- ¼-⅓ cup pure maple syrup

1. Preheat oven to 400°F. Thoroughly coat the molds of 2 mini-Bundt pans with nonstick cooking spray or oil. Sprinkle molds evenly with granulated sugar, tapping out the excess. (If you only have 1 pan, bake the recipe in 2 batches.)

2. In a mixing bowl, whisk flour, baking powder, baking soda, salt and cinnamon; set aside. In another bowl, whisk egg, brown sugar, apple butter or fruit puree fat replacement, maple syrup, cider, yogurt and oil. Add the dry ingredients to the wet ingredients and stir just until moistened.

3. Spoon about 2 generous tablespoons of batter into each prepared mold, smoothing the surfaces.

4. Bake for 10 to 12 minutes, or until the tops spring back when touched lightly. Loosen edges and turn the doughnuts out onto a wire rack to cool. (If baking in 2 batches, cool the pan, clean it, then recoat it with cooking spray or oil and sugar.)

TO MAKE MAPLE GLAZE:

In a bowl, combine confectioners' sugar and vanilla. Gradually whisk in enough maple syrup to make a smooth, thick glaze. When the doughnuts are completely cool, set them, fluted-side up, on a wire rack over wax paper. Spoon some glaze over each dough-nut, letting it drip down the sides. (*Alternatively, dip the doughnuts in glaze.*)

Makes 1 dozen doughnuts.

285 calories per doughnut: 3 grams protein, 4 grams fat (0 grams saturated fat), 61 grams carbohydrate; 265 mg sodium; 18 mg cholesterol; 1 gram fiber.

 NUTRITION BONUS: Apple butter also works well in other spiced baked goods, such as gingerbread, hermits and apple cakes.

Chocolate Doughnuts

2	tablespoons plus ½ cup granulated sugar
1½	cups all-purpose white flour
⅓	cup unsweetened cocoa powder, preferably Dutch-process
1½	teaspoons baking powder
½	teaspoon baking soda
½	teaspoon salt
1	large egg
1	large egg white
½	cup packed light brown sugar
¾	cup nonfat plain yogurt *or* buttermilk
¼	cup canola oil
1	teaspoon pure vanilla extract

GLAZE
1¼	cups confectioners' sugar
1	teaspoon pure vanilla extract
2-3	tablespoons low-fat milk

1. Preheat oven to 400°F. Thoroughly coat the molds of 2 mini-Bundt pans with nonstick cooking spray or oil. Sprinkle molds evenly with 2 tablespoons of the granulated sugar, tapping out the excess. (If you only have 1 pan, bake the recipe in 2 batches.)

2. In a mixing bowl, whisk together flour, cocoa, baking powder, baking soda and salt.

3. In another bowl, whisk egg and egg white until frothy. Add brown sugar and the remaining ½ cup granulated sugar; whisk until smooth. Add yogurt or buttermilk, oil and vanilla and whisk until blended. Add the dry ingredients and stir with a rubber spatula just until moistened.

4. Spoon about 2 generous tablespoons of batter into each prepared mold, smoothing the surfaces.

WHAT IS UNBLEACHED FLOUR?

There is a great deal of controversy surrounding the merits of bleached and unbleached flour. The debate has little to do with the nutrition profiles of either. Flour boasting an "un-bleached" label may conjure up a superior nutritional image, but both bleached and unbleached flour are refined flours made from the starchy part of the wheat kernel after it has been stripped of its fiber- and nutrient-rich components.

The color of flour has no practical or nutritional significance; white flour is bleached simply to appeal to consumers who desire whiter baked products. Bleaching removes the light yellow color of flour. Although flour loses the yellow tinge naturally over time, most flour producers use chlorine dioxide, a suspected carcinogen, to speed the bleaching process. The chemical residue that remains falls well below FDA limits. Opponents of bleaching claim that it is unnecessary and imparts a slightly medicinal taste to food. Unless cooks desire the whitest possible baked goods, unbleached flour is an appropriate, less-processed option.

5. Bake for 8 to 10 minutes, or until the tops spring back when touched lightly. Loosen edges and turn the doughnuts out onto a wire rack to cool. (If baking in 2 batches, cool the pan, clean it, then recoat it with cooking spray or oil and sugar.)

TO MAKE GLAZE:

In a bowl, whisk confectioners' sugar, vanilla and enough of the milk to make a smooth, thick glaze. When the doughnuts are completely cool, set them, fluted-side up, on a wire rack over wax paper. Spoon some glaze over each doughnut, letting it drip down the sides. (*Alternatively, dip the doughnuts in glaze.*)

Makes 1 dozen doughnuts.

220 calories per doughnut: 3 grams protein, 5 grams fat (0.5 gram saturated fat), 41 grams carbohydrate; 185 mg sodium; 19 mg cholesterol; 0 grams fiber.

 NUTRITION BONUS: Because of its tiny fat content, cocoa is a health-conscious chocoholic's friend.

Honey-Glazed Cinnamon Doughnuts

1¾ cups all-purpose white flour
2 tablespoons plus ¾ cup granulated sugar
2 tablespoons ground cinnamon
1 teaspoon baking powder
½ teaspoon baking soda
½ teaspoon salt
¾ cup buttermilk
½ cup dark molasses
3 large egg whites
3 tablespoons canola oil
1½ cups confectioners' sugar, sifted
2 tablespoons honey

1. Preheat oven to 400°F. Thoroughly coat the molds of 2 mini-Bundt pans with nonstick cooking spray or oil. Sprinkle molds evenly with 2 tablespoons of the granulated sugar, tapping out the excess. (If you only have 1 pan, bake the recipe in 2 batches.)

2. In a large mixing bowl, whisk flour, the remaining ¾ cup granulated sugar, cinnamon, baking powder, baking soda and salt. Make a well in the dry ingredients and set aside. In another bowl, whisk buttermilk, molasses, egg whites and oil. With a rubber spatula, fold buttermilk mixture into the dry ingredients just until blended.

3. Spoon about 2 generous tablespoons of batter into each prepared mold, smoothing the surfaces.

4. Bake for 8 to 10 minutes, or until the tops spring back when touched lightly. Loosen edges and turn the doughnuts out onto a wire rack to cool. (If baking in 2 batches, cool the pan, clean it, then recoat it with cooking spray or oil and sugar.)

5. In a bowl, whisk confectioners' sugar, honey and about 1 tablespoon hot water to make a smooth, thick glaze. When the doughnuts are completely cool, set them, fluted-side up, on a wire rack over wax paper. Spoon some glaze over each doughnut, letting it drip down the sides. (*Alternatively, dip the doughnuts in glaze.*)

Makes 1 dozen doughnuts.

245 calories per doughnut: 3 grams protein, 4 grams fat (0.4 gram saturated fat), 50 grams carbohydrate; 195 mg sodium; 1 mg cholesterol; 1 gram fiber.

Ⓝ NUTRITION BONUS: These doughnuts have *no* added cholesterol-raising saturated or hydrogenated fats.

Poppy Seed Doughnuts

2 tablespoons plus 1¼ cups sugar
2 tablespoons poppy seeds
2 cups all-purpose white flour
1½ teaspoons baking powder
1½ teaspoons baking soda
½ teaspoon salt
1 large egg
1 cup nonfat plain yogurt
3 tablespoons canola oil
2 teaspoons grated lemon zest
1 teaspoon pure vanilla extract

1. Preheat oven to 400°F. Thoroughly coat the molds of 2 mini-Bundt pans with nonstick cooking spray or oil. Sprinkle molds evenly with 2 tablespoons of the sugar, tapping out the excess. (If you only have 1 pan, bake the recipe in 2 batches.)

2. In a small dry skillet, stir poppy seeds over medium heat until they are fragrant, about 1 minute. Transfer to a bowl. Add flour, baking powder, baking soda and salt; whisk to blend and set aside.

3. In a large mixing bowl, whisk egg until frothy. Add the remaining 1¼ cups sugar, yogurt, oil, lemon zest and vanilla; mix well. Add the dry ingredients and stir with a rubber spatula just until moistened.

4. Spoon about 2 generous tablespoons of batter into each prepared mold, smoothing the surfaces.

5. Bake for 8 to 12 minutes, or until the tops spring back when touched lightly. Loosen edges and turn the doughnuts out onto a wire rack to cool. (If baking in 2 batches, cool the pan, clean it, then recoat it with cooking spray or oil and sugar.)

Makes 1 dozen doughnuts.

205 calories per doughnut: 4 grams protein, 5 grams fat (0.5 gram saturated fat), 38 grams carbohydrate; 255 mg sodium; 18 mg cholesterol; 1 gram fiber.

Ⓝ NUTRITION NOTE: With 4 grams of fat in a tablespoon, poppy seeds can be an unexpected source of fat in baked goods. Lightly toasting poppy seeds enhances their flavor, so you can get away with a small amount in a recipe.

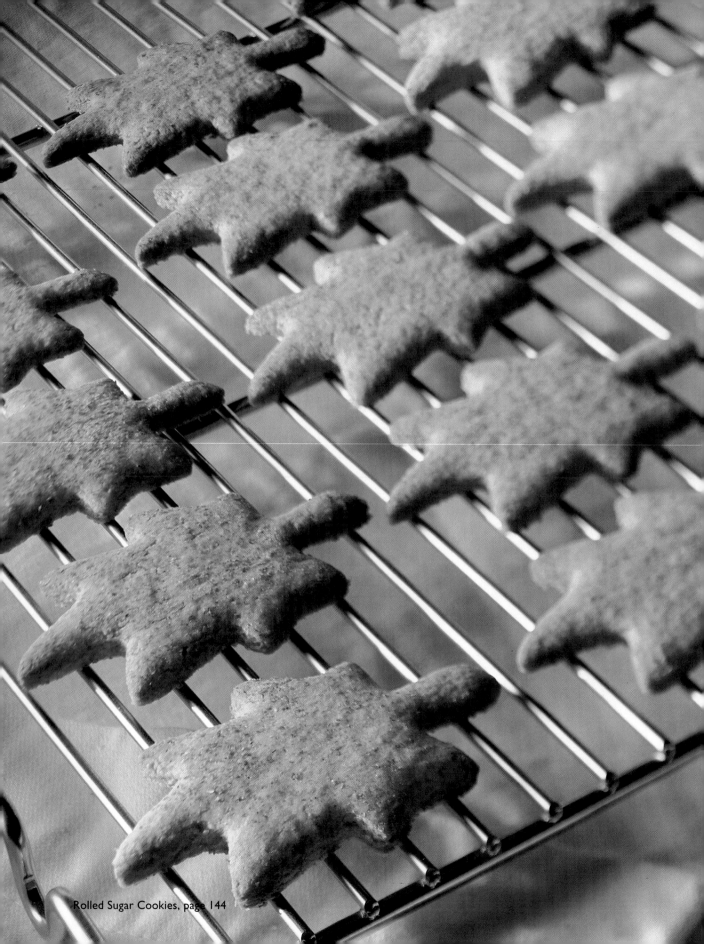

Rolled Sugar Cookies, page 144

THE TECHNIQUES

75 Reducing the saturated fat in
rolled cookies

76 Rescuing a high-fat cookie with
cornstarch

77 Cutting the fat with pumpkin puree

78 Crafting crisp cookies from phyllo

79 Baking bars with graham cracker crumbs

80 Using low-fat granola to make healthier
granola bars

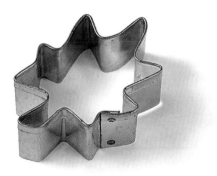

COOKIES & BARS

CRISP, CHEWY, TENDER, BUTTERY:
THESE ARE THE WORDS WE USE TO
DESCRIBE THE BEST HOME-BAKED
cookies and bars. It's that combination of sweetness, buttery flavor and satisfying texture that
keeps you reaching for seconds or thirds. But these
same qualities are hard to come by in low-fat
cookie makeovers, which can run to gummy or
tough or bland. And while we might tolerate a
so-so cookie from a package, a homemade cookie
has got to be better than mediocre or it's not worth
the time and the effort. With six years of practice,
the EATING WELL Test Kitchen has learned more
than a few tricks when it comes to cookies. All the
while we have kept three things in mind: cut
the fat (particularly saturated fat), maintain the
original texture and, most of all, don't compromise
the flavor.

75 Focus on reducing *saturated* fat in rolled cookies.

Most cookies pack a double fat whammy. Not only are they high in total fat, but, because they contain solid fats like butter and shortening, much of their fat is saturated. Our recipes not only cut down the fat, but increase the proportion of more healthful monounsaturated fat by using a combination of butter and canola oil. The technique described in the box on the opposite page makes rolling and cutting the low-fat doughs easy—and mess-free.

F FAT SAVINGS: An old-fashioned rolled sugar cookie contains about 70 calories and 3 grams of fat (2 saturated). An Eating Well sugar cookie has 50 calories and 2 grams of fat (only 0.6 gram saturated).

Rolled Sugar Cookies

Working from a recipe for classic rolled sugar cookies, we replaced its ½ cup butter with 2 tablespoons canola oil plus 2 tablespoons butter, browned to maximize its flavor. In addition, we increased the vanilla because low-fat baked goods tend to taste a little flat unless the flavorings are boosted.

½ cup sugar
2 tablespoons butter, browned (*see Technique 81, page 154*)
2 tablespoons canola oil
1 large egg
1½ teaspoons pure vanilla extract
¾ cup whole-wheat flour
¾ cup unsifted cake flour
1 teaspoon baking powder
¼ teaspoon salt

1. Position oven rack in the upper third of the oven and preheat to 350°F. Lightly oil 2 baking sheets or coat them with nonstick cooking spray.
2. In a mixing bowl, combine sugar, browned butter and oil and beat with an electric mixer until smooth. Mix in egg and vanilla; beat until smooth.
3. Sift the flours, baking powder and salt together into the sugar/egg mixture; mix on low speed until just combined. Divide the dough in half and press each piece into a disk. Roll the dough out to an even ⅛-inch thickness and freeze (*see box, page 145*).
4. Cut out cookies with small (2- to 2½-inch) cookie cutters. Place the cookies about ½ inch apart on the prepared baking sheets.
5. Bake in the upper third of the oven, 1 sheet at a time, for 5 to 7 minutes, or until slightly golden on the edges. Do not overbake. Transfer cookies to wire racks to cool. (*The cookies will keep for up to 3 days in a tightly covered cookie tin. Freeze for longer storage.*)
Makes about 2½ dozen cookies.

50 calories per cookie: 1 gram protein, 2 grams fat (0.6 gram saturated fat), 8 grams carbohydrate; 40 mg sodium; 9 mg cholesterol; 1 gram fiber.

N NUTRITION BONUS: The whole-wheat flour in this recipe adds 1 gram of fiber per cookie.

Gingerbread Men

The aroma of baking gingerbread cookies is sure to draw a crowd to the kitchen.

4 cups sifted all-purpose white flour
1 teaspoon baking soda
1 teaspoon ground cinnamon
1 teaspoon ground ginger
½ teaspoon ground cloves
½ teaspoon salt
¾ cup packed brown sugar
¼ cup canola oil
3 tablespoons butter, softened
½ cup unsulfured molasses
2 large egg whites
Icing for Cookies (*recipe follows*)

1. In a bowl, whisk flour, baking soda, cinnamon, ginger, cloves and salt.
2. In a mixing bowl, using an electric mixer, cream brown sugar, oil and butter until light and fluffy,

about 3 minutes. Gradually beat in molasses until smooth. Beat in egg whites one at a time. With the mixer on low speed, add the dry ingredients in 4 additions just until combined.

3. Divide the dough into thirds; roll out to an even $\frac{1}{16}$-inch thickness and freeze (*see box at right*).

4. Position oven rack in the upper third of the oven and preheat to 375°F. Lightly oil 2 or 3 baking sheets or coat them with nonstick cooking spray. Cut out cookies with a small gingerbread-man cutter. Transfer to a prepared sheet, spacing them about 1 inch apart.

5. Bake for 6 to 8 minutes, or until firm to the touch and just starting to brown on the edges. Transfer the cookies to wire racks to cool.

6. Decorate the cookies with icing. (*The cookies will keep in a tightly covered cookie tin for 1 week. Freeze for longer storage.*)

Makes about 6 dozen 3-inch cookies.

50 calories per cookie:
I gram protein, I gram fat
(0.4 gram saturated fat),
8 grams carbohydrate;
35 mg sodium; I mg
cholesterol; 0 grams fiber.

N NUTRITION BONUS: Low-fat
Christmas cookies are much appreciated at a time of year when so many offerings are so high in fat.

Icing for Cookies

1¾	cups confectioners' sugar
1½	tablespoons light corn syrup
½	teaspoon pure vanilla extract
1-2	drops pure orange extract *or* lemon extract (optional)

Sift confectioners' sugar into a bowl. Stir in corn syrup, vanilla, orange or lemon extract, if using, and 1½ tablespoons hot water; mix until smooth. If the icing is too thick, add a few more drops of water.

Makes about ¾ cup.

20 calories per teaspoon: 0 grams protein, 0 grams fat, 6 grams carbohydrate; 0 mg sodium; 0 mg cholesterol; 0 grams fiber.

? WHAT'S THE BEST WAY TO ROLL OUT COOKIES?

Most recipes for gingerbread men and other cut-out cookies instruct you to chill the dough, then roll the hard lump to an even thickness. Instead, we do the opposite, rolling the dough between sheets of parchment paper and then freezing it.

1. Begin by dividing the dough into two or three manageable portions. Place a 14-by-18-inch sheet of parchment or wax paper on the work surface and set a portion of dough on top, flattening it slightly. Cover with a second sheet of parchment or wax paper. With a rolling pin, roll the dough out, inverting occasionally and smoothing out any wrinkles 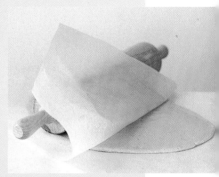 that form in the paper. Transfer the dough to a baking sheet, with the paper still attached. Repeat the rolling process with the dough that remains and stack on the baking sheet with the other dough sheet. Freeze the dough, baking sheet and all, for at least 1 hour and for up to 3 days.

2. When you are ready to bake the cookies, carefully peel off one of the sheets of paper from a rolled portion of dough and set the paper back in place. (Leave the remaining dough in the freezer.) Lay the dough, loosened sheet down, on a flat work surface. Peel off the top sheet of paper and set aside to use again. Cut out cookies with a cookie cutter. If the dough is too firm to cut out, let stand a few minutes to warm up slightly. Using a metal spatula, transfer the cookies from the paper to a baking sheet. Repeat the process with the remaining dough. Gather all the scraps and reroll between sheets of the reserved paper. Freeze briefly on a baking sheet until firm enough to cut out.

Linzer Cookies

½ cup sugar
2 tablespoons butter, browned (*see Technique 81, page 154*)
2 tablespoons canola oil
1 large egg
2 teaspoons pure vanilla extract
1¾ cups cake flour
1 teaspoon baking powder
¼ teaspoon salt
¼ cup seedless raspberry jam
   Confectioners' sugar for dusting (optional)

1. In a mixing bowl, combine sugar, browned butter and oil; beat with an electric mixer until smooth. Add egg and vanilla and beat until smooth. Sift the flour, baking powder and salt together into the sugar/egg mixture; mix on low speed just until blended.
2. Divide the dough in half, roll out to an even ¹⁄₁₆-inch thickness, and freeze as directed on page 145.
3. Position oven rack in the upper third of the oven and preheat to 350°F. Lightly oil 2 baking sheets. With a 2-inch round cookie cutter, cut out an even

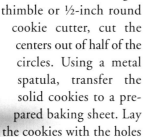

number of circles. Using a thimble or ½-inch round cookie cutter, cut the centers out of half of the circles. Using a metal spatula, transfer the solid cookies to a prepared baking sheet. Lay the cookies with the holes on top of the solid cookies.
4. In a small bowl, whisk raspberry jam until smooth. Spoon ½ teaspoon into the center of each cookie.
5. Bake for 8 to 10 minutes, or until the cookies are firm to the touch and lightly browned on the bottom. Cool on wire racks. Dust with confectioners' sugar, if desired. (*The cookies will keep in a tightly covered cookie tin for 1 week. Freeze for longer storage.*)
Makes about 2½ dozen cookies.

60 calories per cookie: I gram protein, 2 grams fat (0.6 gram saturated fat), 10 grams carbohydrate; 40 mg sodium; 9 mg cholesterol; 0 grams fiber.

 NUTRITION BONUS: If made with a full-fat cookie dough, these cookies would weigh in at 8 grams of fat.

76 Cornstarch comes to the aid of a classic melt-in-your-mouth cookie.

Some call them Mexican wedding cakes, others call them Russian tea cakes; whatever the name, this holiday standard gets its melt-in-your-mouth quality from butter—a lot of butter. Adding cornstarch to the dry ingredients gave a crumbly, melting quality to the cookie, and enabled us to cut back on the butter. The large quantity of nuts in the original can be reduced by toasting them first, which maximizes their flavor and lets you get away with using a smaller amount.

F FAT SAVINGS: The traditional version has 8 grams of fat per cookie; the revision has only 2 grams.

Russian Tea Cakes

1½ cups all-purpose white flour
¼ cup cornstarch
¼ teaspoon salt
1¼ cups confectioners' sugar
5 tablespoons butter, softened
2 tablespoons canola oil
2 tablespoons low-fat milk
1½ teaspoons pure vanilla extract
½ cup walnuts *or* pecans, lightly toasted (*see page 176*) **and finely chopped**

1. Preheat oven to 350°F. In a bowl, whisk flour, cornstarch and salt. Set aside.
2. In a large bowl, using an electric mixer, cream ¾ cup of the confectioners' sugar, butter and oil until smooth and light, about 3 minutes. Add milk and vanilla and beat until smooth. Add the dry ingredients and

walnuts or pecans; blend on low speed just until incorporated.

3. Roll the dough into ¾-inch balls and place on 2 ungreased baking sheets, about 1 inch apart. Bake, 1 sheet at a time, for 10 to 12 minutes, or until very lightly browned on the bottoms.

4. While the cookies are baking, sift the remaining ½ cup confectioners' sugar into a shallow dish. Remove the cookies from the oven and roll them immediately in the sugar, a few at a time. Transfer to wire racks to cool. If desired, sift additional confectioners' sugar over the cookies just before serving. (*The cookies will keep in a tightly covered cookie tin for 1 week. Freeze for longer storage.*)

Makes about 4 dozen cookies.

50 calories per cookie: 1 gram protein, 2 grams fat (0.8 gram saturated fat), 6 grams carbohydrate; 25 mg sodium; 3 mg cholesterol; 0 grams fiber.

Ⓝ NUTRITION BONUS: Walnuts contain linolenic acid, the omega-3 fatty acid from plants.

TECHNIQUE 77
Pumpkin puree cuts fat in a drop cookie.

Working much like a fruit puree (*see Technique 70, page 132*), thick and somewhat sweet pumpkin puree coats the flour and prevents gluten from forming, so you can use much less fat in a recipe. The full flavors in these cookies—spices, molasses, brown sugar— mean they do not need any butter for flavor.

Ⓕ FAT SAVINGS: Half the fat of the average drop cookie and negligible saturated fat.

Pumpkin Drop Cookies

1⅓	cups all-purpose white flour
1	teaspoon baking powder
½	teaspoon baking soda
½	teaspoon salt
1	teaspoon ground cinnamon

> ### ❓ WHY CAN'T I BAKE WITH LIGHT BUTTER?
>
> Reduced-fat or "light" versions of butter and margarine are made by whipping water, air or other fillers into the regular or skim-milk products; the same volume then contains less fat than the original. Because of the added water or fillers, these lighter versions will produce soggier results in baked goods.

½	teaspoon ground ginger
¼	teaspoon ground allspice
¼	teaspoon freshly grated nutmeg
¾	cup canned plain pumpkin puree
¾	cup packed light brown sugar
2	large eggs
¼	cup canola oil
¼	cup dark molasses
1	cup raisins

1. Preheat oven to 350°F. Lightly oil 3 baking sheets or coat them with nonstick cooking spray.

2. In a mixing bowl, whisk flour, baking powder, baking soda, salt, cinnamon, ginger, allspice and nutmeg.

3. In another bowl, whisk pumpkin, brown sugar, eggs, oil and molasses until well combined. Stir the wet ingredients and raisins into the dry ingredients until no traces of dry ingredients remain.

4. Drop the batter by level tablespoonfuls onto the prepared baking sheets, spacing the cookies 1½ inches apart. Bake for 10 to 12 minutes, switching the pans midway, or until firm to the touch and lightly golden on top. Transfer the cookies to a wire rack and let cool. (*The cookies will keep in an airtight container, with wax paper between the layers, for up to 2 days.*)

Makes about 3 dozen cookies.

70 calories per cookie: 1 gram protein, 2 grams fat (0.2 gram saturated fat), 13 grams carbohydrate; 56 mg sodium; 12 mg cholesterol; 0.5 gram fiber.

Ⓝ NUTRITION BONUS: As you might suspect from its orange color, pumpkin puree is an excellent source of beta carotene.

78 Craft crisp cookies using phyllo.

Looking for a perfect crisp cookie to accompany a fruit sorbet? Shocked to learn that the littlest butter cookie can have 4 or 5 grams of fat? An afternoon of experimenting with phyllo dough produced crisp, buttery wafers with less than a gram of fat. The secret lies in lightly brushing the phyllo layers with a mix of melted butter and canola oil, then sprinkling with cinnamon sugar before cutting the stack into wafers.

F FAT SAVINGS: One-fifth the fat of a shortbread or other buttery cookie.

Exposed to air, phyllo dries out quickly and becomes brittle. Keep the stack of phyllo sheets covered with plastic wrap or wax paper and a dampened kitchen towel, removing only one sheet at a time. To keep the pastry brush from soaking up too much oil, dampen it with water before dipping it in the butter/oil mixture. Starting at the center and working toward the edges, brush the phyllo lightly and evenly.

Phyllo Crisps

¼ cup sugar
½ teaspoon ground cinnamon
Pinch of ground cloves
1 tablespoon butter, melted
1 tablespoon canola oil
4 sheets phyllo dough (14x18 inches), thawed if frozen
Confectioners' sugar for dusting

1. Preheat oven to 325°F. Lightly oil a large baking sheet. In a small bowl, combine sugar, cinnamon and cloves. In another small bowl, mix butter and oil.
2. Lay 1 sheet of phyllo on a clean, dry surface. Brush very lightly with some of the butter mixture. Sprinkle about 1 tablespoon of the sugar mixture evenly over the phyllo. Repeat these steps with 3 more phyllo sheets. Cut the phyllo into 4 lengthwise strips; cut each strip into rectangles 1½ inches wide, to make 32 rectangles.
3. With a large metal spatula, carefully transfer half of the rectangles to the prepared baking sheet. Bake for 8 to 12 minutes, or until the cookies are crisp and golden brown. Transfer to a wire rack to cool. Bake the remaining rectangles in the same manner. (*The cookies will keep in an airtight container for up to 3 days.*) Dust with confectioners' sugar before serving.

Makes 32 cookies.

15 calories per cookie: 0 grams protein, 0.6 gram fat (0.2 gram saturated fat), 2 grams carbohydrate; 10 mg sodium; 1 mg cholesterol; 0 grams fiber.

N NUTRITION BONUS: Fresh fruit and two of these cookies would make a nutritionist's dream dessert.

79 Graham cracker crumbs and egg whites combine for a crisp, chewy low-fat bar.

Graham crackers have been doing decades of service as an after-school snack. We discovered that they're a real asset in bar baking. Crumbled and mixed with sugar, 1 egg and 2 egg whites, they produce a crispy and chewy bar.

F FAT SAVINGS: Nutty, chewy, satisfying bars at half the fat of a full-fat bar cookie.

Apple-Walnut Bars

For a good supply of lunchbox treats, make a double batch and freeze individual bars wrapped in aluminum foil.

- ½ cup chopped walnuts
- 32 graham cracker squares
- 1 teaspoon ground cinnamon
- ⅔ cup dried apples
- ½ cup sugar
- 2 large egg whites
- 1 large egg
- 2 teaspoons pure vanilla extract
- ¼ teaspoon salt
- 2 tablespoons confectioners' sugar

1. Preheat oven to 300°F. Spread walnuts in a small baking dish and toast in oven until fragrant and slightly browned, 5 to 7 minutes. Allow to cool, then chop coarsely. Set aside. Lightly oil an 8-by-12-inch baking dish or coat it with nonstick cooking spray. Set aside.

2. In a food processor, process graham crackers and cinnamon until you have fine crumbs. Leaving about ½ cup in the workbowl, transfer the crumbs to another container. Add apples to the workbowl and process until coarsely chopped. Set aside.

3. In a large bowl, combine sugar, egg whites, egg, vanilla and salt. Beat with an electric mixer on high speed until thick, about 3 minutes. Fold in the reserved crumbs, apples and the toasted walnuts just until combined. Transfer batter to the prepared baking dish; smooth the top with a wet rubber spatula. Bake for 30 to 35 minutes, or until the top feels dry and a skewer inserted in the center comes out clean.

4. Let cool completely on a wire rack. Dust lightly with confectioners' sugar and cut into 15 bars. (*The bars will keep in an airtight container for up to 1 week. Freeze for longer storage.*)

Makes 15 bars.

130 calories per bar: 3 grams protein, 4 grams fat (0.5 gram saturated fat), 21 grams carbohydrate; 155 mg sodium; 14 mg cholesterol; 1 gram fiber.

(N) NUTRITION BONUS: More than half of the fat in these bars comes from the walnuts, which are high in heart-healthy monounsaturated and linolenic fatty acids.

TECHNIQUE 80

Use low-fat granola to make healthier bars.

Granola has always had a healthy ring to it. The mix of grains, dried fruits and natural sweeteners just had to be good for you. But old-style granola and granola bars are quite high in fat: often 5 grams of fat in 1 ounce of granola, and 10 to 12 grams of fat in a granola bar. You can make truly healthy granola bars by starting with low-fat granola and using egg whites instead of oil to bind and crisp the mix.

(F) FAT SAVINGS: These bars have one-fifth the fat of a regular granola bar.

Low-Fat Granola Bars

- 1 large egg white, lightly beaten
- 2 tablespoons honey
- 2 teaspoons canola oil
- 1 teaspoon pure vanilla extract
- ½ teaspoon ground cinnamon
- 2 cups low-fat granola
- ¼ cup raisins

1. Preheat oven to 325°F. Lightly oil a 9-inch square baking pan or coat it with nonstick cooking spray.

2. In a small bowl, whisk egg white, honey, oil, vanilla and cinnamon until blended. In a mixing bowl, combine granola and raisins. Stir in the egg white/honey mixture until well coated. With a wet rubber spatula, press granola into the prepared pan.

3. Bake for 15 to 20 minutes, or until lightly browned. Cool in the pan on a wire rack. Cut into 12 bars. (*Wrapped tightly, the bars will keep for up to 5 days.*)

Makes 12 bars.

80 calories per bar: 2 grams protein, 2 grams fat (0.3 gram saturated fat), 16 grams carbohydrate; 40 mg sodium; 0 mg cholesterol; 1 gram fiber.

(N) NUTRITION BONUS: Negligible saturated fat makes these bars an excellent snack choice.

Flavor Boosting
for Low-Fat Desserts

BAKING USED TO BE EASIER. AS LONG AS a recipe had enough butter or cream, it was pretty much guaranteed to taste good. That's because fat not only adds a richness of its own, it acts like a magnifying glass for the other flavors in a recipe. When fat is greatly reduced, the spices, vanilla and other flavorings recede into blandness. If you frequently use EATING WELL recipes, you may have noticed that you are using more spices and vanilla than in the past. As a general rule, we increase spices by 50 percent and double the vanilla when cutting the fat from traditional recipes.

SPICES should be kept in sealed containers at room temperature, out of direct sunlight. After a year on the shelf, they begin to lose their punch, and it's time to replace them. For superior flavor, always grate nutmeg fresh.

———

Banana Spice Cake

Note the large amount of cinnamon and nutmeg called for in this recipe—low-fat cakes need more spices to maintain the same level of flavor as high-fat confections.

2½	cups unsifted cake flour
2	teaspoons baking powder
2	teaspoons baking soda
2	teaspoons ground cinnamon
1	teaspoon freshly grated nutmeg
½	teaspoon ground allspice
½	teaspoon ground ginger
½	teaspoon ground cloves
½	teaspoon salt
3	large egg whites
¼	teaspoon cream of tartar
1¾	cups sugar
1	cup mashed very ripe bananas (2 large bananas)
¼	cup canola oil
2	tablespoons butter, melted
1	large egg yolk
1	tablespoon grated orange zest

2 teaspoons pure vanilla extract
¾ cup buttermilk
Confectioners' sugar for dusting

1. Preheat oven to 350°F. Lightly oil a large (12-cup) Bundt pan or coat it with nonstick cooking spray. Set aside.

2. Sift flour, baking powder, baking soda, cinnamon, nutmeg, allspice, ginger, cloves and salt together into a bowl; set aside.

3. In a clean mixing bowl, beat egg whites with an electric mixer on low speed just until frothy. Add cream of tartar, increase the speed to medium and beat until soft peaks form. Gradually beat in ¾ cup of the sugar, 2 tablespoons at a time, just until firm peaks form. (*See box, page 155.*) Set meringue aside.

4. In a large mixing bowl, combine mashed bananas, oil, melted butter, egg yolk, orange zest, vanilla and the remaining 1 cup sugar; beat to combine. With the mixer on low speed, add the buttermilk and dry ingredients alternately in 2 additions each; beat just until blended. Add a heaping spoonful of the meringue and beat for just a few seconds to lighten the batter. By hand, fold the remaining meringue into the batter.

5. Pour the batter into the prepared pan and bake for 50 to 60 minutes, or until a skewer inserted in the center comes out clean. Cool in the pan on a wire rack for 10 minutes, then turn out onto the rack to cool completely.

6. Before serving, dust the cake with confectioners' sugar and transfer to a cake plate. If you like, serve the cake with a compote of fresh tropical fruits.

Makes 16 servings.

210 calories per serving: 3 grams protein, 6 grams fat (1 gram saturated fat), 39 grams carbohydrate; 250 mg sodium; 18 mg cholesterol; 0 grams fiber.

CITRUS ZEST The aromatic oils, which contribute so much flavor to food, are found in the perfumy outermost skin layer of citrus fruit. For this reason, rely on fresh citrus fruits, rather than bottled juices, in our recipes calling for citrus flavorings.

SPIRITS AND LIQUEURS add a fat-free lift to flavors in desserts. Clear spirits distilled from fruits, such as kirsch (from cherries) or eau-de-vie de framboise (from raspberries), will take the flavor level of fruit desserts up a notch. Brandy and liqueurs add warm, mellow tones to a variety of recipes. (Whenever possible, we do give nonalcoholic alternatives.)

VANILLA Much as salt is in savory cooking, vanilla is the most common flavoring in baking. It adds a sweet smoothness of its own and rounds out the taste of other spices in a particular confection. In low-fat desserts, the quality of the vanilla is important, because without the fat the flavor is more apparent. Avoid imitation extracts, which taste harsh and artificial, and buy only those labeled "pure." For the best vanilla flavor, the EATING WELL Test Kitchen prefers extracts made from Madagascar Bourbon vanilla beans.

You can also make your own vanilla extract: Slit 4 whole vanilla beans and steep them in a jar with 2 cups vodka or brandy for at least 2 weeks.

Whole vanilla beans easily lend their flavor to sugar. Bury 1 bean in 2 cups of sugar for 2 weeks. Use the sugar for delicately flavored cookies, custard sauces, and for sprinkling on fresh fruits.

Raspberry Cloud Cake, page 160

THE TECHNIQUES

81 Switching from butter to a pear
puree cuts fat in a pound cake

82 Baking angel food and chiffon
cakes

83 Using cake flour and pastry
flour for tender cakes

84 Beating egg whites to make a
meringue topping

TECHNIQUES
81-84
CAKES

THERE IS ALWAYS THE TEMPTATION
WHEN YOU ARE ABOUT TO BAKE A
CAKE FOR A SPECIAL OCCASION TO
rely on a tried-and-true high-fat recipe. But
low-fat baking does not have to be harder
or unreliable or result in a less-than-
stupendous cake; these recipes are
proof of that. In the EATING WELL
Test Kitchen, we love baking cakes,
and we don't mind having to test
and retest to get them just right so
they work for you. And remember, it is
truly a gift of love to bake a cake that does
not have 20 or 25 grams of fat in a slice.

81 Canned pears replace almost all of the butter in a remarkable pound cake.

TECHNIQUE

The requisite 2 cups of butter and 9 egg yolks gave traditional pound cake an extraordinary richness and a fine, dense crumb that was perfect for slicing. A puree made from canned pears imitates that fine texture without adding fat. To provide buttery richness, the small amount of butter in the recipe is browned to bring out its flavor, making a little go a long way.

F FAT SAVINGS: Pound cake made the traditional way has 21 grams of fat per slice; our pound cake has 3.

To bring out the flavor of butter, melt it over low heat and cook, swirling the pan, until the butter turns a nutty brown, about 1 minute.

Pound Cake

2   16-ounce cans pears in light syrup, drained
3   tablespoons butter, browned
    (*see photograph above*)
1   tablespoon canola oil

3½ cups sifted cake flour
1   teaspoon salt
1   teaspoon baking powder
½   teaspoon baking soda
1¾ cups sugar
1   cup buttermilk
1   tablespoon pure vanilla extract
1   tablespoon grated lemon zest
2   large eggs, separated
2   large egg whites

1. In a food processor or blender, puree drained pears. Transfer the puree to a heavy saucepan and stir over medium-low heat until it has reduced to 1 cup, 10 to 15 minutes. Transfer the puree to a mixing bowl and let cool.

2. Preheat oven to 350°F. Lightly oil a 10-inch tube pan or coat it with nonstick cooking spray.

3. In a small bowl, combine browned butter and oil; set aside.

4. Sift cake flour, salt, baking powder and baking soda into a bowl and set aside.

5. In a mixing bowl, combine the reserved pear puree, 1½ cups of the sugar, buttermilk, vanilla, lemon zest, egg yolks and the butter/oil mixture and whisk until smooth. Add the dry ingredients in 2 additions, folding with a whisk just until blended.

6. In a clean mixing bowl, with clean beaters, beat the 4 egg whites until soft peaks form. While continuing to beat, slowly add the remaining ¼ cup sugar and beat until stiff, but not dry, peaks form.

7. With a rubber spatula, gently fold the beaten whites into the batter. Pour the batter into the prepared pan. Bake for 40 to 45 minutes, or until a skewer inserted in the center comes out clean. Let cool in the pan for 5 minutes, then turn out onto a wire rack to cool, right-side up. (*The cake can be made in advance and stored in the freezer for up to 1 month.*)

Makes one 10-inch cake, for 20 thin slices.

195 calories per slice: 3 grams protein, 3 grams fat (1.4 grams saturated fat), 39 grams carbohydrate; 190 mg sodium; 26 mg cholesterol; 0.5 gram fiber.

N NUTRITION BONUS: Dress up this cake with fresh berries or sliced fruit and you still have a very low-fat dessert.

82

TECHNIQUE

For low-fat cakes, bake angel food or chiffon.

Get out the mixer, wipe out the bowl, add the eggs and start beating. Two standards in the American cake repertoire are naturals for the low-fat cook. Angel food cake, made with upwards of a dozen egg whites, has no fat—you should always look to angel food when baking for someone on a very low-fat diet. Angel food's cousin, chiffon cake, does contain whole eggs and some oil, but no butter. Usually, chiffons are made with 5 or 6 whole eggs; we like to cut back the whole eggs to 3 and lighten the batter with 7 egg whites.

F FAT SAVINGS: Every egg yolk eliminated from a cake recipe reduces the fat by 5 grams.

Angel Food Cake with Eggnog Spices

1	cup sifted cake flour
1	teaspoon freshly grated nutmeg
½	teaspoon ground cinnamon
¼	teaspoon ground mace
¼	teaspoon ground allspice
⅛	teaspoon ground cloves
⅛	teaspoon salt
1½	cups sugar
12	large egg whites, at room temperature
1	teaspoon cream of tartar
1	teaspoon pure vanilla extract
	Confectioners' sugar for dusting

1. Preheat oven to 350°F. In a bowl, whisk flour, nutmeg, cinnamon, mace, allspice, cloves and salt. Add ½ cup of the sugar; whisk again and set aside.

2. Place egg whites in a large, grease-free bowl and beat with an electric mixer until frothy. Add cream of tartar and continue beating until soft peaks form. Add vanilla and gradually add the remaining 1 cup

❓ WHAT IS THE BEST WAY TO BEAT EGGS?

PROPER TEMPERATURE The proteins in eggs are far more elastic at room temperature than when cold, which means they will beat up more quickly and to greater height. Take the eggs out of the refrigerator 30 minutes before using.

CLEAN BEATERS Beat egg whites in a clean metal or glass bowl with clean beaters. Even a trace of grease will prevent the whites from beating to their maximum volume.

CAREFUL SEPARATION A bit of yolk in the egg whites will also prevent them from whipping up properly. When separating several eggs, first drop the white into a small bowl before pouring it into the large mixing bowl with the other whites. That way if a little yolk does get into one egg, as often happens, it won't spoil the whole batch.

EXTRA STRENGTH Cream of tartar will strengthen egg whites, enabling them to mount to greatest volume. Before beating, add ¼ teaspoon for every 4 egg whites. Beating whites in a copper bowl has the same effect as using cream of tartar.

sugar, a few tablespoons at a time; beat just until stiff, but not dry, peaks form. Do not overbeat.

3. Sift one-third of the dry ingredients over the beaten egg whites and fold in gently. Repeat in 2 more additions.

4. Pour the batter into an ungreased 10-inch tube pan. Smooth the top and run a small knife or spatula through the batter to remove any air pockets.

5. Bake for 45 minutes, or until a skewer inserted in the center comes out clean and the top springs back when touched lightly. Invert the pan over the neck of a bottle and let the cake cool completely.

6. With a knife, loosen the edges of the cake and invert onto a cake plate. Dust with confectioners' sugar.

Makes 1 large cake, for 12 servings.

145 calories per serving: 4 grams protein, 0 grams fat, 32 grams carbohydrate; 80 mg sodium; 0 mg cholesterol; 0 grams fiber.

N NUTRITION BONUS: A fat-free cake with the rich taste of eggnog is a treat everyone can enjoy.

Mocha Confetti Cake

CAKE

- 2 tablespoons instant coffee powder, preferably instant espresso
- 2 teaspoons pure vanilla extract
- ¼ cup canola oil
- 3 large eggs, separated
- ¾ cup semisweet chocolate chips
- 1½ cups sugar
- 1⅓ cups unsifted cake flour
- 1 teaspoon baking powder
- 7 large egg whites, at room temperature
- ½ teaspoon cream of tartar
- ¼ teaspoon salt

GLAZE

- 1 teaspoon instant coffee powder
- 1½ tablespoons Kahlúa *or* other coffee liqueur
- 1 cup confectioners' sugar
- ¼ cup semisweet chocolate chips, melted

TO MAKE CAKE:

1. Preheat oven to 350°F. Line the bottom of an ungreased angel food cake pan with parchment or wax paper: First place the pan on a piece of the paper and trace a circle. Cut out the circle and cut a circle out of the center the width of the tube.

2. In a small bowl, stir coffee powder, vanilla and ¼ cup warm water until the coffee dissolves. Whisk in oil and 3 egg yolks; set aside. In a food processor, pulse chocolate chips until finely chopped; set aside. Sift ¾ cup of the sugar, flour and baking powder into a bowl; set aside.

3. In a mixing bowl, beat the 10 egg whites, cream of tartar and salt with an electric mixer on low speed until frothy. Gradually increase the mixer speed to medium-high and beat until soft peaks form. While still beating, slowly add the remaining ¾ cup sugar and beat until semi-stiff peaks form. With a rubber spatula, fold the egg yolk/coffee mixture into the beaten egg whites followed by the chopped chocolate chips. Sprinkle about ⅓ cup of the reserved flour mixture over the top and gently fold in; repeat with the remaining flour, adding ⅓ cup at a time.

4. Pour the batter into the prepared pan. Bake for 55 to 65 minutes, or until a skewer inserted in the center of the cake comes out clean. Invert the cake to cool completely, about 2 hours. (If the cake pan has no "legs," invert it over the neck of a bottle.)

5. With a narrow, sharp knife, loosen the cake from the side and center tube of the pan. Turn the cake out onto a wire rack and peel off the paper. Turn the cake right-side up.

Mocha Confetti Cake: Bake one for Father's Day.

TO MAKE GLAZE:

1. In a small bowl, dissolve coffee powder in 1 tablespoon hot water. Add coffee liqueur. Whisk in confectioners' sugar until smooth, adding a little more liqueur if the glaze is too thick. Holding the spoon a few inches above the cake, drizzle thin lines of glaze over the top of the cake, tilting the cake to let some of the glaze drip down the side.

2. Put melted chocolate chips in a small plastic bag and snip a tiny hole in one corner of the bag. Squeeze the chocolate out in thin lines over the glaze.

3. Transfer the cake to a serving plate and let the glaze and chocolate firm up for about 30 minutes before serving.

Makes one 10-inch tube cake, for 16 servings.

255 calories per serving: 4 grams protein, 9 grams fat (0.5 gram saturated fat), 43 grams carbohydrate; 90 mg sodium; 40 mg cholesterol; 0 grams fiber.

Ⓝ NUTRITION BONUS: Chiffon cakes rely on vegetable oil for moistness so they are typically low in saturated fat. Canola oil makes them even more heart-healthy because it is rich in monounsaturated fat.

83 Use cake and pastry flours for tender cakes.

TECHNIQUE

How many cake recipes in your card file begin with the instructions "Cream ¾ cup butter until soft"? Besides adding moistness and flavor, the butter in cakes keeps them tender by coating the flour particles and preventing gluten from developing. Very low-fat cakes baked with all-purpose flour develop an undesirable sturdiness. Flours milled from softer wheat, such as cake flour, pastry flour and whole-wheat pastry flour, will help to remedy this problem. Cake flour is sold in supermarkets; pastry flours can be purchased at whole-foods stores and through baking-supply catalogs.

Ⓕ FAT SAVINGS: A typical yellow cake (without frosting) has about 12 grams of fat in a slice; ours have 7.

ⓘ WHAT IS GLUTEN?

When the protein in wheat flour combines with liquid in a recipe, the elastic substance that forms is called gluten. While elasticity is desirable in yeast doughs that are kneaded and stretched, it can translate to rubberiness in cakes and quick breads. Lower-protein flours, such as cake flour and pastry flour, help produce tender baked goods. Protein levels in flours range from 8% for cake flour and 9% for pastry flour to nearly 12% in all-purpose flour.

Buttermilk Cake with Strawberries

Mascarpone (Italian cream cheese) is blended with drained nonfat yogurt for a smooth, creamy cake filling.

BUTTERMILK CAKE
- 2 tablespoons fine dry breadcrumbs
- 1 tablespoon butter
- 2 tablespoons canola oil
- ⅓ cup buttermilk
- 1½ cups unsifted cake flour
- 2 teaspoons baking powder
  Pinch of salt
- 2 large eggs, at room temperature
- ¾ cup sugar
- 2 teaspoons pure vanilla extract

ORANGE-MASCARPONE FILLING
- 2 cups nonfat vanilla yogurt, drained overnight in the refrigerator (*see Technique 52, page 104*)
- ¼ cup mascarpone (Italian cream cheese)
- 2 tablespoons confectioners' sugar
- 1½ teaspoons grated orange zest

ORANGE SYRUP & STRAWBERRY LAYERS
- ¼ cup sugar
- ¼ cup fresh orange juice
- ¼ cup Grand Marnier *or* other orange liqueur
- 4 cups fresh strawberries, hulled and sliced
- ½ cup red currant jelly

TO MAKE CAKE:

1. Preheat oven to 350°F. Lightly oil a 9-inch round cake pan or coat it with nonstick cooking spray. Add breadcrumbs, tilting the pan to evenly coat the inside. Tap out the excess.

2. In a small saucepan, melt butter over medium-low heat. Cook, swirling the pan, until the butter turns a nutty brown, about 30 seconds. (*See Technique 81, page 154.*) Pour the butter into a small bowl. Whisk in oil, then buttermilk; set aside.

3. Sift flour, baking powder and salt into a small bowl; set aside.

4. In a mixing bowl, combine eggs and sugar. Beat with an electric mixer on high speed until the mixture is thick and pale and falls in a ribbon when the beaters are lifted, about 5 minutes. Beat in vanilla.

5. Sift half of the reserved dry ingredients over the egg mixture and fold in with a rubber spatula. Fold in half of the reserved buttermilk mixture. Repeat with the remaining dry ingredients and buttermilk mixture.

6. Pour the batter into the prepared pan. Bake for 20 to 25 minutes, or until a skewer inserted in the center comes out clean. Let the cake cool in the pan on a wire rack for 5 minutes, then turn out of the pan and place right-side up on the rack to cool completely.

TO MAKE FILLING & SYRUP & ASSEMBLE CAKE:

1. In a bowl, whisk drained yogurt, mascarpone, confectioners' sugar and orange zest until smooth.

2. In a small saucepan over low heat, dissolve sugar in ½ cup water. Simmer gently for 5 minutes. Remove from the heat and stir in orange juice and liqueur.

3. With a long serrated knife, cut the cake horizontally into 2 layers using a gentle sawing motion. With a pastry brush, brush all of the syrup on the cut sides of the cake. Place the bottom layer on a cake plate, cut-side up. Spread half of the orange-mascarpone filling over the bottom layer. Arrange about

A birthday in June calls for Buttermilk Cake with Strawberries.

one-third of the sliced strawberries in an even layer on top. Spread with the remaining filling. Place the second cake layer on top, cut-side down.

4. In a small saucepan, melt red currant jelly over low heat. Brush the top of the cake lightly with about 2 tablespoons of the melted jelly. Arrange the remaining sliced strawberries in rows on top. Overlap the slices and reverse the direction of the slices in each row. Cover the cake with plastic wrap and place in the refrigerator to chill for at least 1 hour.

5. Just before serving, remelt the remaining red currant jelly and brush it over the strawberries on top of the cake.

Makes one 9-inch cake, for 12 servings.

285 calories per serving: 5 grams protein, 7 grams fat (1 gram saturated fat), 50 grams carbohydrate; 120 mg sodium; 46 mg cholesterol; 2 grams fiber.

Ⓝ NUTRITION BONUS: Bakery cakes festooned with shortening roses are a nutritional nightmare. A slice of cake with only 1 gram of saturated fat is reason to celebrate.

Lemony Yellow Cake with Blackberry Sauce

    2 tablespoons fine dry breadcrumbs
    ⅓ cup low-fat milk
    3 tablespoons canola oil
    1½ cups unsifted cake flour
    2 teaspoons baking powder
       Pinch of salt
    2 large eggs, at room temperature
    1 large egg yolk, at room temperature
    ¾ cup granulated sugar
    1 tablespoon fresh lemon juice
    2 teaspoons grated lemon zest
    1 teaspoon pure vanilla extract
       Blackberry Sauce (*recipe follows*)
       Confectioners' sugar for dusting

1. Preheat oven to 350°F. Lightly oil a 9-inch round cake pan or coat it with nonstick cooking spray. Add breadcrumbs, tilting the pan to evenly coat the inside. Tap out the excess.

2. In a measuring cup, combine milk and oil. Sift flour, baking powder and salt into a bowl; set aside.

3. In a mixing bowl, combine eggs, egg yolk, sugar and lemon juice. Beat with an electric mixer on high speed until the mixture is thick and pale and falls in a ribbon when the beaters are lifted, about 5 minutes. Beat in lemon zest and vanilla.

4. Sift half of the reserved dry ingredients over the beaten egg mixture and fold in with a rubber spatula until blended. Fold in half of the milk mixture. Repeat these steps with the remaining dry ingredients and milk mixture.

5. Pour the batter into the prepared pan. Bake for 20 to 25 minutes, or until a skewer inserted in the center comes out clean. Let the cake cool in the pan on a wire rack for 5 minutes, then turn out of the pan and place right-side up on the rack to cool completely.

6. Meanwhile, make Blackberry Sauce.

7. Dust the cake with confectioners' sugar, slice and serve with the Blackberry Sauce alongside.

Makes one 9-inch cake, for 8 servings.

220 calories per slice (without sauce): 4 grams protein, 7 grams fat (1 gram saturated fat), 36 grams carbohydrate; 130 mg sodium; 80 mg cholesterol; 0.5 gram fiber.

Blackberry Sauce

    1½ pints blackberries
    2 tablespoons blackberry brandy *or* vodka
    2 tablespoons fresh orange juice
    3 tablespoons honey

Pick over and reserve 1 cup of the smallest and most attractive berries. In a food processor, puree the remaining 2 cups of berries with brandy or vodka, orange juice and honey. Transfer the mixture to a sieve set over a bowl. Press the puree through the sieve and discard the seeds. (*The sauce can be made up to 8 hours ahead and stored, covered, in the refrigerator.*) Stir the remaining berries into the sauce just before serving.

Makes about 2 cups.

15 calories per tablespoon: 0 grams protein, 0 grams fat, 4 grams carbohydrate, 0.1 gram alcohol; 1 mg sodium; 0 mg cholesterol; 1 gram fiber.

Ⓝ NUTRITION BONUS: Simple fruits are an appealing and healthful way to dress up a cake. Blackberries are high in fiber.

Pumpkin-Cranberry Cake

An ideal cake to make when you are expecting a crowd.

2½ cups whole-wheat pastry flour *or* 1 cup whole-wheat flour and 1⅔ cups cake flour
2 cups cornmeal, preferably stone-ground
2½ teaspoons baking soda
1¼ teaspoons baking powder
1 teaspoon ground cinnamon
½ teaspoon ground allspice
1 teaspoon salt
2 large egg whites
2 cups packed light *or* dark brown sugar
1 15-ounce can plain pumpkin puree
1 cup low-fat plain yogurt
⅓ cup canola oil
2 teaspoons grated orange *or* lemon zest (optional)
1½ cups dried cranberries *or* raisins
Confectioners' sugar for dusting

1. Preheat oven to 350°F. Coat a 12-cup Bundt pan with nonstick cooking spray and set aside.
2. In a large bowl, whisk flour, cornmeal, baking soda, baking powder, cinnamon, allspice and salt.
3. In a medium bowl, whisk egg whites, brown sugar, pumpkin, yogurt, oil and orange or lemon zest, if using, until well combined. Stir the pumpkin mixture and dried cranberries or raisins into the dry ingredients with a rubber spatula just until completely blended.
4. Pour the batter into the prepared pan, smoothing the top with the spatula. Bake for 50 to 60 minutes, or until a skewer inserted in the center comes out clean.
5. Let the cake cool in the pan on a wire rack for 5 minutes, then turn out of the pan and place right-side up on the rack to cool. Dust the top with confectioners' sugar.

Makes 1 large cake, for 24 servings.

220 calories per serving: 4 grams protein, 4 grams fat (0.4 gram saturated fat), 45 grams carbohydrate; 195 mg sodium; 1 mg cholesterol; 3 grams fiber.

N NUTRITION BONUS: Whole-wheat pastry flour—the whole-grain equivalent of cake flour—adds fiber and a rich, nutty taste.

TECHNIQUE 84

Beat egg whites to make a meringue topping, a nonfat alternative to buttercream.

After having baked a lovely, low-fat cake, it is a shame to encase it in a high-fat frosting, and there are alternatives to buttercream. Sweet, fluffy meringue has no fat and inevitably brings out many oohs and ahs. Because of the slight risk of salmonella contamination, we use a cooked meringue here, and you will need an instant-read thermometer to accurately gauge the temperature.

F FAT SAVINGS: Buttercream frosting (consisting of butter or shortening, sugar and eggs) will easily add 10 grams of fat to your piece of cake—more if you demand one of the frosting roses. Meringue toppings add no fat.

Raspberry Cloud Cake

Pureed fresh raspberries delicately flavor the meringue topping and tint it a delicious pink color.

ALMOND CAKE
6 ounces almond paste (½ cup plus 1 tablespoon)
½ cup granulated sugar
¼ teaspoon salt
⅔ cup sifted cake flour
6 large egg whites
Pinch of cream of tartar

RASPBERRY FILLING & MERINGUE
5 cups fresh raspberries
⅓ cup seedless raspberry preserves
3 large egg whites
½ cup sugar
¼ teaspoon cream of tartar
Confectioners' sugar for dusting

TO MAKE CAKE:

1. Preheat oven to 325°F. Line the bottoms of two 9-inch round cake pans with parchment paper or wax paper. Lightly coat the paper and the pan sides with nonstick cooking spray. Dust with flour, tapping out the excess, and set aside.

2. In a food processor or blender, combine almond paste, ¼ cup of the granulated sugar, salt and ⅓ cup water. Process until smooth. Add flour and pulse just until combined. Transfer the mixture to a large bowl.

3. In a clean mixing bowl, beat egg whites and cream of tartar with an electric mixer on high speed until frothy. While continuing to beat, slowly add the remaining ¼ cup sugar. Continue to beat on high speed until soft peaks form.

4. Whisk one-fourth of the beaten egg whites into the almond paste mixture to lighten it. With a rubber spatula, fold in the remaining egg whites just until combined.

5. Spread the batter in the prepared pans. Bake for 15 to 18 minutes, or until the cake layers are just beginning to color and feel firm when lightly pressed in the center.

6. Dust a large piece of parchment paper or wax paper with confectioners' sugar. Run a knife around the outside edge of each cake layer and invert onto the paper. Lift off the rounds of paper from the cake bottoms. Let the cake layers cool to room temperature.

TO FILL CAKE & MAKE RASPBERRY MERINGUE:

1. In a saucepan over medium heat, stir 3 cups of the raspberries until juicy. Transfer to a fine sieve set over a bowl. With a rubber spatula, press the raspberries through the sieve, extracting all the pulp, and discard the seeds.

2. Return the raspberry puree to the saucepan. Cook over medium-low heat, stirring, until thick and reduced to ½ cup, 5 to 10 minutes. Set aside ¼ cup of the puree in a small bowl. Add raspberry preserves to the puree remaining in the saucepan. Whisk over low heat until smooth and slightly reduced, about 2 minutes. Transfer to a large bowl to cool to room temperature.

3. Set aside about 30 of the best-looking raspberries to use as a garnish. Gently fold the rest of the raspberries into the cooled raspberry preserve mixture in the large bowl.

4. With a wide spatula, invert one of the cooled cake layers onto a *heatproof* serving plate. Spread the raspberry mixture evenly over the top. Set the second cake layer on top. Set aside.

5. Bring about 1 inch of water to a gentle simmer in a saucepan. In a heatproof mixing bowl large enough to fit over the saucepan, combine egg whites, sugar and cream of tartar. Set the bowl over the barely simmering water and beat with an electric mixer on low speed, moving the beaters around the bowl constantly, until an instant-read thermometer registers 140°F. (This will take 3 to 5 minutes.)

6. Increase the mixer speed to high and continue beating over the heat for a full 3½ minutes. Remove the bowl from the heat and beat the meringue until it has cooled to room temperature, about 5 minutes. On low speed, beat in the reserved ¼ cup of raspberry puree.

7. Preheat the broiler. Put about ⅔ cup of the meringue into a pastry bag fitted with a medium star tip. Spread the remaining meringue on the sides and top of the cake. Smooth the sides and top with a long metal spatula. Pipe swirls of meringue around the edge of the cake. (*Alternatively, if you don't have a pastry bag and tip, make swirls of meringue with the back of a spoon.*)

8. With the cake about 2 inches below the heat source, broil until the top is lightly browned, about 1 minute. Let cool briefly, then decorate with the reserved raspberries. (*At this point, the cake can be covered with a domed cake cover and refrigerated for up to 1 day.*)

9. Just before serving, lightly dust the top with confectioners' sugar.

Makes one 9-inch cake, for 10 servings.

245 calories per serving: 6 grams protein, 5 grams fat (0.5 gram saturated fat), 47 grams carbohydrate; 105 mg sodium; 0 mg cholesterol; 4 grams fiber.

Ⓝ NUTRITION BONUS: Unlike most cakes that are high in saturated fat because of butter, this cake is enriched with almond paste, a source of heart-healthy monounsaturated fat.

Key Lime Cake

Veiled in swirls of pale meringue, this golden cake with the hidden Key lime filling is ideal for a shower luncheon or rehearsal dinner.

KEY LIME FILLING

- ¾ cup sugar
- 1 large egg
- 1 large egg white
- ¼ cup fresh *or* bottled Key lime juice
- 2 teaspoons grated lime zest
- 2 tablespoons cornstarch

A slice of Key Lime Cake has only 2 grams of fat.

CAKE

- ⅓ cup low-fat milk
- ¾ cup plus 2 tablespoons unsifted cake flour
- 1 teaspoon baking powder
- ¼ teaspoon freshly grated nutmeg
- 2 large eggs, at room temperature
- 2 large egg whites, at room temperature
- 1 cup sugar
- 2 teaspoons fresh *or* bottled Key lime juice
- 2 teaspoons pure vanilla extract

MERINGUE

- ¾ cup sugar
- 3 large egg whites, at room temperature
- ¼ teaspoon cream of tartar
- 1 teaspoon pure vanilla extract
  Fresh lime slices for garnish

TO MAKE KEY LIME FILLING:

1. In a small saucepan, whisk sugar, egg and egg white until well combined. Whisk in lime juice, lime zest and ½ cup water. Stir over low heat until the sugar dissolves. Remove the pan from the heat.

2. In a small bowl, stir together cornstarch and ¼ cup water; whisk into the egg mixture. Return to the heat, increase the heat to medium-high and continue whisking until the filling comes to a boil and thickens. Whisk for 30 seconds longer and remove from the heat. Transfer the filling to a small bowl and place a piece of wax paper or plastic wrap directly on the surface to prevent a skin from forming. Refrigerate until cool, about 1 hour.

TO MAKE CAKE:

1. Preheat oven to 350°F. Line the bottom of a 9-inch round cake pan with parchment or wax paper. Lightly oil or coat the paper and inside of the pan with nonstick cooking spray.

2. In a small pan, heat milk until steaming; remove from the heat, cover and set aside. Sift flour, baking powder and nutmeg into a bowl; set aside.

3. In a mixing bowl, beat eggs and egg whites with an electric mixer on low speed until frothy. Add sugar and beat on medium speed until the eggs are very fluffy and pale, a full 3½ minutes. Add lime juice, vanilla and the reserved dry ingredients. Beat on low speed just until the flour is incorporated. Beat in the hot milk (the batter will be thin).

4. Pour the batter into the prepared pan. Bake for 23 to 25 minutes, or until the top feels firm when touched lightly and a skewer inserted in the center of the cake comes out clean. Let the cake cool in the pan for 5 minutes. Run a knife around the inside of the pan to loosen the edges. Turn the cake out of the pan and set it right-side up on a wire rack to cool completely.

TO FILL CAKE & MAKE MERINGUE:

1. To cut a depression in the cake for the filling, hold scissors with the tips angled slightly down toward the center of the cake and snip a ¼-inch-deep circle around the cake, ½ inch in from the cake's rim. With a serrated knife, cut horizontally to the center of the cake, angling down toward the center to create the depression but leaving the bottom of the cake intact. Lift off the cake "lid." Set the cake bottom on a large ovenproof plate or baking sheet. Spread the chilled lime filling in the depression and replace the cake lid on top.

2. Preheat oven to 375°F. Bring about 1 inch of water to a simmer in a large saucepan. Put sugar, egg whites, cream of tartar and 3 tablespoons of water in a metal bowl that will fit over the saucepan. Set the bowl over the gently simmering water and beat with an electric mixer on low speed, moving the beaters around the bowl constantly, until an instant-read thermometer registers 140°F, 3 to 5 minutes. Increase the mixer speed to high and continue beating over the heat for 3½ minutes. Remove the bowl from the heat and beat until the meringue is cool, about 5 minutes. Beat in vanilla.

3. With a spatula, spread the meringue over the sides and top of the filled cake, mounding it toward the center and swirling it in peaks. Bake for 10 minutes, or until the meringue is golden.

4. Place the cake on a wire rack and let cool to room temperature, about 1 hour. If the cake is on a baking sheet, transfer it to a serving plate. Serve immediately, or cover carefully with plastic wrap that has been lightly sprayed with nonstick spray and refrigerate for up to 8 hours. Just before serving, garnish with lime slices.

Makes one 12-inch cake, for 10 servings.

265 calories per serving: 5 grams protein, 2 grams fat (0.5 gram saturated fat), 59 grams carbohydrate; 90 mg sodium; 64 mg cholesterol; 0 grams fiber.

Ⓝ NUTRITION BONUS: Instead of frosting, which often doubles the fat in a slice of cake, the refreshing lime filling adds smooth contrast without fat.

Almond-Scented Peach & Cherry Pie, page 167

THE TECHNIQUES

85 Switching to a healthier fat in pie crusts

86 Making low-fat crusts with cookie and graham cracker crumbs

87 Cutting back on butter in phyllo crusts

88 Using apple-juice concentrate in a streusel topping

89 Choosing meringue for a fat-free pie shell

TECHNIQUES
85-89
PIES
Pastries

A HOMEMADE PIE IS MEANT TO BE SHARED. WHETHER IT'S A WARM APPLE PIE ON A CRISP autumn afternoon or a brilliant rhubarb tart to celebrate the glories of spring, a good pie fosters good conversations. But can pies be part of a healthy diet?

On one hand, pies are a great way to use lots of fruits in season. On the other hand, their crusts are a concentrated source of saturated fat and calories. You don't have to abandon this most American of desserts, however. By paying attention to the amount and the kind of fat you add to a pie crust, and by keeping the fillings on the light side, pies slide into the low-fat range—now *there's* something to talk about.

85 Switch to a healthier fat in pie crusts.

Pie bakers (and pie eaters) debate the merits of butter vs. lard vs. shortening in pie crusts. But there is no debate from the nutrition experts—all three are high in saturated fat, which should be kept to a minimum in the diet. That's hard to do when it comes to pie crust, where recipes call for up to ½ cup of fat for every 1 cup of flour. At EATING WELL, we keep that ratio to ¼ cup of fat to 1 cup of flour, and replace most of that saturated fat with monounsaturated fat.

Even this reduced-fat crust is still a little too rich in fat to consider making a two-crust pie. An easy solution is to bake a one-crust pie, leaving the pretty filling unadorned.

F FAT SAVINGS: The Eating Well crust has half the fat of other pie crusts. The reduction in saturated fat is even more impressive: the fat in the high-fat crust is 60% saturated; in the Eating Well crust, it is 16% saturated.

1. A light touch is best when mixing pie crust. Use a fork to combine the flour and the butter/oil mixture. Then add ice water, 1 tablespoon at a time, just enough so the dough holds together.

2. Gather the pie dough into a ball and flatten it into a disk. Set the dough on 2 overlapping lengths of plastic wrap on the work surface. Cover with 2 more sheets of plastic wrap. With a rolling pin, roll the dough into a circle 12 to 13 inches in diameter. Remove the top sheets of plastic. Invert the dough into the pie pan. Gently press the dough into the pan.

3. Remove the remaining plastic wrap. Fold the edges of the dough under at the rim and crimp. Cover loosely with plastic wrap and refrigerate for 15 minutes. Fill or blind-bake the pie shell as directed in the recipe. Empty pie shells can be made in advance and frozen for 1 month.

Almond-Scented Peach & Cherry Pie

The fact that peaches and sour cherries are both ripe at the same time is a propitious coincidence for pie bakers.

CRUST
1¼   cups all-purpose white flour
  1   tablespoon sugar
  ¼   teaspoon salt
  ¼   cup canola oil
  1   tablespoon butter, browned
     (*see Technique 81, page 154*)
  2   tablespoons Amaretto, other almond-flavored liqueur *or* water

FILLING
  1   pound tart cherries, pitted (3 cups)
  ½   cup plus 2 tablespoons sugar
  5   tablespoons fresh lemon juice
  2   tablespoons Amaretto, other almond-flavored liqueur *or* water
  2   tablespoons cornstarch
  1   teaspoon grated lemon zest
  3   pounds peaches (about 8 peaches)

TO MAKE CRUST:
1. Preheat oven to 375°F. Lightly oil a 9-inch pie pan or spray it with nonstick cooking spray.

2. In a medium bowl, whisk flour, sugar and salt. In a small bowl, combine oil and browned butter; with a fork, stir into dry ingredients. Stir in Amaretto, followed by just enough water, 1 or 2 tablespoons, so the dough holds together. (*See Step 1 at left.*) Gather the dough into a ball and press into a flattened disk.

3. Roll out the dough into a circle about 13 inches in diameter and line the pie pan. (*See Steps 2 and 3 at left.*)

4. Line the pastry shell with a piece of aluminum foil or parchment paper and fill with pie weights or dried beans. Bake for 15 minutes, remove weights and foil or paper and bake for 8 to 10 minutes more, or until the crust is golden. Cool the pie crust on a wire rack while you make the filling. Increase oven temperature to 450°F.

TO MAKE FILLING:
1. In a saucepan, combine cherries, ½ cup of the sugar and 2 tablespoons of the lemon juice. Heat over low heat, stirring occasionally, until the sugar dissolves. Simmer the cherries until very tender, 7 to 10 minutes. In a small bowl, whisk Amaretto and cornstarch and add to the cherries. Increase heat to medium and cook, stirring constantly, until thick and glossy, about 1 minute. Remove from the heat and stir in lemon zest. Let cool to room temperature, about 1 hour.

2. Meanwhile, bring a large pot of water to a boil. Immerse peaches for 30 seconds; remove with a slotted spoon. Let cool briefly, then slip off skins.

3. Pit the peaches and slice into wedges. Combine with the remaining 2 tablespoons sugar and 3 tablespoons lemon juice. Transfer to a baking sheet (with sides) that is just large enough to hold the peaches in a single layer. Roast the peaches in the upper third of the 450°F oven, stirring often, until they are tender and caramelized, about 20 minutes. Let cool for about 15 minutes.

4. Spoon the cooled cherry filling into the baked crust. Arrange the roasted peaches on top. Let sit for 30 minutes before serving.

Makes 8 servings.

340 calories per serving: 4 grams protein, 9 grams fat (1.5 grams saturated fat), 63 grams carbohydrate; 85 mg sodium; 4 mg cholesterol; 3 grams fiber.

Ⓝ NUTRITION BONUS: There are two servings of fruit in every slice of this pie.

Rhubarb Tart

Making a thick puree with some of the rhubarb gives this out-of-the-ordinary tart intense color and flavor.

FILLING
  1   orange, scrubbed
  9   cups (about 3 pounds) finely diced red rhubarb (¼-inch dice)
1¼   cups sugar

CRUST
1¼   cups all-purpose white flour
  1   tablespoon sugar
  ¼   teaspoon salt
  ¼   cup canola oil
  1   tablespoon butter, browned
     (*see Technique 81, page 154*)

TO MAKE FILLING:

1. Use a vegetable peeler or sharp paring knife to pare 2 or 3 long strips of zest from the orange. Slice the zest into thin julienne strips, then cut into tiny dice.

2. Set aside 3 cups of the rhubarb, covered, in the refrigerator. In a wide heavy-bottomed saucepan, combine the remaining 6 cups rhubarb, sugar and 2 tablespoons of the diced orange zest. Bring to a boil, then reduce the heat to low and simmer gently. Cook, stirring often to prevent scorching, until the puree has reduced to about 1⅔ cups, 40 to 50 minutes. Transfer the puree to a bowl and let cool to room temperature. (*The puree can be made up to 2 days ahead and stored, covered, in the refrigerator.*)

TO MAKE CRUST:

1. Position oven rack in the lower third of the oven and set a large baking sheet on it; preheat to 400°F. Lightly oil a 10½-inch tart pan with a removable bottom or coat it with nonstick cooking spray; set aside.

2. In a medium bowl, whisk flour, sugar and salt. In a small bowl, combine oil and browned butter. Using a fork, slowly stir the oil/butter mixture into the dry ingredients until the mixture is crumbly. Gradually stir in enough ice water (2 to 3 tablespoons) so that the dough holds together and is not at all crumbly. (*See Step 1 on page 166.*) Press the dough into a flattened disk.

3. Roll out the dough into a circle 14 inches in diameter. Press into the pan and remove the plastic wrap. Fold in the overhanging edge of the crust to form a sturdy edge, patching any thin spots with scraps. (*See Steps 2 and 3 on page 166.*)

TO ASSEMBLE & BAKE TART:

Combine the raw and cooked rhubarb and spread it in the crust. Place the tart pan on the preheated baking sheet and bake for 35 to 40 minutes, or until the crust is golden and the filling bubbles at the edges. Let the tart cool to room temperature before serving.

Makes one 10½-inch tart, for 8 servings.

290 calories per serving: 3 grams protein, 9 grams fat (1.5 grams saturated fat), 53 grams carbohydrate; 90 mg sodium; 4 mg cholesterol; 1 gram fiber.

Ⓝ NUTRITION BONUS: This dessert is rich in potassium (420 milligrams) and calcium (125 milligrams).

A thick, ruby fruit puree gives Rhubarb Tart its intense flavor.

86 Bind cookie-crumb and graham cracker crusts with egg white, not butter.

Some of the quickest, easiest crusts around are made with wafer cookie or graham cracker crumbs held together with melted butter. We have found that the substitution of 1 egg white for ¼ cup of the butter (⅔ of the total) in a typical crust recipe produces a nearly identical crust with much less fat.

F FAT SAVINGS: The switch to the lower-fat crumb crusts cuts about 4 grams of fat per serving.

Latte Mousse Pie

You will need an instant-read thermometer to make sure the eggs are cooked to the proper temperature.

PIE CRUST

1¾ cup chocolate wafer crumbs (about 35 wafers)
1 large egg white, lightly beaten
1 tablespoon butter, melted
1 tablespoon canola oil

LATTE MOUSSE

1½ teaspoons unflavored gelatin
2 large eggs
2 teaspoons instant coffee granules dissolved in ¼ hot cup water
3 tablespoons plus ½ cup sugar
1 teaspoon pure vanilla extract
2 large egg whites
¼ teaspoon cream of tartar
¼ cup whipping cream
Cinnamon *or* cocoa powder for garnish

TO PREPARE CRUST:

1. Position oven rack in the lower third of the oven; preheat to 350°F. Lightly oil a 9-inch pie pan or coat it with nonstick cooking spray; set aside.

2. In a mixing bowl, combine chocolate wafer crumbs, egg white, butter and oil; with fingertips or fork, blend until thoroughly combined. Press the mixture evenly into the bottom and up the sides of the pie pan. Bake for 10 minutes, or until slightly puffed. Cool on a wire rack.

TO PREPARE MOUSSE FILLING & ASSEMBLE PIE:

1. Place 1½ tablespoons cold water in a small glass bowl. Sprinkle gelatin evenly over the water and let stand for 2 minutes to soften. Dissolve the softened gelatin in a microwave for about 20 seconds. Set aside.

2. Bring about 1 inch of water to a simmer in a large saucepan. In a heatproof bowl large enough to fit over the saucepan, combine whole eggs, coffee and 3 tablespoons sugar. Whisk constantly over the simmering water until the mixture thickens and an instant-read thermometer registers 160°F. Remove the bowl from the heat; whisk in dissolved gelatin and vanilla. Let cool for 20 minutes.

3. In a second heatproof mixing bowl large enough to fit over the saucepan, combine ½ cup sugar, egg whites, cream of tartar and 1½ tablespoons water. Set the bowl over the barely simmering water and beat with an electric mixer at low speed, moving the beaters around the bowl constantly, until the instant-read thermometer registers 140°F. Increase the mixer speed to high and continue beating for 3½ minutes. Remove the bowl from the heat and beat the meringue until cool, about 4 minutes. Set aside.

4. In a small chilled bowl, beat whipping cream until soft peaks form. Set aside.

5. Whisk one-fourth of the meringue into the coffee mixture to lighten it. Very gently whisk in the remaining meringue. Fold in the whipped cream. Pour the mousse into the pie crust. Chill for at least 4 hours. Just before serving, place a paper doily over the pie and sift cinnamon or cocoa liberally over the top. Carefully remove the doily and serve.

Makes one 9-inch pie, for 10 servings.

215 calories per serving: 4 grams protein, 9 grams fat (3.5 grams saturated fat), 31 grams carbohydrate; 205 mg sodium; 57 mg cholesterol; 1 gram fiber.

N NUTRITION BONUS: The beaten egg whites in the filling help keep the fat in this treat to a minimum.

Fresh Fruit Tart

The choice of fruit topping is yours. A mix of colors is fun; try red raspberries or strawberries, yellow peaches and a burst of green kiwi.

CRUST

1	large egg white
1½	cups graham cracker crumbs
1	tablespoon butter, melted
1	tablespoon canola oil

FILLING

1½	cups low-fat vanilla yogurt
2	tablespoons fresh orange juice
1	teaspoon unflavored gelatin
¼	cup whipping cream
2	tablespoons confectioners' sugar
3	tablespoons apricot preserves *or* red currant jelly, for glaze (optional)
4-5	cups fresh fruit, such as strawberries, raspberries, peaches *and/or* kiwis

TO MAKE CRUST:

1. Before you begin making the crust, there is advance preparation for the filling. Place a fine-mesh stainless-steel sieve over a bowl and spoon in yogurt; place in the refrigerator to drain for 1 hour. (*See Technique 52, page 104.*)

2. Preheat oven to 300°F. Lightly oil a 10-inch tart pan with a removable bottom or coat it with nonstick cooking spray.

3. In a small mixing bowl, lightly beat egg white. Add cracker crumbs, butter and oil; blend with a fork to thoroughly combine. Press the mixture evenly into the prepared tart pan, extending the crust 1 inch up the pan sides. Bake for 10 minutes, or until the crust is dry and crisp to the touch. Cool on a wire rack.

TO MAKE FILLING:

1. Pour orange juice into a large heatproof bowl. Sprinkle gelatin over the surface and allow to soften for 2 minutes. Set the bowl in a skillet of simmering water and stir the orange juice to completely dissolve the gelatin. (*Or use a microwave-safe bowl and heat in the microwave for about 25 seconds.*) In another bowl, beat whipping cream and sugar to soft peaks.

2. With a rubber spatula, fold the drained yogurt into the gelatin mixture. Gently fold in the whipped

cream. Pour the filling into the cooled tart shell and chill in refrigerator for 20 to 30 minutes, or until partially set.

TO ASSEMBLE TART:

1. If you plan to glaze the fruit, melt apricot preserves or red currant jelly in a small saucepan over low heat; if using preserves, strain through a fine sieve set over a small bowl. Set aside to cool slightly.

2. Trim or slice fruits as necessary and arrange on the chilled filling. Brush the fruits with the apricot glaze or currant jelly, if using. Return the tart to the refrigerator to chill until the filling has set completely, about 4 hours.

Makes one 10-inch tart, for 12 slices.

160 calories per serving: 4 grams protein, 6 grams fat (2 grams saturated fat), 2 grams carbohydrate; 125 mg sodium; 9 mg cholesterol; 2 grams fiber.

Ⓝ NUTRITION BONUS: Counting calories? This dessert has surprisingly few.

TECHNIQUE

87 Cutting back on butter in phyllo crusts.

Many-layered phyllo pastries are impressive and actually quite easy to make, but traditional recipes tell you to generously brush melted butter between each layer; the butter adds flavor and prevents the layers from sticking together in a solid lump during baking. We are able to greatly cut back on the amount of butter by brushing the phyllo layers very, very lightly with a mixture of melted butter and canola oil and then sprinkling with fine dry breadcrumbs. Remember to thaw frozen phyllo several hours ahead of when you plan to use it. (*For more tips on working with phyllo, see Technique 78, page 148.*)

Ⓕ FAT SAVINGS: Traditional phyllo pastries call for about 1 tablespoon of butter to be brushed between each layer of phyllo; done the Eating Well way, you will use only ½ teaspoon of melted butter and oil.

Pear Mincemeat Strudel

Fresh pears and lemon juice lighten jarred mincemeat.

1 cup prepared mincemeat
2 ripe but firm pears, peeled, cored and diced
1 tablespoon brandy
1 tablespoon fresh lemon juice
2 tablespoons canola oil
1 tablespoon butter, melted
8 sheets phyllo dough (14x18 inches), thawed if frozen
3 tablespoons fine dry breadcrumbs
Confectioners' sugar for dusting

1. Preheat oven to 375°F. Lightly oil a baking sheet or spray it with nonstick cooking spray; set aside.

2. In a large bowl, gently combine mincemeat, pears, brandy and lemon juice. In a small bowl, combine oil and melted butter.

3. Unroll phyllo onto a clean, dry surface. Cover with a sheet of wax paper and then a damp kitchen towel. Place a dry kitchen towel with a long edge toward you on the work surface. Sprinkle the towel with 1 teaspoon breadcrumbs. Lay 1 sheet of phyllo on the towel. (Keep the stack of phyllo sheets covered to prevent them from drying out while you are working.)

4. Starting at the center and then working toward the outside edges, lightly brush the phyllo sheet with the oil/butter mixture. Sprinkle with 1 teaspoon breadcrumbs. Lay another sheet of phyllo on top; brush with more oil/butter and sprinkle with breadcrumbs. Repeat with the remaining 6 sheets of phyllo, lightly brushing with oil/butter and sprinkling with breadcrumbs between each layer. Be sure to reserve a little of the oil/butter for the top of the strudel once it is rolled.

5. Mound the filling in a 3-inch-wide strip along the long edge of the phyllo stack, leaving a 2-inch border at the bottom and at the sides. Fold the short edges in and, starting at the long edge nearest you, roll the filling and phyllo into a cylinder, using the towel to help lift as you roll. Roll up firmly but not too tightly, to allow a little room for expansion.

6. Carefully transfer the strudel, seam-side down, to the prepared baking sheet. Brush the top with the remaining oil/butter. With a serrated knife, cut several slits diagonally across the top of the strudel.

7. Bake the strudel for 40 to 50 minutes, or until the

Pear Mincemeat Strudel and Eggnog Ice Cream (*page 199*) marry rich Old World flavors with a modern low-fat sensibility.

phyllo is golden and the filling is bubbling. Use a wide metal spatula to transfer the strudel to a serving platter. Dust with confectioners' sugar. Serve warm or at room temperature, accompanied by Eggnog Ice Cream (*page 199*). (*The strudel is best served within a few hours of baking, because the phyllo becomes soggy over time. If necessary, recrisp the strudel by reheating at 350°F for 15 to 20 minutes before serving.*)

Makes 8 servings.

110 calories per serving: 1 gram protein, 5 grams fat (1.2 grams saturated fat), 15 grams carbohydrate; 60 mg sodium; 4 mg cholesterol; 1 gram fiber.

Ⓝ NUTRITION BONUS: Compared to a mince pie baked in a traditional crust, this is a far healthier choice.

Plum Ruffle Pie

Phyllo ruffles give an airy, informal look to the pie.

PLUM FILLING

   2 **pounds ripe red plums, thinly sliced (about 6 cups)**
   1 **tablespoon fresh lemon juice**
   ⅔ **cup sugar**
   ⅓ **cup flour**
   ½ **teaspoon ground cinnamon**
   ⅛ **teaspoon ground ginger**

CRUST

   1 **tablespoon butter, melted**
   1 **tablespoon canola oil**
   9 **sheets phyllo dough (14x18 inches), thawed if frozen**
   2 **tablespoons fine dry breadcrumbs**
      Confectioners' sugar for dusting

1. Position oven rack in the lower third of the oven and set a baking sheet on it; preheat to 400°F. Lightly oil a 9-inch pie pan or coat it with nonstick cooking spray; set aside.

2. In a large bowl, toss plums with lemon juice. In a small bowl, combine sugar, flour, cinnamon and ginger; add to the plums and toss to coat evenly.

3. In a small bowl, combine butter and oil. Unroll phyllo onto a baking sheet or a clean, dry surface; keep covered with wax paper and a slightly damp kitchen towel to prevent dough from drying out.

Center one sheet in the pie pan, letting edges of phyllo hang over the sides. Sprinkle the phyllo in the pan with ½ teaspoon of the butter/oil mixture. Brushing from the center toward the edge, use a pastry brush to distribute the mixture evenly. Sprinkle with ½ teaspoon breadcrumbs. Repeat with 7 more sheets of phyllo, setting each sheet down at a 45° angle to the previous one. Over the eighth layer, sprinkle all the remaining breadcrumbs. (Reserve the remaining 2 teaspoons of the butter/oil mixture and the ninth phyllo sheet.)

4. Spoon the plum filling into the crust. Lift an overhanging corner of phyllo, twist it once near its base, and set it gently onto the filling with the fluted point ruffling up. Continue twisting the remaining corners in the same fashion; the first few twists should be set toward the center of the pie to allow room near the edge of the pan for the final twists. (If two layers stick together, simply twist both together.) When you are done, there will be a small circle of uncovered filling at the center of the pie. Tuck any leftover drapes into the sides of the pan.

5. Cut the last phyllo sheet in half lengthwise, then in half crosswise. Pinch at the center of each quarter, gathering it to form a tuft, and set lightly, with the pinched end down, in center of pie. (Do not worry if some of the plum filling is still visible between the tufts; this allows steam to escape.) Brush the phyllo ruffles carefully with the remaining butter/oil mixture.

6. Place the pie pan on the preheated baking sheet and bake for 10 minutes. Reduce oven temperature to 350°F and continue baking for 50 to 60 minutes, or until the pastry is golden brown and the filling is bubbling. (If the ruffles become too dark before the filling is done, cover loosely with aluminum foil, shiny side up.)

7. Transfer the pie to a wire rack and let cool to room temperature. Dust with confectioners' sugar just before serving.

Makes one 9-inch pie, for 8 servings.

230 calories per serving: 2 grams protein, 3 grams fat (1 gram saturated fat), 52 grams carbohydrate; 75 mg sodium; 4 mg cholesterol; 3 grams fiber.

Ⓝ NUTRITION BONUS: This pie is one way to take advantage of healthful plums when they're abundant and inexpensive.

Sweet Cheese Strudel

Serve the strudel at brunch, or dress it up at dinner with a strawberry puree.

CHEESE FILLING

- ⅓ cup sugar
- 2 teaspoons cornstarch
- 1 egg white, lightly beaten
- 1 teaspoon pure vanilla extract
- ½ teaspoon grated lemon zest
- 1 cup part-skim ricotta cheese, preferably without added gums or stabilizers
- ½ cup raisins

STRUDEL

- 1 tablespoon canola oil
- ½ tablespoon butter, melted
- 8 sheets phyllo dough (14x18 inches), thawed if frozen
- 2 tablespoons fine dry breadcrumbs
  Confectioners' sugar for dusting

TO MAKE FILLING:

In a small bowl, combine sugar, cornstarch, egg white, vanilla and lemon zest; stir gently until well combined. With a rubber spatula, gently fold in ricotta cheese just until combined. Gently fold in raisins. Set aside.

TO MAKE STRUDEL:

1. Preheat oven to 350°F. Lightly oil a large baking sheet or coat it with nonstick cooking spray.

2. In a small bowl, combine oil and butter. Unroll phyllo onto a clean, dry surface; cover with wax paper and then a slightly damp tea towel to prevent the dough from drying out.

3. Lay one sheet of phyllo on the prepared baking sheet. Sprinkle with ½ teaspoon of the oil/butter mixture and spread it thin with a pastry brush. (Not all the phyllo will be covered.) Sprinkle with ½ teaspoon breadcrumbs. Repeat with 7 more sheets of phyllo, aligning each sheet over the previous ones. Over the eighth layer, sprinkle all the remaining breadcrumbs; reserve the remaining oil/butter mixture.

4. Gently spoon the cheese filling in a long, 12-by-2-inch mound along one long edge of the phyllo layers, leaving a 2-inch border between the mound and the short edges of the phyllo. Fold up the long edge and loosely roll up the strudel. (Do not roll too tightly; the filling will expand during baking.) Set the strudel seam-side down on the baking sheet. Fold and tuck the open ends securely but not tightly beneath the roll.

5. Brush the strudel with the remaining oil/butter mixture. With a sharp paring knife, make four short (1-inch) diagonal slashes along the top of the strudel to allow steam to escape. Bake for 35 to 40 minutes, or until the phyllo is golden brown. Carefully transfer the strudel to a wire rack and let cool completely. Just before serving, dust with confectioners' sugar.

Makes 8 servings.

165 calories per serving: 5 grams protein, 5 grams fat (2.1 grams saturated fat), 25 grams carbohydrate; 110 mg sodium; 11 mg cholesterol; 1 gram fiber.

Ⓝ NUTRITION BONUS: Part-skim ricotta has about half the fat of whole-milk ricotta.

TECHNIQUE 88
Substitute apple-juice concentrate for butter in a streusel topping.

Butter in a streusel topping loosely holds the flour and sugar together—and adds about 5 grams of unwanted fat to every slice of pie. We find that apple-juice concentrate mixed with a little canola oil does the job quite deliciously.

Ⓕ FAT SAVINGS: Traditional streusel toppings call for 4 to 6 tablespoons of butter; we use 1 tablespoon of oil and some fat-free apple-juice concentrate.

Apple-Cranberry Streusel Pie

CRUST

- 1 cup all-purpose white flour
- 1 tablespoon granulated sugar
- ¼ teaspoon salt
- 3 tablespoons canola oil
- 1 tablespoon butter, browned
  (*see Technique 81, page 154*)

STREUSEL TOPPING

- ½ cup plus 1 tablespoon rolled oats
- ½ cup all-purpose white flour
- ½ cup packed light brown sugar
- ¼ teaspoon ground cinnamon
- 2 tablespoons apple-juice concentrate
- 1 tablespoon canola oil

FILLING

- ½ cup granulated sugar
- 3 tablespoons all-purpose white flour
- 2 pounds flavorful tart apples, such as Northern Spy, Cortland *or* York, peeled, cored and sliced (about 6 cups)
- 1 cup dried cranberries
  Grated zest and juice of 1 lemon

TO MAKE CRUST:

1. Lightly oil a 9-inch pie pan or coat it with nonstick cooking spray. In a medium bowl, whisk flour, sugar and salt. In a small bowl, combine oil and browned butter. Using a fork, slowly stir the oil/butter mixture into the dry ingredients until the mixture is crumbly. Gradually stir in enough cold water (1 to 2 tablespoons) so that the dough holds together easily. (*See Step 1 on page 166.*) Press the dough into a flattened disk.

2. Roll out the dough into a circle about 13 inches in diameter and line the pie pan. (*See Steps 2 and 3 on page 166.*) Position oven rack in the lower third of the oven; preheat to 350°F.

TO MAKE STREUSEL TOPPING:

In a bowl, combine ½ cup of the oats, flour, brown sugar and cinnamon. Add apple-juice concentrate and oil and work in with your fingertips until small crumbs form. Set aside.

TO MAKE FILLING & ASSEMBLE PIE:

1. In a small bowl, stir together sugar and flour. In a mixing bowl, toss apples and cranberries with lemon zest and juice. Sprinkle the sugar mixture over the apples and toss well. Pile the filling in the pie shell.

2. Spread the reserved streusel topping evenly over the apples and sprinkle the remaining tablespoon of oats over the top. Set the pie on a baking sheet to catch any drips.

3. Bake for 55 to 65 minutes, or until the fruit is bubbling at the edges and is easily pierced with a skewer in the center. Check the pie toward the end of the baking time; if the crust or the topping is becoming too dark, cover the pie loosely with foil.

Makes one 9-inch pie, for 8 servings.

405 calories per serving: 4 grams protein, 9 grams fat (1.2 grams saturated fat), 81 grams carbohydrate; 80 mg sodium; 2 mg cholesterol; 4 grams fiber.

Ⓝ NUTRITION BONUS: Oats and dried cranberries add fiber to this autumn dessert.

TECHNIQUE 89
Choose meringue for a fat-free pie shell.

There *is* an option for pie lovers on very low-fat diets: meringue baked in a pie pan has no fat whatsoever.

Ⓕ FAT SAVINGS: A full-fat pie crust adds 14 grams of fat to your slice of pie; the Eating Well crust adds 7 grams and this meringue crust adds 0.

Lemon Dream Pie

MERINGUE PIE SHELL

- Canola oil for brushing foil
- 3 large egg whites, at room temperature
- ¼ teaspoon cream of tartar
- ½ cup granulated sugar
- ¾ teaspoon pure vanilla extract
- ⅓ cup confectioners' sugar, sifted

LEMON FILLING

- ½ cup granulated sugar
- 2 large eggs
- 2 large egg whites
- 6 tablespoons fresh lemon juice
- 2 teaspoons grated lemon zest
- 2 tablespoons butter
- 4 cups fresh raspberries
  Confectioners' sugar for dusting

TO MAKE MERINGUE PIE SHELL:

1. Position oven rack in the center of the oven; preheat to 275°F. Line a 9-inch deep-dish pie pan with aluminum foil, dull-side up. Lightly brush foil with oil.

2. In a large, grease-free mixing bowl, beat egg whites with an electric mixer on low speed for 30 seconds. Gradually raise the speed to high and continue beating until the whites are frothy and opaque. Add cream of tartar and beat until the whites just begin to form soft peaks. Immediately begin adding sugar a bit at a time. Beat in vanilla. Continue to beat until the meringue stands in stiff, but not dry, peaks. Fold confectioners' sugar into the meringue evenly.

3. Spoon the meringue into the prepared pie pan and use the back of the spoon to hollow out the center and spread the mixture up the sides to form a pie shell.

4. Bake for 1 hour. Lower the heat to 250°F and bake 30 to 40 minutes longer, or until the meringue is firm, dry and just beginning to brown. Transfer to a wire rack and let cool thoroughly. Lift the meringue and foil away from the pie pan and gently peel off the aluminum foil. (*Cooled meringue may be placed in an airtight container and stored for up to 1 week.*)

TO MAKE LEMON FILLING:

1. Have a medium bowl ready. In a heavy saucepan, whisk sugar, eggs, egg whites, lemon juice and lemon zest until well combined. Add butter and cook over low heat, whisking constantly, until the mixture has thickened and bubbled several times, about 5 minutes. (The filling must be thoroughly thickened but not allowed to scramble.)

2. Immediately transfer the filling to the bowl. Place a piece of plastic wrap directly on the surface to prevent a skin from forming and refrigerate until completely chilled, about 1 hour. (*The filling can be made up to 1 day ahead and refrigerated until just before serving.*)

TO ASSEMBLE PIE:

Spoon the chilled lemon filling into the meringue shell and fill the center with fresh raspberries. Dust lightly with confectioners' sugar.

Makes 8 servings.

195 calories per serving: 4 grams protein, 4 grams fat (2.2 grams saturated fat), 37 grams carbohydrate; 80 mg sodium; 61 mg cholesterol; 3 grams fiber.

Ⓝ NUTRITION BONUS: Not only is the crust fat-free, the filling has a healthy dose of vitamins and minerals from the raspberries.

Meringue Shells with Summer Berries

3 large egg whites, at room temperature
¼ teaspoon cream of tartar
⅛ teaspoon salt
¾ cup sugar, preferably instant-dissolving
½ teaspoon pure vanilla extract
3 cups raspberries, blackberries, strawberries *and/or* other seasonal berries
2 tablespoons crème de cassis *or* vodka

1. Preheat oven to 275°F. Line 2 baking sheets with parchment paper or aluminum foil and set aside.

2. In a large mixing bowl, combine egg whites, cream of tartar and salt. Beat with an electric mixer until soft peaks form. Add ¼ cup of the sugar and beat for 30 seconds. Gradually beat in the remaining ½ cup sugar. Add vanilla and beat for 7 to 10 minutes longer, stopping occasionally to scrape down the sides of the bowl, until all the sugar is dissolved and the meringue is stiff and shiny.

3. Spoon the meringue into a pastry bag fitted with a ½-inch plain or star tip. Pipe six 3-inch round disks, then pipe a wall around the edge of each disk. (*Alternatively, drop 6 large spoonfuls of meringue, evenly spaced, onto the prepared baking sheets. With the back of a spoon, form the meringue into little nests about 3 inches in diameter.*)

4. Bake for about 1 hour, or until crisp and firm. While still warm, remove from the baking sheet and let cool on a wire rack. (*Meringues can be made ahead and stored in an airtight container for up to 2 weeks.*)

5. Just before serving, combine berries and crème de cassis or vodka. Spoon the fruit into the shells and serve.

Makes 6 servings.

135 calories per serving: 2 grams protein, 0 grams fat, 31 grams carbohydrate; 75 mg sodium; 0 mg cholesterol; 2 grams fiber.

Ⓝ NUTRITION BONUS: Meringue shells filled with plump, juicy berries make a fat-free indulgence to please every diner.

Flavorful Nuts

NUTS NOT ONLY ADD RICH, nutty flavor, they provide satisfying textural contrast in baked goods. A concentrated source of protein, calories and fat, ½ cup of nuts in a recipe will contribute more than 8 grams of protein, 350 calories and 36 grams of fat to the total count. Translate that to the average batch of cookies and you raise the fat count by 1 gram per cookie.

In the EATING WELL Test Kitchen, in order to maximize the effect of a reduced quantity of nuts, we often toast them. This brings out their rich flavor, deepens their color and increases their crunchiness. If you do a side-by-side taste test, a cookie or a bar made with toasted nuts does taste nuttier.

Toasting can be done on the stovetop or in the oven, but we find that the oven's even heat means nuts are less likely to scorch—and the oven is usually turned on when you are getting ready to bake.

THERE IS GOOD news about the oil in nuts: Although they're certainly not low in fat, nuts can help lower blood cholesterol because nut oils are rich in monounsaturated fat, which lowers cholesterol when it replaces saturated fat. And that's exactly what we do in our recipes—replace cholesterol-raising saturated fats with heart-healthy monounsaturated fats. Nuts are also rich sources of trace minerals and flavor.

THE BEST WAY TO STORE NUTS is to keep them in their shells. This keeps them from light, humidity and exposure to the air, all factors that hasten rancidity. Once nuts are shelled, keep them in an airtight container in the freezer. Whenever you are baking with nuts, be sure to taste a couple before adding to the batter; nuts can develop an off taste when old or improperly stored.

One pound of nuts in the shell yields about ½ pound of shelled nuts.

WALNUT AND HAZELNUT OILS ARE pressed from toasted nuts. Buy nut oils in small bottles or cans and store in the refrigerator, as nut oil becomes rancid more quickly than other oils. When a recipe contains nuts, using a small amount of nut oil heightens the flavor. These oils are high in heart-healthy monounsaturated fats.

Above: Hazelnuts
Left: Toasted pine nuts
Right: Walnuts

TO TOAST NUTS

Spread almonds, walnuts, pecans, hazelnuts or pine nuts in a single layer in a metal baking pan. Toast in a 350°F oven for 5 to 8 minutes, shaking the pan once or twice to ensure even browning. Once the nuts are fragrant and lightly browned, transfer them to a plate or dish. Do not overbrown nuts, because they tend to continue to darken and become crisper as they cool.

Apple-Walnut Upside-Down Cake

APPLE TOPPING

  ¾ cup sugar
3-4 Golden Delicious apples, peeled and thinly sliced (4 cups)
  1 tablespoon fresh lemon juice

WALNUT CAKE

  ¾ cup walnut halves, lightly toasted
  ⅔ cup unsifted cake flour
  1 teaspoon baking powder
  ¼ teaspoon salt
  2 large egg whites
  ⅔ cup sugar
  2 large eggs
  1 teaspoon pure vanilla extract

TO MAKE APPLE TOPPING:

1. Preheat oven to 375°F. Lightly oil a 9-inch round cake pan with sides at least 2 inches high or coat it with nonstick cooking spray.

2. In a heavy-bottomed saucepan, combine sugar and ¼ cup water. Bring to a simmer over low heat, stirring occasionally. Increase the heat to medium-high and cook, without stirring, until the syrup turns a deep amber color, about 5 minutes. (Swirl the pan if the syrup is coloring unevenly.) Immediately pour the syrup into the prepared cake pan.

3. In a bowl, toss apple slices with lemon juice. Evenly press the apples into the warm caramel and set aside.

TO MAKE WALNUT CAKE:

1. In a food processor, combine walnuts, flour, baking powder and salt; process until the walnuts are ground to a coarse meal.

2. In a mixing bowl, beat the 2 egg whites with an electric mixer until soft peaks form. One tablespoon at a time, beat in ⅓ cup of the sugar, continuing to beat until the egg whites are stiff and glossy; set aside.

3. In a separate mixing bowl, beat the 2 whole eggs with the remaining ⅓ cup sugar until thick and pale, about 5 minutes. Beat in vanilla.

4. Whisk one-fourth of the reserved beaten egg whites into the whole-egg mixture. Sprinkle half of the dry ingredients over the top and fold in gently using a rubber spatula. Fold in the remaining beaten whites, followed by the remaining dry ingredients.

5. Spread the batter over the fruit in the pan. Bake for 40 to 45 minutes, or until the top springs back when lightly touched and a skewer inserted in the center comes out clean. Let cool in the pan for 5 minutes, then invert onto a serving plate, setting any stray apples back in place. Serve warm or at room temperature.

Makes one 9-inch cake, for 10 servings.

225 calories per serving: 5 grams protein, 6 grams fat (0.7 gram saturated fat), 41 grams carbohydrate; 110 mg sodium; 43 mg cholesterol; 2 grams fiber.

One-Bowl Chocolate Cake, page 180

THE TECHNIQUES

90 Switching from high-fat chocolate to Dutch-process cocoa powder

91 Cutting the fat in chocolate cheesecake

92 Substituting dried cherries for coconut in chewy chocolate cookies

93 Using nonfat sweetened condensed milk in ice cream and hot fudge sauce

TECHNIQUES
90-93
Chocolate

THE COOKS IN EATING WELL'S TEST KITCHEN FIND THAT REDUCING fat in chocolate desserts makes for very satisfying work. Not only do they feel a great sense of accomplishment once the slice of chocolate cheesecake weighs in at only nine grams of fat, they will have had the opportunity to taste-test all the versions along the way.

Chocolate desserts present several challenges for fat-busting. Chocolate itself contains fat in the form of cocoa butter; the switch from chocolate to lower-fat cocoa is the first step in cutting the fat. But cocoa butter isn't the only culprit. High-fat butter, cream and eggs have an affinity for chocolate and must be reduced without losing flavor. That has been done successfully in these recipes.

90 Switch from chocolate to cocoa powder— and make it Dutch-process cocoa for the fullest flavor.

The choice for low-fat bakers is clear: 1 ounce of premium unsweetened chocolate has 16 grams of fat, while 3 tablespoons of cocoa (equivalent to 1 ounce of chocolate in terms of flavor) has only 1.5 grams of fat. To keep the chocolate flavor intense and rich, we prefer Dutch-process cocoa.

F FAT SAVINGS: Using cocoa in place of chocolate not only allows you to control the amount of fat in chocolate desserts, the fat you do add can be heart-healthy rather than saturated.

One-Bowl Chocolate Cake

This cake is dark, moist, rich—and easy.

- ¾ cup plus 2 tablespoons all-purpose white flour
- ½ cup granulated sugar
- ⅓ cup unsweetened cocoa powder, preferably Dutch-process
- 1 teaspoon baking powder
- 1 teaspoon baking soda
- ½ teaspoon salt
- ½ cup buttermilk
- ½ cup packed light brown sugar
- 1 large egg, lightly beaten
- 2 tablespoons canola oil
- 1 teaspoon pure vanilla extract
- ½ cup hot strong black coffee
  Confectioners' sugar for dusting

1. Preheat oven to 350°F. Lightly oil a 9-inch round cake pan or coat it with nonstick cooking spray. Dust the pan with flour, tapping out the excess.

2. In a mixing bowl, whisk flour, granulated sugar,

? WHAT IS DUTCH-PROCESS COCOA POWDER?

"Dutching" is a process that neutralizes the natural acidity in cocoa powder, resulting in a more mellow chocolate flavor with a darker color. The cocoa is widely available. Imported Dutch-process cocoa is available in specialty-food stores, while domestic brands can be found in supermarkets.

cocoa powder, baking powder, baking soda and salt. Add buttermilk, brown sugar, egg, oil and vanilla. Beat with an electric mixer on medium speed for 2 minutes. Add hot coffee and beat to blend. (The batter will be quite thin.)

3. Pour the batter into the prepared pan. Bake for 30 to 35 minutes, or until a skewer inserted in the center comes out clean. Cool the cake in the pan on a wire rack for 10 minutes; remove from the pan and let cool completely. Dust the top with confectioners' sugar before slicing.

Makes one 9-inch cake, for 12 servings.

110 calories per serving: 2 grams protein, 3 grams fat (0.5 gram saturated fat), 18 grams carbohydrate; 205 mg sodium; 18 mg cholesterol; 0 grams fiber.

N NUTRITION BONUS: Cake mixes may be easier but they contain hydrogenated fats.

Cocoa Fudge

- 3 cups sugar
- ⅔ cup unsweetened cocoa powder, preferably Dutch-process
- ¼ teaspoon salt
- 1½ cups low-fat milk
- 2 tablespoons butter
- 1 tablespoon canola oil
- 1 teaspoon pure vanilla extract

1. Line the bottom and sides of an 8-inch square baking pan with a sheet of aluminum foil. Lightly oil the foil or spray it with nonstick cooking spray. Set aside.

2. In a large (3½-quart) heavy saucepan, whisk sugar,

cocoa and salt. Slowly stir in milk. Place the saucepan over medium heat and bring to a boil, stirring continuously with a wooden spoon. Once the mixture comes to a boil, stop stirring. Boil, without stirring, until the fudge reaches the soft-ball stage (when a small amount dropped into ice water forms a very soft ball) or 234°F on a candy thermometer, about 10 minutes. Remove from the heat and add butter, oil and vanilla but do not stir. Let cool to lukewarm, about 45 minutes.

3. With a wooden spoon, stir the fudge vigorously until it begins to thicken and just loses its gloss, 1 to 2 minutes. Quickly pour into the foil-lined pan and spread evenly; let cool. Invert onto a cutting board, remove the foil and cut the fudge into 36 squares. (*The fudge may be wrapped in plastic wrap and stored at room temperature for up to 1 week.*)

Makes 36 squares.

80 calories per square: I gram protein, I gram fat (0.5 gram saturated fat), 17 grams carbohydrate; 28 mg sodium; 2 mg cholesterol; 0 grams fiber.

 NUTRITION BONUS: Most recipes for fudge call for regular milk and much more butter. Using low-fat milk and replacing some of the butter with canola oil gives this fudge a better nutrition profile.

Marbled Cheesecake Brownies

CHEESECAKE TOPPING
- 8 ounces reduced-fat cream cheese, at room temperature
- ⅔ cup sugar
- ½ teaspoon pure vanilla extract
- 1 large egg
- 1 large egg white
- 1 tablespoon all-purpose *or* cake flour

BROWNIE
- 1 cup sifted cake flour
- ½ cup unsweetened cocoa powder, preferably Dutch-process
- ½ teaspoon salt
- 1½ cups packed light brown sugar
- ¼ cup canola oil
- ¼ cup buttermilk
- 1 large egg

- 2 large egg whites
- 1 tablespoon instant coffee granules
- 2 teaspoons pure vanilla extract

TO MAKE TOPPING:
With an electric mixer, beat cream cheese until smooth and creamy, about 1 minute. Add sugar and vanilla; beat until sugar dissolves completely, 2 to 3 minutes. Beat in egg, then egg white. Continue beating another 3 minutes. Add 1 tablespoon flour on low speed and beat just until blended. Set aside.

TO MAKE BROWNIE:
1. Preheat oven to 350°F. Lightly oil an 8-by-12-inch baking pan or coat it with nonstick cooking spray. Dust with flour, tapping out the excess. Set aside.

2. In a small bowl, whisk together flour, cocoa and salt. In a large bowl, beat together brown sugar, oil, buttermilk, egg, egg whites, coffee granules and vanilla on high speed until smooth, making sure no

Marbled Cheesecake Brownies: Two delicious vices in one.

lumps of brown sugar remain. Add the dry ingredients and beat on low speed just until blended.

3. Pour three-fourths of the brownie batter into the prepared pan, spreading it into the corners. Carefully pour the cheesecake topping evenly over the brownie batter. Dot the cheesecake layer with large spoonfuls of the remaining brownie batter. Without disturbing the bottom brownie layer, swirl the top two layers with a table knife. Bake for 40 to 50 minutes, or just until the top is set. Let cool completely in the baking pan on a wire rack. Cut into 16 bars.

Makes 16 bars.

220 calories per bar: 4 grams protein, 7 grams fat (2 grams saturated fat), 34 grams carbohydrate; 155 mg sodium; 37 mg cholesterol; 0 grams fiber.

Ⓝ NUTRITION BONUS: Reduced-fat cream cheese has 30 to 50 percent less fat than full-fat cream cheese.

Chocolate-Banana Soufflés

  3 tablespoons granulated sugar, plus extra for preparing soufflé dishes
  ⅓ cup unsweetened cocoa powder, preferably Dutch-process
  3 tablespoons cornstarch
  ¼ cup light brown sugar
  ¼ teaspoon salt
  ¼ cup plus 2 teaspoons low-fat milk
  2 teaspoons instant coffee granules, preferably espresso
  2 ounces semisweet chocolate, chopped
  ½ cup mashed ripe banana (1 medium banana)
  2 teaspoons pure vanilla extract
  5 large egg whites
    Pinch of cream of tartar
    Confectioners' sugar for dusting

1. Preheat oven to 350°F. Coat six 6-ounce soufflé dishes with nonstick cooking spray. Dust with granulated sugar, tapping out the excess. Set aside.

2. Sift cocoa and cornstarch into a large bowl. Stir in brown sugar and salt. Stir in ¼ cup milk and set aside.

3. Dissolve the coffee powder in 2 teaspoons of the milk. In a medium bowl, melt the chocolate over a pan of barely simmering water, stirring often. Re-move the bowl from the water and stir in the coffee mixture. Whisk in mashed banana and vanilla.

4. Gradually stir the banana mixture into the cocoa mixture. Place egg whites in a clean, grease-free mixing bowl. With an electric mixer, beat on low speed until frothy. Add cream of tartar, raise the speed to medium and whip until soft peaks form. Gradually add the remaining 3 tablespoons sugar and beat on medium-high speed until stiff peaks form.

5. Stir one-fourth of the egg whites into the chocolate mixture. Gently but quickly fold in the remaining whites. Spoon into the prepared soufflé dishes. Bake until puffed and browned, about 25 minutes. Sift a little confectioners' sugar over the top and serve immediately.

Makes 6 servings.

185 calories per serving: 5 grams protein, 3 grams fat (0.2 gram saturated fat), 36 grams carbohydrate; 145 mg sodium; 0 mg cholesterol; 1 gram fiber.

Ⓝ NUTRITION BONUS: A lot of chocolate flavor for relatively few calories.

TECHNIQUE

91 Cut the fat in chocolate cheesecake.

Homemade chocolate cheesecake that is smooth and creamy and under 10 grams of fat per slice? Impossible!

Most of the fat in a chocolate cheesecake comes from cream cheese. We have found that 2 parts pureed cottage cheese blended with 1 part reduced-fat cream cheese gives the same rich dairy flavor with one-fifth the fat of regular cream cheese. For the chocolate flavor, we switched from semisweet chocolate to cocoa, extending it with 2 ounces of bittersweet chocolate. To further boost the chocolate intensity, we added some strong coffee.

Ⓕ FAT SAVINGS: The full-fat original of our chocolate cheesecake tipped the scale at 27 grams of fat per slice; this far healthier version has 9 grams of fat.

Chocolate Cheesecake

CRUST

1 cup chocolate wafer crumbs (about 20 wafers)

1 tablespoon brown sugar

1 tablespoon canola oil

1 teaspoon instant coffee granules dissolved in 2 teaspoons hot water

FILLING

24 ounces low-fat (1%) cottage cheese (3 cups)

12 ounces reduced-fat cream cheese (1½ cups), cut into pieces

1 cup packed brown sugar

½ cup granulated sugar

¾ cup unsweetened cocoa powder, preferably Dutch-process

¼ cup cornstarch

1 large egg

2 large egg whites

2 tablespoons instant coffee granules dissolved in 2 tablespoons hot water

2 teaspoons pure vanilla extract

¼ teaspoon salt

2 ounces bittersweet (*not* unsweetened) *or* semisweet chocolate, melted

16 chocolate-covered coffee beans (optional)

TO MAKE CRUST:

1. Preheat oven to 325°F. Spray a 9-inch springform pan with non-stick cooking spray. Wrap the outside bottom of the pan with a double thickness of aluminum foil to keep out water while the cheesecake is baking.

2. In a small bowl, combine chocolate wafer crumbs, sugar, oil and coffee; blend with a fork or your fingertips. Press the mixture into the bottom of the prepared pan. Cover and set aside.

TO MAKE FILLING & BAKE CHEESECAKE:

1. In a food processor, puree cottage cheese until very smooth, stopping once or twice to scrape down the sides of the workbowl. (If using a small food processor, transfer the cottage cheese to the mixing bowl of an electric mixer.) Add cream cheese, brown sugar, granulated sugar, cocoa and cornstarch. Process (or beat with an electric mixer) until smooth. Add egg, egg whites, coffee, vanilla, salt and melted chocolate and blend well. Pour the batter into the crust-lined pan.

2. Place the cheesecake in a shallow roasting pan and pour in enough boiling water to come ½ inch up the side of the springform pan. Bake for about 50 minutes, or until the edges are set but the center still jiggles when the pan is tapped.

3. Turn off the oven. Spray a knife with cooking spray and quickly run it around the edge of the cake. Let the cake cool in the oven, with the door ajar, for 1 hour. Transfer from the water bath to a wire rack and remove foil. Let cool to room temperature, about 2 hours. Refrigerate, uncovered, until chilled, then

This luscious Chocolate Cheesecake tastes—even feels—decadent.

cover with plastic wrap and refrigerate for up to 2 days.

4. Before serving, garnish the cheesecake with chocolate-covered coffee beans, if using.

Makes 1 cheesecake, for 16 servings.

220 calories per serving: 10 grams protein, 9 grams fat (5 grams saturated fat), 27 grams carbohydrate; 400 mg sodium; 24 mg cholesterol; 1 gram fiber.

Ⓝ NUTRITION BONUS: The cottage cheese in this recipe gives you 24 milligrams of calcium per serving.

92 Use dried cherries to reduce the fat in chocolaty cookies.

No one will believe that these cookies are low in fat. Similar to chocolate macaroons, they're chewy and rich, chocolaty *and* full of coconut. To eliminate some of the fat contributed by the coconut (sweetened flaked coconut has 24 grams of fat per cup), we replace half of it with chopped dried cherries, which are virtually fat-free. In addition, nonfat sweetened condensed milk was substituted for the full-fat version, cutting another 25 grams of fat.

Ⓕ FAT SAVINGS: High-fat chocolate macaroons weigh in at 5 or 6 grams of fat each; made the Eating Well way, the toll is only 1 gram.

Chocolate-Cherry Chews

1 cup dried cherries, chopped
¼ cup cranberry juice
¾ cup unsweetened cocoa powder, preferably Dutch-process
½ cup nonfat sweetened condensed milk
½ cup cherry *or* apple butter
1 tablespoon pure vanilla extract
2 cups sweetened flaked coconut

1. Preheat oven to 350°F. Lightly oil 2 baking sheets

or coat them with nonstick cooking spray; set aside.

2. In a small saucepan, combine cherries and cranberry juice. Bring to a simmer over low heat and cook, stirring frequently, for 2 minutes, or until all the juice has been absorbed. Set aside to cool.

3. In a mixing bowl, combine cocoa, condensed milk, cherry or apple butter and vanilla. With an electric mixer, beat until smooth and blended. Add the plumped cherries and 1⅔ cups of the coconut; stir just until combined.

4. Using 2 small spoons, form and drop 1-inch mounds onto the prepared baking sheet. Sprinkle the remaining coconut over the cookies. Bake for 8 to 10 minutes, or until the cookies are no longer sticky and the coconut has begun to brown. (Do not overbake; the cookies firm up slightly as they cool.) Transfer to a wire rack to cool completely.

Makes 3 dozen cookies.

55 calories per cookie: 1 gram protein, 1 gram fat (0 grams saturated fat), 9 grams carbohydrate; 12 mg sodium; 0 mg cholesterol; 0 grams fiber.

Ⓝ NUTRITION BONUS: Although coconut oil is high in saturated fat, coconut flakes are a less-concentrated source.

93 Nonfat sweetened condensed milk cuts fat in chocolate desserts.

Chocolate isn't the only source of fat in chocolate desserts. It's often the cream, butter or egg yolks that put chocolate confections off limits. The new nonfat version of sweetened condensed milk comes in handy when it comes to chocolate. Thick and sweet, it gives a smooth luster and creamy mouthfeel to chocolate ice cream and fudge sauce—without adding any fat.

Ⓕ FAT SAVINGS: A nice big scoop of full-fat chocolate ice cream has about 15 grams of fat; the Eating Well recipe has one-third that amount without any reduction in flavor.

Chocolate Ice Cream

1½ teaspoons unflavored gelatin
2½ cups low-fat milk
1 14-ounce can nonfat sweetened condensed milk
¼ cup unsweetened cocoa powder, preferably Dutch-process
¼ cup dark corn syrup
1 ounce unsweetened chocolate, coarsely chopped
1 teaspoon pure vanilla extract

1. In a small bowl, sprinkle gelatin over 1 tablespoon water; let stand until softened, 1 minute or longer.
2. In a heavy saucepan, combine ½ cup of the low-fat milk, condensed milk, cocoa and corn syrup; whisk until smooth. Bring to a simmer over medium heat, whisking constantly. Remove from the heat and add chocolate and the softened gelatin; stir until the chocolate has melted. Transfer the mixture to a bowl. Gradually whisk in the remaining 2 cups milk and vanilla until smooth. Cover and chill until cold, about 1 hour.
3. Pour into the canister of an ice cream maker and freeze according to the manufacturer's directions. If necessary, place the ice cream in the freezer to firm up before serving in chilled dessert dishes. (*Use within hours of freezing, if possible, or store in the freezer for up to 4 days. If the ice cream becomes very hard in the freezer, let it soften for 20 minutes before scooping.*)

Makes about 1 quart, for 6 servings.

320 calories per serving: 11 grams protein, 5 grams fat (1 gram saturated fat), 60 grams carbohydrate; 149 mg sodium; 16 mg cholesterol; 0 grams fiber.

NUTRITION BONUS: Sweetened condensed milk is a concentrated source of calcium.

Hot Fudge Sauce

½ cup low-fat milk
⅓ cup unsweetened cocoa powder, preferably Dutch-process
¼ teaspoon instant coffee granules dissolved in 1 tablespoon hot water
½ cup nonfat sweetened condensed milk
⅓ cup sugar
1 teaspoon pure vanilla extract
2 tablespoons semisweet chocolate chips
Pinch of salt

In a small heavy saucepan, whisk together milk, cocoa and coffee until smooth. Whisk in condensed milk and sugar. Whisking constantly, bring to a simmer over low heat; scrape bottom of pan frequently with whisk to prevent sauce from sticking and scorching. Continue to simmer for 1 minute, whisking constantly. Remove from heat and stir in vanilla, chocolate chips and salt. (*Stored in a glass jar, sauce can be refrigerated for up to 2 weeks. Reheat in microwave or by placing jar in a pot of simmering water.*)

Makes about 1½ cups sauce.

40 calories per tablespoon: 1 gram protein, 1 gram fat (0 grams saturated fat), 8 grams carbohydrate; 10 mg sodium; 1 mg cholesterol; 0 grams fiber.

NUTRITION BONUS: Hot fudge sauce is also a low-fat way to add a chocolate kick to a plain piece of cake.

Roasting
Brings Out the Goodness of Fruits

FEW THINGS TASTE BETTER THAN A piece of perfectly ripened fruit. Except, perhaps, that same fruit after it has been roasted in a hot oven. Roasting lightly caramelizes the natural sugars in fruits and enhances their marvelous aroma. The technique is easy enough for weeknights and sophisticated enough for more formal dinners. Combine roasted fruits for a compote and serve over frozen yogurt.

Roasted Pineapple

1   whole pineapple (2½-3 pounds)
2   tablespoons brown sugar

Preheat broiler. Trim leaves and bud end from pineapple. With a sharp, serrated knife, cut into ½-inch-thick slices. Set slices in a single layer on a baking sheet. Sprinkle with brown sugar. (Cover the pineapple slices only; any sugar on the sheet may burn.) Broil, rearranging slices as needed for even cooking, for 10 to 15 minutes. Turn the slices over and continue broiling on the other side for 5 to 10 minutes, until the pineapple is tender and golden brown.

Makes 6 servings.

110 calories per serving: I gram protein, I gram fat (0 grams saturated fat), 28 grams carbohydrate; 4 mg sodium; 0 mg cholesterol; 2 grams fiber.

Roasted Apples

2-3   cooking apples, such as Golden Delicious *or* Rome Beauty (about 1 pound)
1   tablespoon fresh lemon juice
2   tablespoons sugar

Preheat oven to 425°F. Peel, core and cut apples into ½-inch-thick slices. In a large bowl, toss the slices with lemon juice; add sugar and toss once again. Transfer to a baking pan large enough to hold slices in a single layer. Roast for 25 to 30 minutes, stirring occasionally to prevent scorching, until apples are tender and golden brown.

Makes 4 servings.

90 calories per serving: 0 grams protein, 1 gram fat (0 grams saturated fat), 24 grams carbohydrate; 1 mg sodium; 0 mg cholesterol; 3 grams fiber.

Roasted Pears

2-3 pears (about 1 pound)
1 tablespoon fresh lemon juice
2 tablespoons sugar

Preheat oven to 425°F. Peel, core and cut pears into ½-inch-thick slices. In a large bowl, toss the pear slices with lemon juice; add sugar and toss once again. Transfer to a baking pan large enough to hold the slices in a single layer. Roast for 25 to 30 minutes, stirring occasionally to prevent scorching, until the pears are tender and golden brown.

Makes 4 servings.

90 calories per serving: 1 gram protein, 1 gram fat (0 grams saturated fat), 23 grams carbohydrate; 1 mg sodium; 0 mg cholesterol; 3 grams fiber.

Roasted Plums

4-5 ripe plums (about 1 pound)
½ tablespoon fresh lemon juice
1 tablespoon sugar

Preheat oven to 425°F. Slice plums in half and remove pits. In a large bowl, toss the plums with lemon juice; add sugar and toss once again. Arrange the plums cut-side up in a shallow baking dish. Roast for 20 to 25 minutes, or until tender. If the juices in the pan begin to burn, add a

little water and cover the pan loosely with aluminum foil. Let cool slightly before serving.

Makes 4 servings.

105 calories per serving: 1 gram protein, 1 gram fat (0 grams saturated fat), 25 grams carbohydrate; 0 mg sodium; 0 mg cholesterol; 4 grams fiber.

Roasted Peaches

4 ripe peaches (about 1¼ pounds)
½ tablespoon fresh lemon juice
1 tablespoon sugar

Preheat oven to 425°F. Cut peaches in half and remove pits. In a large bowl, toss the peach halves with lemon juice; add sugar and toss once again. Arrange halves cut-side up in a baking dish. Roast for 20 to 25 minutes, or until the peaches are tender. If the juices in the pan begin to burn, add a little water and cover the pan loosely with aluminum foil.

Makes 4 servings.

60 calories per serving: 1 gram protein, 0 grams fat, 16 grams carbohydrate; 0 mg sodium; 0 mg cholesterol; 2 grams fiber.

Double Raspberry Soufflés, page 192

THE TECHNIQUES

94 Substituting meringue for whipped
cream in a luscious mousse

95 Combining meringue and fruit in a
fat-free soufflé

96 Draining low-fat vanilla yogurt for a
creamy effect

97 Switching to low-fat cottage cheese
in a creamy pumpkin cheesecake

98 Reducing the fat in a classic Christmas
pudding

99 Making fat-free frozen yogurt in minutes

100 Using nonfat sweetened condensed milk
to make very low-fat ice cream

TECHNIQUES
94-100
Classic DESSERTS

AN AIRY SOUFFLÉ, A
CLOUDLIKE MOUSSE
OR SOME CREAMY, RICH
ice cream—these are the sorts of confections that
once took a lot of work. Whether it was beating
egg whites by hand to stiff peaks or cranking the
ice cream freezer until it would turn no more,
these light desserts were not to be undertaken
lightly. Electric mixers, food processors and small,
handy ice cream freezers have eased the work load
considerably. And EATING WELL's healthy cooking
techniques have greatly lessened the considerable
fat burden.

94 Substitute meringue for whipped cream to make light, luscious mousse.

Most often a mousse owes its light, airy texture to whipped cream. That fluffy cream is a tremendous source of fat, however. By folding meringue into the mousse base you achieve the same light effect. (We use a *cooked* meringue to avoid a salmonella risk.) To recreate the luxurious feel of a mousse, we add a tiny amount of whipped cream.

F **FAT SAVINGS:** When a mousse depends on whipped cream and egg yolks for richness, its fat count can reach 30 grams per serving. Our velvety mousses have 5 to 6 grams.

To ensure a safe cooked meringue, beat the meringue in a mixing bowl set over a pan of simmering water. Beat slowly until an instant-read thermometer reads 140°F. Increase mixer speed to high and beat for 3½ minutes.

Apricot Amaretti Mousse

1½	cups apricot nectar
¾	cup dried apricots
½	cup fresh lemon juice
2	tablespoons apricot *or* peach brandy
1	teaspoon unflavored gelatin
½	cup sugar
2	large egg whites
⅛	teaspoon cream of tartar
⅓	cup whipping cream
6	amaretti cookies, crumbled

1. In a small saucepan, combine apricot nectar and dried apricots. Bring to a boil, reduce heat to low and simmer just until the apricots are tender, about 20 minutes.

2. Meanwhile, in a small bowl, combine lemon juice and liqueur. Sprinkle with gelatin and set aside to soften.

3. Transfer the hot apricots and their cooking liquid to a food processor. Add softened gelatin; process to a smooth puree. Set a fine-mesh stainless-steel sieve over a large bowl, transfer the apricot puree to the sieve and work it through with a rubber spatula. (Discard coarse pulp.) Let the puree cool to room temperature.

4. In a large saucepan, bring about 1 inch of water to a simmer. In a heatproof mixing bowl large enough to fit over the saucepan, combine sugar, egg whites, cream of tartar and 3 tablespoons of water. Set the bowl over the barely simmering water and beat with an electric mixer on low speed, moving the beaters around the bowl constantly, until an instant-read thermometer registers 140°F. (This will take 2 to 4 minutes.) Increase the mixer speed to high and continue beating over the heat for a full 3½ minutes. Remove the bowl from the heat and beat the meringue until cool, about 4 minutes.

5. In a chilled bowl, whip cream to soft peaks. Whisk about one-fourth of the meringue into the cooled apricot mixture to lighten it, then fold in the remaining meringue with a rubber spatula. Fold in the whipped cream.

6. Divide the mousse among 6 dessert dishes or stemmed glasses. Cover loosely and refrigerate until set, about 4 hours. (*The mousse can be stored, covered,* *in the refrigerator for up to 2 days.*) Garnish with crumbled amaretti cookies before serving.

Makes 6 servings.

225 calories per serving: 3 grams protein, 6 grams fat (3 grams saturated fat), 42 grams carbohydrate; 40 mg sodium; 21 mg cholesterol; 2 grams fiber.

NUTRITION BONUS: Apricots and apricot nectar are rich in carotenoids and potassium.

Lemon Mousse

Yellow food coloring (optional)
1 teaspoon unflavored gelatin
2 large eggs
¼ cup plus ⅔ cup sugar
½ cup fresh lemon juice
1 tablespoon grated lemon zest
3 large egg whites
¼ teaspoon cream of tartar
¼ cup whipping cream
Lemon slices for garnish

1. Bring about 1 inch of water to a simmer in a large saucepan. Place 3 tablespoons cold water in a small bowl. If using food coloring, add about 3 drops to the water. Sprinkle in gelatin and let stand for 2 minutes to soften. Dissolve the softened gelatin in the microwave or over the simmering water. Set aside.

2. In a heatproof bowl large enough to fit over the saucepan of simmering water, combine whole eggs, ¼ cup sugar, lemon juice and lemon zest. Set the bowl over the barely simmering water and whisk slowly and constantly until the mixture thickens and reaches 160°F. Remove the bowl from the heat and whisk in the dissolved gelatin. Let cool for 20 minutes.

3. Meanwhile, in another heatproof mixing bowl large enough to fit over the saucepan of water, combine the remaining ⅔ cup sugar, egg whites, cream of tartar and 3 tablespoons of water. Set the bowl over the barely simmering water and beat with an electric mixer on low speed, moving the beaters around the bowl constantly, until an instant-read thermometer registers 140°F. (This will take 3 to 5 minutes.) Increase the mixer speed to high and continue beating over the heat for a full 3½ minutes. Remove the bowl

from the heat and beat the meringue until cool, about 4 minutes.

4. In a chilled bowl, whip cream to soft peaks. Set aside. Whisk about one-fourth of the meringue into the cooled lemon mixture to lighten it, then fold in the remaining meringue with a whisk. With a rubber spatula, fold in the whipped cream.

5. Divide the mousse among 6 dessert dishes or stemmed glasses. Cover loosely and refrigerate until set, about 3 hours. (*The mousse can be stored, covered, in the refrigerator for up to 2 days.*) Garnish with lemon slices before serving.

Makes 6 servings.

185 calories per serving: 5 grams protein, 5 grams fat (2 grams saturated fat), 33 grams carbohydrate; 53 mg sodium; 82 mg cholesterol; 0 grams fiber.

NUTRITION BONUS: A small amount of whipping cream goes a long way in this velvety mousse.

Light, refreshing Lemon Mousse is perfect after a big meal.

TECHNIQUE

95 Combine meringue and fruit for a fat-free dessert soufflé.

Fruit soufflés can be made with or without pastry cream, which adds egg yolks and whole milk. The pastry cream makes the soufflé sturdier, but not necessarily tastier. We have found that as long as the eggs are stiffly beaten and the oven has been thoroughly preheated, fruit soufflés are a breeze, and their fresh fruit flavors really come through.

F FAT SAVINGS: Made with egg yolks and whole milk, a fruit soufflé has 6 to 8 grams of fat per serving; once they are eliminated, it is a fat-free dessert.

Double Raspberry Soufflés

If you prefer, you may sprinkle 1 teaspoon sugar over the berries in each dish instead of liqueur.

BERRY LAYER
- 6 teaspoons sugar
- 3 cups fresh *or* frozen unsweetened raspberries
- 6 teaspoons crème de cassis *or* eau-de-vie de framboise (optional)

SOUFFLE
- 3 cups fresh *or* frozen unsweetened raspberries
- 1 tablespoon crème de cassis *or* eau-de-vie de framboise (optional)
- 4 large egg whites, at room temperature
  Pinch of salt
- ⅓ cup sugar
  Confectioners' sugar for dusting

TO MAKE BERRY LAYER:
Preheat oven to 375°F. Coat six 8-ounce soufflé dishes with nonstick cooking spray. Add 1 teaspoon sugar to each cup and swirl to coat the inside. Distribute raspberries in the bottom of the dishes and sprinkle each with 1 teaspoon of the liqueur.

TO MAKE SOUFFLES:
1. In a saucepan, stir raspberries over low heat until juicy (for fresh) or thawed (for frozen). Transfer to a stainless-steel sieve set over a bowl. With a spoon, press the berries through the sieve to remove seeds.

2. Return the puree to the saucepan. Bring to a simmer and stir over medium heat until very thick and reduced to ¼ cup, about 10 minutes. (Reduce the heat as the mixture thickens.) Stir in 1 tablespoon liqueur, if using, and set aside to cool slightly.

3. In a mixing bowl, beat egg whites and salt with an electric mixer on high speed until soft peaks form. Continuing to beat, gradually add sugar and beat until stiff peaks form. Whisk about one-fourth of the beaten whites into the reserved raspberry puree to lighten it, then pour the mixture over the remaining whites. With a rubber spatula, gently fold the puree and whites together until evenly blended. Spoon the soufflé mixture into the dishes, spreading to the edges of the dishes.

4. Set the dishes on a baking sheet and bake for 10 minutes, or until lightly browned. Dust with confectioners' sugar and serve immediately.

Makes 6 individual soufflés.

150 calories per soufflé: 3 grams protein, 0 grams fat, 32 grams carbohydrate; 37 mg sodium; 0 mg cholesterol; 6 grams fiber.

N NUTRITION BONUS: Each serving contains a full cup of raspberries, with their complement of vitamins and minerals.

Grand Marnier Soufflé

- ½ cup sugar, plus extra for preparing soufflé dish
- 2 tablespoons cornstarch
- 1 cup fresh orange juice
- 1 tablespoon fresh lemon juice
- 2 teaspoons grated orange zest
- 3 tablespoons orange marmalade
- 2 tablespoons Grand Marnier *or* other orange liqueur
- 5 large egg whites, at room temperature
- ¼ teaspoon cream of tartar
  Pinch of salt
  Confectioners' sugar for dusting

1. In a small heavy saucepan, combine ¼ cup of the sugar and cornstarch. Gradually stir in orange juice, lemon juice and orange zest. Bring to a boil, stirring constantly. Cook, stirring, for 45 to 60 seconds, until the mixture is thick. Remove from the heat and stir in marmalade and orange liqueur. Transfer the soufflé base to a bowl and let cool to room temperature.

2. Position oven rack in the lower third of the oven; preheat to 350°F. Lightly coat a 1½-quart soufflé dish with vegetable oil or nonstick cooking spray. Dust with sugar, tapping out the excess.

3. In a large mixing bowl, beat egg whites with an electric mixer on medium speed until foamy. Add cream of tartar and salt; gradually increase speed to high and beat until soft peaks form. Gradually add the remaining ¼ cup sugar and beat until stiff peaks form.

4. Whisk about one-fourth of the beaten egg whites into the cooled soufflé base to lighten it; gently fold it back into the remaining whites. Turn into the prepared dish and smooth the top.

5. Bake the soufflé until puffed and lightly browned, about 35 minutes. Dust with confectioners' sugar and serve immediately.

Makes 6 servings.

130 calories per serving: 3 grams protein, 0 grams fat, 30 grams carbohydrate; 90 mg sodium; 0 mg cholesterol; 0.5 gram fiber.

Ⓝ NUTRITION BONUS: Soufflés are a dieter's friend with their rich, elegant taste and low-calorie profile.

TECHNIQUE

96

Drain low-fat vanilla yogurt for a creamy effect.

Draining yogurt for 1 hour will reduce its volume by about 30 percent; the drained yogurt has more body, and it can be blended with a small amount of whipped cream to use as an accompaniment for fruit desserts.

Ⓕ FAT SAVINGS: Whipped cream has 5.6 grams of fat in a 2-tablespoon dollop; Eating Well's Cream Topping (*page 194*) has 2 grams of fat in the same-sized dollop.

Ⓠ ## HOW MUCH FAT IS IN WHIPPED CREAM?

While whipped cream often has the effect of lightening desserts by making them fluffier and lighter-looking, it certainly weighs them down in terms of fat grams. Depending on the brand, 1 cup of whipping or heavy cream has 80 to 90 grams of fat. It doubles in volume when whipped, but even then it still brings a lot of fat grams to a pie, sundae or mousse.

Plum Fool

1	pound plums, pitted and sliced (about 2½ cups)
¼-½	cup sugar
½	teaspoon grated fresh ginger
½	teaspoon ground cinnamon
1½	cups low-fat vanilla yogurt
⅓	cup whipping cream

1. Set aside a few plum slices for garnish. In a small heavy saucepan, combine the remaining plum slices, ¼ cup sugar, ginger and cinnamon. Bring to a simmer, stirring, over medium heat, and cook for 15 to 20 minutes, or until the mixture has softened into a chunky puree. Taste and add more sugar, if desired. Transfer to a bowl and chill until cool, about 1 hour.

2. Meanwhile, set a fine-mesh stainless-steel sieve over a bowl. Spoon in yogurt and let drain in the refrigerator until reduced to 1 cup, about 1 hour. (*See Technique 52, page 104.*)

3. In a chilled bowl, whip cream to soft peaks. With a rubber spatula, gently fold in drained yogurt. Fold this mixture into the fruit puree, leaving distinct swirls. Spoon into 6 individual dessert dishes and cover with plastic wrap. Refrigerate for at least 1 hour or up to 2 days. Garnish with plum slices before serving.

Makes 2½ cups, for 6 servings.

170 calories per serving: 2 grams protein, 5 grams fat (3 grams saturated fat), 32 grams carbohydrate; 40 mg sodium; 18 mg cholesterol; 2 grams fiber.

Ⓝ NUTRITION BONUS: Plums are a fairly good source of vitamin C and fiber.

Blueberry-Lemon Pudding

 3 cups low-fat vanilla yogurt
 2 cups fresh blueberries
 3 tablespoons fresh lemon juice
 2 tablespoons sugar
 1½ teaspoons grated lemon zest

1. Set a fine-mesh stainless-steel sieve over a bowl. Spoon in yogurt and let drain in the refrigerator until reduced to 1 cup, about 1 hour. (*See Technique 52, page 104.*)

2. Meanwhile, combine blueberries, lemon juice, sugar and lemon zest in a saucepan. Stir over medium heat until the berries just begin to break down, 2 to 3 minutes. Transfer to a bowl and refrigerate.

3. Just before serving, add the drained yogurt to the cooled berries and stir to combine.

Makes 4 servings.

250 calories per serving: 10 grams protein, 3 grams fat (1.3 grams saturated fat), 47 grams carbohydrate; 125 mg sodium; 10 mg cholesterol; 2 grams fiber.

Ⓝ NUTRITION BONUS: Reduced-fat yogurts usually have more calcium than milk because milk solids are added as a thickener.

Cream Topping

Perfect for strawberry shortcake.

 1½ cups low-fat vanilla yogurt
 ½ cup light whipping cream
 1 tablespoon confectioners' sugar
 1 tablespoon Grand Marnier *or* other orange liqueur (optional)

1. Set a fine-mesh stainless-steel sieve over a bowl. Spoon in yogurt and let drain in the refrigerator until reduced to 1 cup, about 1 hour. (*See Technique 52, page 104.*)

2. In a chilled bowl, whip cream to soft peaks. Add the drained yogurt, sugar and liqueur, if using; fold gently to mix. (*Store in the refrigerator for up to 8 hours.*)

Makes about 2 cups.

20 calories per tablespoon: 1 gram protein, 1 gram fat (1 gram saturated fat), 1 gram carbohydrate; 9 mg sodium; 4 mg cholesterol; 0 grams fiber.

TECHNIQUE 97
Switch to low-fat cottage cheese in a cheesecake.

Fat-busting in a dessert as rich as pumpkin cheesecake requires more than one technique. We began with the crust, moistening the gingersnap crumbs with 1 tablespoon canola oil instead of 3 tablespoons butter. We replaced 60 percent of the full-fat cream cheese with pureed 1% cottage cheese. The original recipe had called for full-fat sour cream; the reduced-fat variety performed just as well. We eliminated 2 egg yolks without ill effect.

Ⓕ FAT SAVINGS: The original model for this recipe contained 27 grams of fat per serving (16 grams saturated); our makeover has only 8 grams of fat, 4 saturated.

Marbled Pumpkin Cheesecake

CRUST
 1 cup gingersnap cookie crumbs (about 20 cookies)
 1 tablespoon canola oil
FILLING
 20 ounces low-fat (1%) cottage cheese (2½ cups)
 12 ounces reduced-fat cream cheese (1½ cups), softened
 1 cup sugar
 4 tablespoons cornstarch
 1 large egg
 2 large egg whites
 8 ounces reduced-fat sour cream (1 cup)
 1½ teaspoons pure vanilla extract
 ¼ teaspoon salt
 1 teaspoon fresh lemon juice
 ¾ cup canned plain pumpkin puree
 3 tablespoons dark brown sugar
 2 tablespoons unsulfured molasses

1 teaspoon ground cinnamon
1 teaspoon ground ginger
½ teaspoon freshly grated nutmeg
⅛ teaspoon ground cloves

TO MAKE CRUST:

1. Preheat oven to 325°F. Lightly oil a 9-inch spring-form pan or coat it with nonstick cooking spray. Wrap the outside bottom of the pan with a double thickness of aluminum foil to keep out water while the cheesecake is baking.

2. In a small bowl, combine crumbs and oil. Press the mixture into the bottom of the prepared pan. Cover and set aside.

TO MAKE FILLING & BAKE CHEESECAKE:

1. In a food processor, puree cottage cheese until very smooth, stopping once or twice to scrape down the sides of the workbowl. (If using a small food processor, transfer the cottage cheese to the mixing bowl of an electric mixer.) Add cream cheese, sugar and 3 tablespoons of the cornstarch. Process (or beat with an electric mixer) until smooth. Add egg and egg whites, sour cream, vanilla and salt and blend well. Measure 3½ cups of the batter into a separate bowl; stir in lemon juice and set aside.

2. To the filling remaining in the food processor or mixing bowl, add pumpkin, brown sugar, molasses, cinnamon, ginger, nutmeg, cloves and the remaining 1 tablespoon cornstarch; blend well.

3. Pour about 1 cup of the vanilla filling into the center of the crust. Then pour about 1 cup of the pumpkin filling into the center of the vanilla filling. Add the remaining fillings in the same manner, alternating cups of vanilla and pumpkin filling. Concentric circles of vanilla and pumpkin will form as the fillings spread over the crust. To create a marbled effect, gently swirl a knife or skewer through the fillings without disturbing the crust.

4. Place the cheesecake in a shallow roasting pan and pour in enough boiling water to come ½ inch up the side of the springform pan. Bake for about 50 minutes, or until the edges are set but the center still jiggles when the pan is tapped.

5. Turn off the oven. Spray a knife with cooking spray and quickly run it around the edge of the cake. Let cake cool in the oven, with the door ajar, for 1 hour. Transfer from the water bath to a wire rack and remove foil. Let cool to room temperature, about 2 hours. Refrigerate, uncovered, until chilled, then cover with plastic wrap and refrigerate for up to 2 days.

Makes 1 cheesecake, for 16 servings.

215 calories per serving: 9 grams protein, 8 grams fat (4 grams saturated fat), 28 grams carbohydrate; 350 mg sodium; 27 mg cholesterol; 0 grams fiber.

Ⓝ NUTRITION BONUS: Canned pumpkin is a rich source of carotenoids, which are fat-soluble and best absorbed along with some amount of dietary fat.

Our lightened Marbled Pumpkin Cheesecake ends a feast gracefully.

98 Trim the fat from a Christmas pudding and its accompanying sauce.

It's hard to know how to begin cutting the fat from very traditional recipes. Take steamed puddings; many old recipes call for 1 pound of chopped suet! We found fruit puree to be the ideal fat buster in a moist pudding: almost any commercial fruit puree, such as prune pie filling (Lekvar), apple butter or fruit puree fat replacement, works well in the intensely spiced dessert.

Steamed puddings are usually served with a hard sauce whose three ingredients are butter, sugar and brandy. To avoid adding even more fat to your holiday dessert, try our easy Caramel-Orange Sauce instead.

F FAT SAVINGS: A traditional steamed pudding has about 25 grams of fat per slice; the hard sauce adds another 3 grams. The revised pudding has 6 grams and the new sauce adds just 1 more.

Christmas Steamed Pudding

1	cup golden raisins
1	cup dark raisins
3	tablespoons brandy
⅓	cup chopped pecans
1	cup all-purpose white flour
1	cup breadcrumbs made from day-old firm white sandwich bread (3-4 slices)
1½	teaspoons baking powder
1	teaspoon baking soda
1½	teaspoons ground cinnamon
½	teaspoon ground ginger
¼	teaspoon ground cloves
½	teaspoon salt
2	large eggs
¾	cup granulated sugar
½	cup packed brown sugar
¾	cup prune pie filling (Lekvar), fruit puree fat replacement *or* apple butter
¼	cup canola oil
1½	teaspoons grated orange zest
1	tablespoon fresh orange juice
1½	cups grated carrots (3-4 medium)

FOR SERVING

	Candied Orange Zest (*page 198*)
¼	cup brandy
	Caramel-Orange Sauce (*recipe follows*)

Christmas Steamed Pudding makes an impressive holiday dessert, with all the traditional richness but just one-fourth the original fat.

1. Lightly oil a 2-quart pudding mold or deep heat-proof bowl or spray it with cooking spray. Cut a piece of parchment or wax paper to fit over the top, and spray 1 side of the paper with cooking spray. Select a pot that is tall enough to hold the mold comfortably and place a trivet or rack in it. Put a teakettle of water on to heat for steaming the pudding.

2. In a bowl, combine golden and dark raisins and brandy; cover and set aside.

3. Toast pecans in a small dry skillet, stirring over medium heat until fragrant, 2 to 3 minutes. Set aside.

4. In a bowl, whisk flour, breadcrumbs, baking powder, baking soda, cinnamon, ginger, cloves and salt.

5. In a large mixing bowl, whisk eggs. Add granulated sugar and brown sugar, prune pie filling (or fruit puree fat replacement or apple butter), oil, orange zest and juice; whisk until smooth. Add the dry ingredients and stir with a wooden spoon until blended. Stir in carrots, the plumped raisins (and liquid) and the toasted pecans.

6. Spoon the batter into the prepared mold. (The mold should be about two-thirds full.) Set the prepared circle of parchment or wax paper, sprayed-side down, on top. Cover with the lid or a double thickness of aluminum foil, securing with string or masking tape. Set the mold in the pot and pour in enough boiling water to come halfway up the sides of the mold. Bring the water to a simmer; reduce heat to low, cover the pot and steam the pudding for 2 hours. (Add more water to maintain level during steaming, if necessary.) The top of the pudding should spring back when touched lightly, and the sides should pull away slightly from the sides of the mold.

7. Transfer the mold to a wire rack, uncover and let stand for 10 to 15 minutes before unmolding. (*If you like, the pudding can be made up to 1 month in advance. Unmold it, sprinkle with ½ cup brandy, wrap tightly in plastic wrap and store in a cool, dry place. To heat before serving, unwrap and put back in the mold; steam for 45 minutes.*)

8. To serve, unmold the pudding onto a serving platter and garnish with Candied Orange Zest. Warm brandy in a small saucepan over low heat. (Do not boil.) Carefully ignite the brandy and pour over the warm pudding. Serve with warm Caramel-Orange Sauce.

Makes 16 servings.

295 calories per serving: 3 grams protein, 6 grams fat (0.9 gram saturated fat), 56 grams carbohydrate, 2 grams alcohol; 185 mg sodium; 28 mg cholesterol; 2 grams fiber.

 NUTRITION BONUS: The saturated fat in this recipe has been slashed by 95 percent.

Caramel-Orange Sauce

1   cup sugar
¾   cup fresh orange juice
2   teaspoons butter
1   tablespoon brandy

1. In a small heavy saucepan, combine sugar and ⅓ cup water. Bring to a boil over medium-high heat, stirring to dissolve the sugar. Cook, without stirring, until the syrup turns deep amber, 5 to 12 minutes.

2. Remove from the heat and carefully pour in orange juice. Stand back, as the caramel may sputter. Return to low heat and stir until all the caramel has dissolved. Remove from the heat and swirl in butter. Stir in brandy and let cool slightly before serving. (*The sauce can be made up to 1 week ahead and stored, covered, in the refrigerator. Warm in the microwave or on the stovetop before serving.*)

Makes about 1⅓ cups, for 16 servings.

55 calories per serving: 0 grams protein, 1 gram fat (0.3 gram saturated fat), 13 grams carbohydrate; 5 mg sodium; 1 mg cholesterol; 0 grams fiber.

Candied Orange Zest

1 orange, scrubbed
½ cup sugar

With a vegetable peeler, remove long strips of zest from the orange. Using a chef's knife, cut the strips lengthwise into julienne strips. Place the strips in a saucepan, cover with cold water and bring to a simmer; cook for 5 minutes. Drain and return the orange zest to the pan. Add sugar and ½ cup water; bring to a simmer. Cook over low heat until the strips of zest are translucent and tender, about 10 minutes. With a fork, remove the strips of candied zest to a piece of wax paper to cool. (*Candied orange zest can be stored in an airtight container for up to 2 weeks.*)

TECHNIQUE 99 — Make healthy frozen treats with a fresh taste using fruit and nonfat yogurt.

Even if you do not own an ice cream maker, you can still enjoy homemade frozen yogurt that is much better than anything you can buy. The trick is to start with unsweetened frozen fruit and use your food processor to whirl in yogurt or buttermilk for an instant fat-free frozen treat. This technique works well with a variety of fruits: try sliced peaches, nectarines or melon balls (alone or in combination). Look for IQF (individually quick-frozen) fruits at your supermarket or better yet, use seasonal fruits you freeze yourself. Seedy fruits, such as raspberries, should be pureed and strained to remove the seeds.

F FAT SAVINGS: Commercial strawberry frozen yogurts range from fat-free to 4.5 grams of fat for a similar-size serving. But none has the very fresh taste of frozen yogurt you make yourself.

Strawberry Frozen Yogurt

1 16-ounce package IQF (individually quick-frozen) unsweetened strawberries (about 3½ cups)
½ cup sugar, preferably instant-dissolving
½ cup nonfat plain yogurt *or* buttermilk
1 tablespoon fresh lemon juice

In a food processor, combine frozen strawberries and sugar. Pulse until coarsely chopped. Combine yogurt or buttermilk and lemon juice; with the machine running, gradually pour the mixture through the feed tube. Process until smooth and creamy, scraping down the sides of the workbowl once or twice. (*The frozen yogurt should be firm enough to be served directly from the food processor, but if it is a little soft, let it harden in the freezer for about 30 minutes.*)

Makes about 3 cups, for 4 servings.

150 calories per serving: 2 grams protein, 0 grams fat, 38 grams carbohydrate; 25 mg sodium; 1 mg cholesterol; 3 grams fiber.

N NUTRITION BONUS: There are 4 ounces of strawberries in every serving of this refreshing dessert.

Banana Frozen Yogurt

The tiny amount of fat in this dessert comes from the bananas.

- 3 large bananas
- ½ cup sugar, preferably instant-dissolving
- ½ teaspoon ground cinnamon
- ½ cup nonfat plain yogurt *or* buttermilk
- 1 tablespoon fresh lemon juice

1. Line a baking sheet with wax paper. Peel and slice bananas into ¼-inch-thick rounds. Spread the rounds on the baking sheet, cover with more wax paper and freeze until solid, 1½ to 2 hours.

2. In a food processor, combine the frozen bananas, sugar and cinnamon. Pulse until coarsely chopped. Combine yogurt or buttermilk and lemon juice; with the machine running, gradually pour the mixture through the feed tube. Process until smooth and creamy, scraping down the sides of the workbowl once or twice. (*The frozen yogurt should be firm enough to be served directly from the food processor, but if it is a little soft, let it harden in the freezer for about 30 minutes.*)

Makes about 3 cups, for 4 servings.

215 calories per serving: 3 grams protein, 1 gram fat (0.2 gram saturated fat), 53 grams carbohydrate; 25 mg sodium; 1 mg cholesterol; 2 grams fiber.

Ⓝ NUTRITION BONUS: Bananas are a good source of potassium.

Mixed Berry Frozen Yogurt

- 2 cups fresh *or* frozen and thawed berries (raspberries, blackberries *and/or* blueberries)
- 1 small banana
- ¼ cup frozen orange-juice concentrate
- 1 cup nonfat plain yogurt *or* buttermilk
- ¼ cup brown sugar
- ½ teaspoon pure vanilla extract

1. In a food processor, puree berries until smooth. Transfer to a stainless-steel sieve set over a bowl. With a spoon, work the puree through the sieve to remove seeds. Pour the puree into an ice cube tray and freeze. Slice banana and freeze at the same time.

2. In a food processor, combine the frozen berry puree, banana slices and orange-juice concentrate. Pulse until coarsely chopped.

3. Combine yogurt or buttermilk, brown sugar and vanilla; with the machine running, gradually pour the mixture through the feed tube. Process until smooth and creamy, scraping down the sides of the workbowl once or twice. (*The frozen yogurt should be firm enough to be served directly from the food processor, but if it is a little soft, let it harden in the freezer for about 30 minutes.*)

Makes about 4 cups, for 4 servings.

150 calories per serving: 4 grams protein, 0 grams fat, 34 grams carbohydrate; 50 mg sodium; 1 mg cholesterol; 3 grams fiber.

Ⓝ NUTRITION BONUS: This frozen treat has 3 grams of fiber per serving.

TECHNIQUE

100 Nonfat sweetened condensed milk cuts the fat in ice cream.

The small ice cream makers that fit in your freezer have made making ice cream a whole lot easier. But some of the old recipes—ones that required making a custard sauce and then chilling it—were time-consuming. And all of those old recipes, whether custard-based or cream-based, were high in fat. We have found that nonfat sweetened condensed milk gives ice creams an old-fashioned creaminess.

Ⓕ FAT SAVINGS: The fat content of premium ice creams varies greatly, anywhere from 7 to 17 grams of fat in a 4-ounce scoop. These Eating Well ice creams have 1 or 2 grams of fat in the same amount.

Eggnog Ice Cream

- 1 tablespoon brandy *or* rum
- 2 teaspoons pure vanilla extract
- 1½ teaspoons unflavored gelatin

3   cups low-fat milk
2   large egg yolks
1   14-ounce can nonfat sweetened condensed milk
1   teaspoon freshly grated nutmeg

1. In a small bowl, combine brandy or rum and vanilla; sprinkle in gelatin and set aside to soften.

2. In a heavy saucepan, heat 1½ cups of the milk over medium heat until steaming. Meanwhile, in a mixing bowl, whisk egg yolks and sweetened condensed milk.

3. Gradually pour the hot milk into the condensed milk/egg yolk mixture, whisking until blended. Return the mixture to the saucepan and cook, stirring with a wooden spoon, until the custard coats the back of the spoon lightly, 3 to 5 minutes. Do not overcook or boil, or the custard will curdle.

4. Strain the custard into a clean bowl. Add the gelatin mixture and whisk until melted. Whisk in nutmeg and the remaining 1½ cups cold milk. Cover and refrigerate until well chilled, about 2 hours.

5. Pour into an ice cream maker and freeze according to manufacturer's directions. If necessary, place the ice cream in the freezer to firm up before serving. (*Use within hours of freezing, if possible, or store in the freezer for up to 4 days. If the ice cream becomes very hard in the freezer, soften it in the refrigerator for about 30 minutes before scooping.*)

Makes about 4 cups, for 8 servings.

205 calories per serving: 8 grams protein, 2 grams fat (1 gram saturated fat), 35 grams carbohydrate; 100 mg sodium; 60 mg cholesterol; 0 grams fiber.

Ⓝ NUTRITION BONUS: Our homemade ice cream is not only lower in fat, it's higher in calcium.

Honey-Crunch Ice Cream

HONEY CRUNCH
1   tablespoon honey
1   teaspoon butter, melted
1   teaspoon milk
1   teaspoon light brown sugar
½   teaspoon pure vanilla extract
¼   cup Grape-Nuts cereal

ICE CREAM
1½ cups whole milk
1   14-ounce can nonfat sweetened condensed milk
1   tablespoon pure vanilla extract
1   tablespoon fresh lemon juice
¼   teaspoon salt

TO MAKE HONEY CRUNCH:

1. Preheat oven to 350°F. Lightly oil a small baking pan or coat it with nonstick cooking spray.

2. In a small bowl, mix honey, butter, milk, brown sugar and vanilla until blended. With a fork, stir in Grape-Nuts until well coated. Spread in a thin layer in the prepared baking pan. Bake, stirring once or twice, for 5 minutes, or until the cereal has darkened and bubbling has subsided. Spread on a plate and let cool completely. Break up any large clumps and set aside. (*The honey crunch can be stored in an airtight container at room temperature for up to 3 days.*)

TO MAKE ICE CREAM:

1. In a large bowl, mix milk, condensed milk and vanilla until blended. For best results, refrigerate the mixture until well chilled, at least 2 hours.

2. Stir lemon juice and salt into the chilled ice cream mixture. Pour into the canister of an ice cream maker and freeze according to manufacturer's directions. Halfway through freezing, when ice cream begins to thicken, sprinkle in honey crunch and continue freezing. If necessary, let the ice cream harden in the freezer for 30 minutes before serving. (*Use within hours of freezing, if possible, or store in the freezer for up to 4 days. If the ice cream becomes very hard in the freezer, soften it in the refrigerator for about 30 minutes before scooping.*)

Makes about 3 cups, for 6 servings.

265 calories per serving: 8 grams protein, 3 grams fat (1.7 grams saturated fat), 52 grams carbohydrate; 225 mg sodium; 13 mg cholesterol; 0 grams fiber.

Ⓝ NUTRITION BONUS: Use Grape-Nuts to add low-fat crunch to other dessert recipes and toppings.

Menus

These 10 menus are offered for inspiration and as a springboard to your own combinations. The recipes were not created specifically for these menus, so in some cases you many need to double the recipes; in others you may have leftovers.

SPRING CELEBRATION
Asparagus with Tangerine & Sesame Seed Dressing, *p.18*
Grilled Mesclun-Stuffed Swordfish, *p.93*
Risotto with Spring Vegetables, *p.127*
Rhubarb Tart, *p.167*

PICNIC ON THE FOURTH
Chili Burgers, *p.78*
Steamed fresh sugar snap peas tossed in Basic Vinaigrette, *p.16*
Potato Salad, *p.27*
Boston Baked Beans, *p.125*
Strawberry Shortcakes, *p.137*

LATE SUMMER LUNCH
Tuna & Tomatoes Provençale, *p.25*
Imported olives, French bread
Plum Fool, *p.193*

HARVEST SUPPER
Pork Medallions with a Port-&-Cranberry Pan Sauce, *p.84*
Ratatouille of Roasted Vegetables, *p.108*
Wide egg noodles
Apple-Walnut Upside-Down Cake, *p.177*

A MEATLESS MEAL
Crostini with Cannellini Beans, *p.126*
Penne with Cremini-Tomato Ragù, *p.50*
Romaine salad with Basil Vinaigrette, *p.18*
French bread
Mocha Confetti Cake, *p.156*
or Banana Spice Cake, *p.150*

DINNER FOR EIGHT

Mixed bitter greens with
Apricot Dressing, *p.18*

Veal Stew, *p.78*

Buttermilk Mashed Potatoes, *p.116*

Double Raspberry Soufflés, *p.192*

HEALTHY HOLIDAY

Roast Turkey with Madeira Gravy
with Corn Bread *&* Apple Stuffing, *p.69*

A favorite cranberry relish

Your choice of Roasted Vegetables, *p.109*

Buttermilk Biscuits, *p.136*

Mixed green salad with
Maple-Balsamic Vinaigrette, *p.17*

Marbled Pumpkin Cheesecake, *p.194*
or Apple-Cranberry Streusel Pie, *p.173*

A CHILI NIGHT

Beef *&* Bean Chili, *p.79*

Warmed corn tortillas, Jícama Slaw, *p.20*

Marbled Cheesecake Brownies, *p.181*

BRUNCH BUFFET

Leek *&* Gruyère Quiche, *p.101*

Rösti Potatoes, *p.117*

Apricot-Nut Bread, *p.135*

Honey-Glazed Cinnamon Doughnuts, *p.141*

Mixed fruit salad with
Poppy Seed Dressing, *p.21*

QUICK CHICKEN DINNER

Honey-Mustard Chicken, *p.67*

Oven Fries, *p.119*

Mixed greens tossed
with Fresh Tomato Vinaigrette, *p.22*

Strawberry Frozen Yogurt, *p.198*

Glossary

NUTRITION TERMS

ANTIOXIDANTS

Generally speaking, antioxidants are chemicals that keep other substances from being oxidized: e.g., the vitamin C in lemon juice is an antioxidant that prevents a sliced apple from turning brown. In the body, antioxidants are thought to disarm free radicals, which are believed to contribute to the development of some cancers, cataracts and atherosclerosis. BETA CAROTENE, vitamins C and E, and many natural plant chemicals are antioxidants.

BETA CAROTENE

Just one member of the huge family of CAROTENOIDS, the pigments in fruits and vegetables that give them an orange or red hue. Carotenoids are thought to help reduce the risk of certain types of cancer.

CALCIUM

The mineral that really does build and maintain strong bones. Inadequate amounts of calcium and lack of exercise contribute to osteoporosis after menopause. Calcium also helps regulate blood pressure and has many other essential roles in the body. The RDA for calcium is 1,200 milligrams for adolescents and postmenopausal women, and 800 milligrams for men and women under the age of 50.

CARBOHYDRATES

Sugars, starches and dietary FIBER derived from plants. Sugars and starches provide 4 calories per gram; fiber is largely undigestible by humans. Sugars are classified as simple carbohydrates; starches and fiber are called complex carbohydrates because they are made up of long chains of sugars. A healthy diet includes generous amounts of complex carbohydrates.

CAROTENOIDS

A huge group (more than 600 have been identified so far) of pigments in plant foods, including BETA CAROTENE and LYCOPENE, many of which act as ANTIOXIDANTS.

CHOLESTEROL

A waxy fatlike substance that is made by the liver and used by the body for a number of vital functions. Too much cholesterol in the blood, however, can contribute to cardiovascular disease. An excess of SATURATED FAT in the diet will raise blood-cholesterol levels. Dietary cholesterol refers to the cholesterol found in foods of animal origin.

ESSENTIAL FATTY ACIDS

The two polyunsaturated fatty acids—LINOLEIC ACID and LINOLENIC ACID—needed in small amounts as essential nutrients. Both are found in vegetables, nuts and vegetable oils.

FAT

A basic component of many foods, containing three types of fatty acids—MONOUNSATURATED, POLYUNSATURATED and SATURATED—in varying proportions. For healthy people, nutritionists recommend a diet that contains no more than 30 percent of calories from fat.

FIBER

The National Cancer Institute recommends 20 to 25 grams of fiber per day. There are two types of fiber: soluble fiber, found in beans, oats and various gums used as food additives, which helps lower blood cholesterol and even out blood-sugar levels; insoluble fiber, found in wheat and other grains, which is important for intestinal health and possibly fights colon cancer.

FIVE-A-DAY

The recommendation from the National Cancer Institute and the USDA that Americans eat at least five servings of fruits and vegetables every day to promote good health and lower the risk of disease.

FOLIC ACID

This B vitamin is critical for preventing neural-tube birth defects, such as spina bifida. It also may protect against some kinds of cancer. And new evidence strongly suggests that folic acid may also lower heart-disease risk. Legumes, leafy green vegetables and oranges are good sources of folic acid.

HDL (HIGH-DENSITY LIPOPROTEIN)

Also known as "good" cholesterol because it speedily and efficiently transports excess cholesterol back to the liver for reprocessing.

HYDROGENATED FATS

To firm up a fat that is normally liquid at room temperature, food manufacturers pump it full of hydrogen atoms. This saturates the fat and produces trans-fatty acids, which are believed to increase the risk of heart disease. Most nutritionists recommend avoiding foods with significant amounts of hydrogenated fats.

LDL (LOW-DENSITY LIPOPROTEIN)

Also known as "bad" cholesterol because it is the type of cholesterol that ends up in arterial plaques.

LINOLEIC ACID

One of the two ESSENTIAL FATTY ACIDS. Corn oil, safflower oil, soybean oil and most POLYUNSATURATED oils are rich in linoleic acid.

LINOLENIC ACID

One of the two ESSENTIAL FATTY ACIDS. Linolenic acid is the plant equivalent of OMEGA-3 FATTY ACIDS found in fish oils. New research suggests that the ratio of linolenic to linoleic acid should be higher than it currently is in the American diet. Sources of linolenic acid are canola oil and walnuts.

LYCOPENE

A CAROTENOID, this red pigment in tomatoes and strawberries is thought to reduce the risk of cancer, particularly prostate cancer.

MONOUNSATURATED FAT

The type of fat that lowers heart-disease risk when it replaces SATURATED FAT in the diet. Olive oil and canola oil are the two richest sources of monounsaturated fat.

OMEGA-3 FATTY ACIDS

A type of fat in fish oil that is believed to lower the risk of arrhythmias and sudden death from heart attacks.

PHYTOCHEMICALS

Phytochemical is a fancy name for a plant chemical that is not necessarily a nutrient, yet fights disease.

POLYUNSATURATED FAT

A type of fatty acid that lowers blood cholesterol when it replaces saturated fat in the diet. Polyunsaturated fats are no longer considered as heart-healthy as monounsaturated fats.

POTASSIUM

A mineral crucial to maintaining the body's fluid balance. All fruits and vegetables are rich in potassium. Dairy products are also a good source.

RDA (RECOMMENDED DIETARY ALLOWANCE)

The amount of an essential nutrient determined by the National Research Council to be adequate for healthy individuals.

SATURATED FAT

One of the three types of fatty acids, found in greatest concentration in animal products and in coconut and palm oils. Saturated fats raise blood cholesterol, contributing to heart disease. For a healthy diet, saturated fat should be kept to a maximum of 10 percent of calories consumed each day.

TOTAL FAT

A person's daily intake of MONOUNSATURATED, POLYUNSATURATED and SATURATED fats. Most major health organizations recommend that for healthy people no more than 30 percent of calories consumed in a day come from fat.

TRACE MINERALS

Copper, manganese, chromium, fluoride, iodine, selenium and molybdenum are minerals the body needs in tiny amounts. The best sources of trace minerals are whole grains, fruits, nuts and vegetables.

A glossary of ingredients begins on the next page.

INGREDIENTS

AMARETTO
An almond-flavored liqueur from Italy, Amaretto is frequently used in desserts and confections.

ANAHEIM PEPPERS
A long, tapered chile pepper available both green and ripe red, also known respectively as the California green chile and Colorado red chile. With a heat level that ranges from mild to moderately hot, it is excellent stuffed and appears frequently in sauces and stews.

ARBORIO RICE
This Italian-grown, medium-grain rice is a must for risotto, for the high-starch kernels contribute to the characteristic creaminess. Arborio is found in most supermarkets, Italian markets and health-food stores.

ARUGULA
Also called rocket, this aromatic green lends a peppery mustard flavor to salads. It is sold in small bunches in supermarkets or farmers' markets. Watercress is a good substitute.

BALSAMIC VINEGAR
A dark, sweet vinegar from Northern Italy that is traditionally made from white grapes and then aged in wood barrels to achieve a rich mellowness. With its extra flavor, balsamic vinegar is perfect for salad dressings and for finishing sauces.

BASMATI RICE
This fragrant, long-grained rice is native to the Middle East and Northern India. Aged to develop its nutty flavor, basmati must be handled carefully to preserve its fine texture. It is available in boxes in the specialty-foods section of the supermarket.

BULGUR
A staple of Middle Eastern cuisines and a nutritious base for pilafs and salads, bulgur is made by precooking, drying and cracking wheat kernels. It can be found in the international- or health-food sections of the supermarket.

CAKE FLOUR
Finely ground from soft wheat, cake flour is used in cakes and pastries to obtain a tender crumb because it is low in gluten, the elastic protein that gives structure to baked goods. Cake flour is often preferred in very light batters because it is bleached. An acceptable substitute can be made by replacing 2 tablespoons in every cup of all-purpose flour with cornstarch.

CANOLA OIL
Obtained from the seeds of the rapeseed plant, canola oil is a versatile, healthy substitute for most other vegetable oils. It is the lowest in saturated fats while containing a high amount of cholesterol-lowering monounsaturated fats and healthful omega-3 fatty acids. With no flavor and a high smoking point, it works well for frying and for dressings and baked goods.

CAPERS
The pickled flower buds of a cliff-clinging bush, capers add their piquancy to many Mediterranean dishes. Those labeled petite nonpareil come from southern France and are the smallest in size; the larger buds, popular throughout Italy and Spain, may need to be chopped before use.

CHINESE CHILE GARLIC PASTE
A thick puree used as a base in many Chinese sauces. Look for this spicy ingredient in the international-foods section of the grocery store or ask for it at Asian markets, where you will find the most flavorful brands.

CHORIZO SAUSAGE
Generously seasoned with garlic, hot paprika and sweet red peppers, this coarse pork sausage appears frequently in Mexican and Spanish cuisine. Look for it near the deli section of the supermarket.

COCONUT MILK
Commonly used in Indian and Southeast Asian cuisines, it adds a characteristic richness to curries and soups. Available at Asian markets and most supermarkets.

COUSCOUS
Resembling a grain, these granules of semolina meal are actually a type of pasta. A staple throughout North Africa, it is traditionally steamed over broth but is now available in a precooked form that only requires five minutes of soaking in hot broth or water. Whole-wheat couscous can be found in health-food stores.

CREME DE CASSIS
A black-currant-flavored liqueur that marries well with berries and is commonly used in desserts.

CREMINI

A cousin of the common white button mushroom, this brown variant is slightly earthier in flavor and firmer in texture. When fully mature, the cremini will open to become a portobello mushroom.

CRYSTALLIZED GINGER

Also termed candied ginger, this is fresh gingerroot that has been cooked in a sugar syrup and then coated with granulated sugar. It lends a spicy-sweet flavor to desserts. Buy it at Asian markets or health-food stores, where it will be less expensive.

DUTCH-PROCESS COCOA POWDER

Significantly lower in fat than chocolate, unsweetened cocoa powder can be used to replace chocolate in desserts. In Dutch-process cocoa, the natural acid has been neutralized, and the cocoa has a darker color and deeper flavor as a result. Often labeled European cocoa, it is available in some supermarkets and in specialty-food stores.

EVAPORATED SKIM MILK

Made by evaporating nearly half the water from fresh skim milk, this thick and slightly sweet canned milk product is a good replacement for cream in desserts where strong flavors will mask the slightly cooked flavor.

EXTRA-VIRGIN OLIVE OIL

Olive oil has long been a foundation of Mediterranean cuisine. Having a high amount of beneficial monounsaturated fat while being extremely low in the undesirable saturated fat, it is now known to be an important ingredient in heart-healthy recipes. Bottled from the first cold pressing of ripe olives, extra-virgin olive oil has a significantly fruitier flavor and darker color than subsequent pressings.

FENNEL

A pale green plant of the parsley family, this vegetable consists of overlapping stems that converge to a bulb-like base. Its delicate anise flavor is essential to Italian cuisine. The feathery leaves can be used for garnish, although often the bulb is sold already trimmed of stem and leaves. Look for fennel in the supermarket produce section where it may be incorrectly labeled sweet anise.

FISH SAUCE

Called *nuoc mam* in Vietnam and *nam pla* in Thailand, fish sauce is a clear, amber liquid derived from fresh anchovies and used as a seasoning and condiment throughout Southeast Asia. Look for it in Asian markets or in the international section of the supermarket, where it sometimes sold as "Thai Seasoning Sauce."

GORGONZOLA

A pungent, creamy, blue-veined cheese from northern Italy made from cow's milk. It is available at any good cheese counter.

GRAND MARNIER

An orange-flavored brandy from France. Popular in desserts, complimenting chocolate as well as citrus flavors.

HABANERO

Ranging from dark green to orange to red in color, this small, lantern-shaped chile pepper is extremely hot, with almost 50 times more heat than the jalapeño. Wash hands and all equipment well after handling. The closely related Scotch bonnet pepper can be substituted.

HAZELNUT OIL

A heart-healthy nut oil obtained from hazelnuts, also known as filberts. It is an excellent addition to breads, cakes and cookies to deepen nutty flavors while cutting back on the amount of nuts in the recipe.

HOISIN SAUCE

Thick, glossy, dark and sweet, hoisin sauce is a fermented soybean paste colored with annato seeds and flavored with garlic and Chinese five-spice. Classically served with Peking duck, it is a popular condiment in China and an important ingredient in glazes for roast pork and poultry.

HOMINY

Whole white or yellow corn that has ripened completely and then been treated with lime; in the process, the kernels become large and puffy. It is commonly served as an accompanying starch or a component of a casserole. A staple in Southern and Southwestern cooking, hominy is widely available dried or canned.

JALAPENO

Dark green, thick-fleshed and ranging from hot to very hot, the jalapeño pepper is very popular and convenient. When ripe, it turns vivid red and takes on a sweetness that is heightened by drying and smoking over mesquite wood; these then are known as chipotle chiles, a base for many Southwestern sauces.

JASMINE RICE

A long-grained, very fragrant rice that is the staple of Southeast Asia, jasmine rice can be found in small boxes in grocery stores and health-food stores as well as in bulk from Asian markets.

KOHLRABI

A member of the same family as broccoli and kale, kohlrabi resembles a turnip in shape, but it is much sweeter and milder in flavor and crisper in texture. Look for it in the produce section of the supermarket from spring to fall.

MACHE

Also known as lamb's lettuce and corn salad, this deep-green herald of spring has a delicate flavor. If you cannot find mâche, substitute young, small spinach leaves.

MADRAS CURRY POWDER

This widely available, turmeric-based curry powder is named for a city in southern India, where spice mixes tend to be very hot. It can be found in the spice section of the supermarket.

MESCLUN

Derived from a word meaning "mix" in southern France, mesclun refers to any colorful mixture of young salad greens, with herbs and edible flowers sometimes added. Look for mesclun in the supermarket produce section or in health-food stores.

PANCETTA

An Italian bacon, pancetta is salted, spiced, then rolled and tied like a sausage. It is an essential flavoring ingredient in many sauces and pasta dishes.

PASTRY FLOUR

Milled from soft wheat, pastry flour is unbleached and has slightly more gluten than cake flour.

PHYLLO

Greek for "leaf," phyllo is a transparently thin sheet of pastry dough, layered in both savory and sweet foods in Middle Eastern and Greek cuisine. Look for it in the frozen-foods section of the supermarket.

PINE NUTS

Also known as pignoli and piñon, these are the small, ivory-colored seeds of various pine trees. Their distinctive light nutty flavor is an important note in many Mediterranean dishes. They can be found in small jars in the international-foods section of the supermarket or in bulk at health-food stores. Store pine nuts in an airtight container in the freezer, for they turn rancid quickly.

POBLANO PEPPERS

A dark green, almost purple chile pepper popular in Mexico, the poblano has wide shoulders tapering 4 to 5 inches to a point. Ranging from medium to hot, they are often filled or used in sauces. Always cooked, poblanos are excellent roasted to bring out their earthy flavor. They are sometimes mistakenly labeled as pasilla peppers; ripened and dried, they are known as ancho chiles.

PORCINI

Meaning "little pigs" in Italian and known as cepes in France, porcini mushrooms have a smooth, dense texture and earthy flavor. Light brown and ranging from 1 to 10 inches in cap diameter, they are not cultivated and thus are both difficult to find and expensive. Dried porcini can be found in some grocery stores and in most specialty-foods stores. Reconstitute in warm water for 30 minutes and use in place of the fresh mushrooms.

PORTOBELLO

A mature cremini, the portobello is a large, dark brown mushroom with a wide, flaring, flat cap. While the stems are usually too woody to eat, the caps have an especially rich and meaty texture.

PROSCIUTTO

A spiced and salt-cured Italian ham that is air-dried then pressed, resulting in a firm, dense texture. Usually sold very thinly sliced, it can be found in specialty-foods stores and Italian markets.

RADICCHIO

A red-leafed member of the chicory family. With its bright colors, crisp leaves and faintly bitter flavor, radicchio is now a popular component of salads. In Italy it is often grilled, sautéed and baked.

RICE VINEGAR

While there are several different rice vinegars used in Asia, the type most commonly seen in the U.S. is the clear, mild Japanese rice vinegar distilled from fermented white rice. It is available in most grocery stores, but cider or white-wine vinegar can be substituted.

RICE WINE
Called sake in Japan, rice wine is in fact distilled from fermented cooked rice. Often combined with soy sauce and sugar in sauces, it adds both rich flavor and brown shine. Look for it in liquor stores, labeled sake or Japanese rice wine.

SCOTCH BONNET
From pale yellow-green to red in color, this pepper resembles the habanero in shape and is almost equal to it in heat. It is essential in Jamaican jerk rub and Caribbean curries.

SERRANO
Dark green ripening to bright red, this 1- to 2-inch chile pepper is cylindrical and tapers to a rounded tip. Its clean heat and high acidity suit it well to such fresh applications as salsas and pickles.

SESAME OIL
Made from crushed white sesame seeds, this nut oil is a dark, deeply flavored seasoning used throughout northern Asia. With a very low smoke-point, it is not used in cooking but rather sprinkled on at the end or added to marinades and dipping sauces. Look for it in the international-foods section of the supermarket or in Asian markets.

SHIITAKE
Available both fresh and dried, the shiitake is a dark brown mushroom with a 3- to 6-inch cap that may have tan cracks. Originally cultivated in Japan, it has a firm texture and a strong flavor that is naturally intensified after drying. Look for fresh mushrooms during spring and autumn; reconstitute the dried mushrooms in warm water and trim the hard stems before using. The shiitake is closely related to the Chinese black mushroom, for which it can be substituted.

SOBA
These thin, buckwheat noodles from Japan are served both cold with a soy-based dipping sauce or hot in a broth. They should be cooked in simmering, not boiling, water and then rinsed well under cold water. Look for soba in health-food stores, Asian markets, or the specialty-foods section of the supermarket.

SUN-DRIED TOMATOES
Though now most often dehydrated by moving air rather than the sun, dried tomatoes are still reduced to the dark red, chewy pieces that contribute intense, sweet tomato flavor to savory dishes.

SWEETENED CONDENSED MILK
Homogenized whole milk and sugar are blended, reduced to a thick syrup, then canned. Used in cookies and confections, it also lends creaminess and body to custards and pie fillings. Look for it in the baking section of the supermarket. It is now available in both low-fat and nonfat versions.

SWISS CHARD
With large, dark green leaves and celery-like stalks of either silvery-celadon or ruby red, Swiss chard approximates spinach in flavor. It is related to the beet and carries a hint of its earthy sweetness; the red variety is stronger in flavor. Despite its name, it was first popular in Southern Italy and France.

TAHINI
A thick paste made from ground sesame seeds, tahini is an important flavoring ingredient in such Middle Eastern appetizers as hummus and baba ghanouj. It is available in health-food stores and in the specialty-foods section of the supermarket.

TEXMATI RICE
A cross of Indian basmati and a native long-grain rice, Texmati is grown here in the U.S. The extra-long-grain basmati rice can also be used. Available in boxes in supermarkets or health-food stores.

WALNUT OIL
Extracted from toasted walnuts, this oil has a delicate nutty flavor and is high in heart-healthy monounsaturated fats. Buy it in small quantities and store in the refrigerator, as nut oils become rancid more quickly than other oils. When a recipe calls for nuts, use a small amount of nut oil to heighten the flavor.

WHOLE-WHEAT PASTRY FLOUR
A fine-textured, soft-wheat flour that includes the wheat germ, giving it a higher fiber content than white flours. Look for it at health-food stores. Store in the freezer.

Recipe Index

Page numbers in italics indicate photographs.
An index of techniques begins on page 220.

Technique Index

It is the editors' hope that readers will use this index not only to locate techniques in this book but also as a tool for building their own low-fat recipes. Page numbers in italics indicate photographs.

A

Apple Butter
reduces fat in cake, 133; in Christmas pudding, 196; in doughnuts, 139; in muffins, 132

Apple-Juice Concentrate
as a substitute for butter in streusel topping, 173

Asian Diet
healthfulness of, 129

B

Bananas
mashed, reduces fat in muffins, 132; in soufflé, 182

Bars
techniques for reducing fat in, 148, 149

Bean Puree
as a low-fat spread, 125; as a sauce for pizza, 55

Beans, Dried
techniques for low-fat cooking of, 121-126

Beans & Grains
a healthy choice, 122

Beef
choosing lean cuts, 74, 76; cooking to medium-rare, 75-77; extending with bulgur or beans, for burgers, 76-78; for meatballs, 42, 42; for meatloaf, 76; extending with vegetables, for chili, 78-79; trimming outside fat, 74, 74

Braising
vegetables, to develop complex flavors, 110

Bread
to thicken soups, 36

Breadcrumbs
add body to pesto, 46; extend a ricotta filling, 45; reduce butter in a phyllo crust, 170

Broth, Canned
skimming fat, boosting flavor, 32, 32

Bulgur
about, 42; reduces fat in meatballs, 42, 42

Butter
browning to enhance flavor, 154, 154; don't use light butter in baking, 147; reducing amount in pie crust, 166, 169, 170; in potato dishes, 116, 117, 118

Buttermilk
about, 20; as a substitute (with cottage cheese) for sour cream, 20; in batter for oven-fried chicken and turkey, 63; in mashed potatoes, 116; in mayonnaise, 22; in salad dressings, 21; tenderizing effect in biscuits and scones, 136

C

Cakes
techniques for reducing fat in, 153-163

Cheese
choosing full-flavored cheeses to boost flavor, 102, 118; choosing part-skim ricotta, 45; techniques to reduce fat in cheese dishes, 101-105

Cherries, Dried
reduce fat in chocolaty cookies, 184

Chicken
leanest cuts, 60; removing skin from pieces, 60, 60; salmonella risk, 61; skinning a whole chicken, 62, 62; techniques for reducing fat in, 59-67

Chocolate Desserts
techniques for reducing fat in, 179-185

Clay-Pot Cooking
keeps chicken moist, 62, 63

Cocoa Powder
choose Dutch-process for fullest flavor, 180; reduces fat in chocolate doughnuts, 140

Condensed Milk, Nonfat Sweetened
in chocolate desserts, 184; in ice cream, 199

Cookies
techniques for reducing saturated fat in, 143-148; techniques for rolling, 145, 145

Cornstarch
cuts fat in a classic cookie, 146

Cottage Cheese
as a substitute for cream cheese in cheesecake, 182, 194; in macaroni & cheese, 102; in quiche, 103; in quick-bread stollen, 138; with buttermilk as a substitute for sour cream, 20

Cream
fat in, 193; substitutes for, 33, 101, 190, 193, 199

Credits

*Our thanks to the fine food writers and photographers whose work
was previously published in* EATING WELL *Magazine.*

RECIPE CONTRIBUTORS

Jeffrey Alford & Naomi Duguid: Dukka, 57

Melanie Barnard: Banana Spice Cake, 150; Blackberry
Sauce, 159; **with Elinor Klivans:** Mocha Confetti
Cake, 156; Key Lime Cake, 162

Dave Berry: Southern-Style Pork Tenderloin, 81; North
Carolina Barbecue Sauce, 82; Southern-Style Black-
Eyed Peas, 126

Mark Bittman: Crisp Rockfish Fillets with Mustard
Sauce, 92; Grilled Mesclun-Stuffed Swordfish, 93;
Pan-Grilled Salmon Fillets with Tomato & Tarragon,
93

Lisa Cherkasky: Gingerbread Men, 144; Russian Tea
Cakes, 146

Natalie Danford: Homemade Chicken Broth, 34

Bharti Kirchner: Swiss Chard & Sweet Pepper Stir-Fry,
113; Mushroom & Pecan Burgers, 115

Mary Ludwig: French Onion Pizza, 53

Marc & Kim Millon: Tuscan Ribollita, 36; Korean
Grilled Beef (Bulgogi), 75

Philip Ogiela: Raspberry Cloud Cake, 160

Steven Raichlen: West Indian Squash Soup, 39; Angel
Food Cake with Eggnog Spices, 155

G. Franco Romagnoli: Basil Pesto, 46; Spinach
Fettuccine with Pesto, 47

Elizabeth Schneider: Beet & Citrus Salad with Creamy
Dressing, 20; Cool Beet Soup with a Chile-Cilantro
Swirl, 38; Penne with Cremini-Tomato Ragù, 50;
Belgian Endive Braised in Cider, 111; Shiitake &
Asparagus Stir-Fry, 112

Regina Schrambling: Roasted Veal Chops with
Gremolata, 83; Braised Fennel with Orange & Olives,
110; Braised Winter Vegetables, 111

Michele Scicolone: Braised Cabbage with Cranberry
Beans & Rice, 122; Crostini with Cannellini Beans,
126

Nina Simonds: Cinnamon Fried Rice, 128

John Willoughby with Chris Schlesinger: Apricot
Dressing, 18; Basil Vinaigrette, 18; Garlic-Lemon
Dressing, 27; Grilled Vegetable Salad, 112

PHOTOGRAPHERS

Angelo Caggiano: page 66

Anita Calero: pages 145, 146

Lois Ellen Frank: page 107

Brian Hagiwara: page 120

Matthew Klein: pages 40, 135, front cover (*right*)

Lori Landau: pages 13, 16, 22, 25, 26, 28, 29, 31, 32,
42, 50, 51, 52, 56, 59, 60, 62, 63, 69, 73, 74, 80, 86,
89, 97, 104, 121, 139, 148, 150, 151 (*upper left*), 153,
154, 166, 176, 177, 179, 186, 187, 189, 190, front
cover (*left*), back cover

Becky Luigart-Stayner: pages 21, 35, 48, 65, 67, 100,
103, 110, 117, 119, 123, 138, 168, 183, 188, 203
(*lower right*), 191, 195

Len Mastri: 41, 151 (*right*)

Steven Mark Needham: pages 19, 54, 68, 114, 124, 127,
137

Victoria Pearson: page 181

Mimi Pfeil: page 82

Alan Richardson: pages 72, 105, 185, 198, 202

Carin & David Riley: pages 156, 158, 162

Maria Robledo: page 84

Matthew Savins: pages 6 (*upper right*), 14, 15, 58, 71,
88, 96, 106, 130, 131, 142, 143, 178, 203 (*upper left*)

Jim Scherer: pages 76, 81

Ellen Silverman: pages 30, 38, 43, 47, 94, 164

Jerry Simpson: page 44

Rick Szczechowski: pages 152, 171, 196, 197

Greens on page 28 courtesy of **Bingham Brook Farm,**
Charlotte, Vermont

Cherry on page 165 courtesy of **Harry & David**

MORE COOKBOOKS FROM

The Eating Well Dessert Cookbook

150 Recipes to Bring Dessert Back Into Your Life
From the Magazine of Food & Health
ISBN 1-884943-09-8   (hardcover) $24.95 / ISBN 1-884943-10-1   (paperback) $16.95

The Eating Well New Favorites Cookbook

More Great Recipes from the Magazine of Food & Health
From the Editors of EATING WELL®
ISBN 1-884943-07-1   (hardcover) $24.95 / ISBN 1-884943-08-X   (paperback) $16.95

The Eating Well Rush Hour Cookbook

Healthy Meals for Busy Cooks
From the Editors of EATING WELL,® The Magazine of Food & Health
ISBN 1-884943-05-5   (hardcover) $24.95 / ISBN 1-884943-06-3   (paperback) $14.95

The Eating Well Recipe Rescue Cookbook

High-Fat Favorites Transformed Into Healthy Low-Fat Favorites
Edited by Patricia Jamieson & Cheryl Dorschner
ISBN 1-884943-00-4   (hardcover) $24.95 / ISBN 1-884943-01-2   (paperback) $15.95

The Eating Well Cookbook

A Deluxe Collection of EATING WELL*'s Finest Recipes*
Edited by Rux Martin, Patricia Jamieson & Elizabeth Hiser
ISBN 1-884943-02-0   (hardcover) $24.95 / ISBN 1-884943-03-9   (paperback) $15.95